THE FINAL PATTERN:

The Critical Need For Critical Thinking

by

T. F. Hanlon

ISBN-13: 978-1-7321044-0-2

ISBN-10: 1732104409

Copyright Pending case number 1-6350864071

Library of Congress Control Number: 2018902996

BISAC   Psychology/cognitive Psychology/cognition

Cover Art: ESB Professional/Shutterstock.com

Cover design: TFHanlon

For HSB, who embodies wisdom; and for RJM,
who prefers not to drink from a firehose.

The enemy is closer wthen you think

PROLOGUE: THE ALIEN PROBE

One day, aliens land a probe on Earth with a kind of video recorder and other sensors. The probe can monitor the surface of the planet without being detected by the human inhabitants. After weeks of observation, the aliens report their findings and analysis back on their world. They describe humans scurrying around the Earth like a colony of ants, impacting their surroundings and their neighbors and doing irrational things, all fueled by what the aliens term "faulty reasoning."

"We note that their beliefs are very much determined by chance, based largely on the immediate environment in which they are raised and in which they live. For example, if their community is near a source of water, they may worship water gods that they think control the water. If the community encourages a peculiar practice, such as scarification, all are expected to partake; and if a member of the community declines the practice, they have a lower status, or are stigmatized or ostracized. Theirs seems to be very much a herd mentality, where conformity not only creates content but seemingly even happiness; the conforming individual becomes accepted by their community, which helps to restore a type of "order," regardless of the seeming foolishness of a given practice.

Their evolution has led to the chance outcome of a brain overwhelmed with the need for pattern-seeking. And if a perceived "pattern" gives the individual a positive feeling, they are more apt to accept their initial interpretation of this pattern over any subsequent analysis or even over actual reality, even when their initial interpretation leads to adverse outcomes to them or their community. However, there is a certain percentage of their population that has recognized these tendencies and subsequently developed a method which largely frees their species from possible misinterpretations. They call this discipline "science," and the practice of it has led to virtually every breakthrough and advancement in their society during their entire history. Even though the vast majority of the inhabitants enjoy the direct benefits of this practice, there are still those individuals who will deny science if it differs with what they wish to believe. In many instances, no amount of clear, demonstrable evidence will shake these individuals from this tendency.

It is significant to note that even among the most experienced practitioners of their science (they are termed "scientists" and "engineers"), there exists a subset that possesses the capacity to set aside this important mental discipline when determining their own opinions and beliefs in non-scientific areas of their lives. And yet this subset seems oblivious to this paradox! A most peculiar species. While the entire species as a whole does seem to be getting more disciplined with their reasoning abilities as time goes by, it is our judgment that their species is still in the early stages of operating their brains with the proper

2

discipline. We recommend that the inhabitants of this planet be given an additional solar century or two to reach the point where they no longer feel the need to hold rallies for reason and science or the need for sociological movements for giving all members of their species equal consideration and rights. Otherwise, the arrival of our society and our advanced abilities may be misinterpreted by some of this species as "magic" or "divinity."

TABLE OF CONTENTS

PREFACE

There have been many books written on the subjects of Critical Thinking, Logic, Science, Reason, and Secular Humanism. How does this book differ from them? How could an area of thinking studied for centuries yield anything new, salient, useful and practical? Why should the reader give yet another book on this subject a moment's consideration?

This book attempts to weave these subjects together in a uniquely accessible way, that is readily <u>applicable to any human idea or endeavor</u>, past, present or future---in essence, a book with ***universal relevance***. At the same time, the author of this book gratefully acknowledges the previous work done by innumerable authors and scholars on which this book draws.

When a doctor diagnoses a malignant cancer that has spread throughout the patient's entire body, it doesn't behoove the patient when the surgeon only removes the cancer from their toe. The rest of the disease remains and will continue its damage until the patient dies. The most effective way of treating and ultimately curing the cancer is approach it body-wide, preferably by attacking the disease at its source; thereby there is at least a chance to eradicate all of the cancer no matter where it may be lurking.

Humans have written innumerable books on how to eliminate a single sociological scourge of humanity. But this isn't likely to be nearly as useful on the whole for the species because there are too many other scourges to address; the damage done by these "cancers" throughout the "body" of humanity has been and continues to be so widespread and pervasive. Occasionally, one scourge, e.g. racism, may be decreased, or at best won't be so overtly manifest, perhaps in one community or one nation; the "cancer" has gone into partial remission. But somehow, after several years or decades, it begins to manifest again, the

6

"cancer" of racism recurs and may even metastasize. Considering how many different scourges that humanity has faced, does the average human have the time, access, and attention span to be able to read enough books about enough of these scourges to take action to eradicate all of them from humanity? On a practical basis, no. No matter how many separate areas of the body are cleared of the maglignancy, enough are left for other cancers to recur again and again...history repeats itself.

The "treatments" for the "cancers" have tried to bludgeon the given scourges down with a kind of "chemotherapy." While the patient may have shown some temporary improvement, they may have still suffered greatly and still cannot be given the "all clear" by the doctor, as the possibility of recurrence is always present. This book aims to attack all of the scourges simultaneously, at their source, by bringing the promise of a kind of "gene therapy" to the "cancers." Instead of forcing the scourges down with force, it instead attempts to elegantly "reprogram" the "genomes" of the scourges to shift their expression from creating further cancer, to instead building normal healthy tissue. As a result, the disease is no longer renewed and shrinks away to nothing, and the patient returns to health.

The ultimate source of all of humanity's human-made scourges is the human brain and its questionable thinking process. If the thinking process can be altered, i.e. "treated," by having its "genome expressed" in a rational rather than irrational manner, the patient, and by extension, all of humanity and the planet will benefit from the cure.

This book was written with the following intentions:

1) That it contains simple wording and maintains clarity; technical terms kept to an absolute minimum; avoiding a didactic tone; instead, any questions to the reader are posed colloquially, as if asking the average person in everyday vernacular;

   a) so that it will be readily understandable by all, formally educated and non-educated, and
   b) so that a translation into any and all other languages will be simplified.

2) That it be written with generic examples and anecdotes whenever possible, so that it shows no bias toward any country, culture or creed; with no one's mindset alienated, there is less chance of the reader prejudicially discounting any valid points.

3) Any human on Earth, past, present or future could recognize themselves represented in its text.

4) That writing from the first person is eliminated to avoid introducing any implied additional bias from the author into the discussion.

5) The emphasis on the style of writing is that it be inclusive, non-threatening, non-alienating; that it be genuinely appealing, even welcoming to any reader, while still being challenging to one's opinions, beliefs and typical ways of thinking.

6) Instead of attempting to argue why one point of view is superior to another point of view (where the details, conflicting definitions and differing interpretations of ideas often bog down any constructive discussion), the approach of this book is to question the epistemology of

all of the viewpoints involved (i.e. the cognitive process by which one arrives at their views). It will save much time if the inherent weaknesses in logic and reasoning that have led to an individual's perspective can be exposed early in a discussion, and the debate can go on to be constructive.

A book about something as universal as the how humans think will have as a direct consequence underline universal relevancy and underline universal appeal. A book cannot have this universality if it is deemed irrelevant based on the reader's circumstances, culture, education or upbringing. So this book deals exclusively with something universal that all humans possess regardless of circumstances, culture, education or upbringing, a human brain.

Since every human thought or idea had its origin inside a human brain, any thought or idea is necessarily limited by the limitations of that organ. The source of each of the human-caused problems faced by humanity can ultimately be traced back to the workings of a human brain. By this very nature, this book may be considered seminal. And while it may sound presumptuous, it may not be overstating the point that by following the tenets of this book, the vast majority of the problems facing humanity could, after a few years or decades, conceivably be abated if not eradicated.

A underline scientific theory is a model created by humans to explain a natural phenomenon in a way understandable by other humans. This construct has proven itself to be reliable, useful, beneficial and can also be predictive. A scientific theory can be applied universally to any phenomenon, in any culture, any country, any planet, or any galaxy for that matter, past, present or future.

While the contents of this book may not be defined as a scientific theory, perhaps the contents can still be considered a kind of theory in that, like a scientific theory, it can be applied universally to any human construct and is extremely useful and beneficial, and in some cases, even predictive.

The author of this book is identified only with the pseudonym "T. F. Hanlon" for the following reasons:

1) The author wishes no individual recognition

2) The author wishes the work to be judged exclusively on its own merits, rather than any imagined/implied "authority" of its author

3) The author wishes to avoid any possible bias from the reader making any judgments of the validity of the enclosed arguments based on any of the following attributes of the author:

    a) the author's gender identification
    b) the author's personal beliefs/biases
    c) the author's nationality/culture/upbringing
    d) the author's education level
    e) the author's proposed mastery of the subject

This book is not intended to be a pathway to truth. It is instead hoped to be a way to avoid untruths that might delay the individual on their own path. By eliminating unnecessary forks in the road and wearisome bogs which might slow the advance, one's pathway to truth will hopefully be simplified and accelerated.

If you've ever been in a difficult situation in your life, you may have thought, "If I could only get out of this bad spot and get to this other place, all my problems would be solved, and I'd finally be happy forever." It's tempting to simplify one's problems to a single phenomenon and then wish to escape that phenomenon. It seems as if you should be able to outrun that problem in your life, that nemesis that you so desperately want to avoid. But it turns out that so much of what creates the problems in your life is very near at hand...or rather, at head; your ultimate enemy is your own brain. In this particular game of "Hot, Warm and Cold" where "Hot" means you're close to discovering the origin of your problem and "Cold" means that you're far away, you have been "on fire" the whole time.

You can't outrun your mind; you can't take a boat or train or jet to get away from it. For your entire life, it will always be with you, lurking behind your eyes, between your ears, ever ready with poorly-reasoned responses to any given situation. And if humankind eventually populates another planet, they won't have to worry about finding hostile inhabitants waiting; they will smuggle in their own worst enemy with them.

> **Where there is great power, there is great responsibility.**
>
> —Winston Churchill (d.1965 Politician, Statesman, Prime Minister, Historian and Writer)

You shouldn't be allowed the convenience of a car without being responsible about how you drive it. The power of this mode of conveyance is great; it can carry you to distant places much faster and more efficiently than walking. But this same power of the car can instantly injure or kill someone, either inside or outside that vehicle, if that power is not adequately controlled. Similarly, each human possesses a brain with the power to do many great things; but when not properly controlled, that same brain can do real lasting damage in uncounted ways, as has been shown throughout human history.

> **The mind is not a vessel to be filled, but a fire to be lighted.**
> —Plutarch (1st-century Greek biographer and essayist)

This is a brilliant thought: that one's actual thinking process is far more important than the facts accumulated; it is the central theme upon which this book is based.

But are all fires constructive? Fire can be harnessed to cook food, melt metals into useful forms and light rooms to enable learning; but left uncontrolled, a fire often burns, maims, destroys, even when the original intent for its creation was good. Here, the mind is similar, capable of critical thought, logic and reasoning and thereby doing much good. But far more often, the mind is left undisciplined, uncontrolled; and when left to itself, it is exceptionally good at misguiding, deluding, and fooling its owner, causing much damage even when its original intent was good.

If you're reading this book, you are quite likely a human. Your ability to read these words and interpret their meaning is dependent upon a 3 pound (1.40 kg) organ located inside your skull: the human brain. Your brain contains 100% of your personality, your thoughts, your memories, your reason and your emotions. Yet, it accounts for only 2% of your body mass. The remaining 98% of your body mass is basically just a physical extension of the processes occurring in that brain. The vast majority of your body is merely a conveyance vehicle for your brain, to move it from one place to another. Your arms and hands allow your brain to alter and interact with its environment. Your other bodily systems (digestive, endocrine, nervous, etc.) nurture your brain and sustain it. The skull around your brain and the skin that surrounds your body are there to protect your brain from trauma and seal off your insides from the pathogens and environmental threats that would do damage to both your body and brain. And your reproductive system exists to improve your chances of passing on your brain genes to another generation of human whose skull will contain a remarkably similar brain.

Say that you were able to place multiple brains in a neat row. You have the brains of a brilliant scientist, an accountant, a mass murderer, a devoted charity worker, a religious terrorist, a popular singer and a sports icon. Their similarity in appearance is so complete that even a forensic pathologist who performs autopsies daily and handles brains routinely wouldn't be able to differentiate between them. Without any face attached to it, without any personality to even form a preliminary and biased opinion about it, you are forced to deal with the fact that every person's brain starts out with basically the same form and potential. Despite superficial differences in bodily appearance, all humans, at their core, are physically alike.

It would be an interesting perspective to imagine all humans as invisible with only their brains still remaining visible. As people go through their daily routines, two brains are seen getting close to one another but stop short as two people kiss; brains are seen bobbing up and down as they walk; multiple brains racing down the road at 50 miles an hour in a line and in opposite directions, ignoring the other brains in the queue and those that it passes; rotating this way and that as each individual takes care of their daily tasks. Yet, this scene, in essence, is what is happening to these brains under the veils of the heads and bodies that encase them.

When the genomes of all existing humans (and those of the past that have been teased out by forensic science) are compared, the similarities are staggering. A uniformity of form and functionality is found, all the more surprising when compared to the presumed "individuality" of each person. But despite the similarity between all people, humanity has come up with countless wholly arbitrary distinctions to use as a shorthand for separating one people from another: skin pigment, stature, "bloodlines," social hierarchy, politics, cultural beliefs, etc. These misleading distinctions are the result of a human brain which has long been described as a "pattern-seeking machine."

Yet, upon closer consideration from the viewpoint of genetics and/or with expanded knowledge, all of these arbitrary distinctions are wiped away in a flood of genetic similarity, much in the same way that the first cosmonauts/astronauts who viewed the Earth from space noted that the arbitrary distinctions and borders between nations and peoples were wiped away with consideration from the unique viewpoint of low Earth orbit; with the added benefit of their expanded knowledge, they were left with a different mindset, literally and figuratively a new worldview. Geneticists have remarked that comparing the genomes of any two people currently on Earth will show a similarity far closer than when comparing the genomes of any two chimpanzees occupying different areas of the same game preserve in Africa. From this more informed mindset, people are all much more alike than they are different, as is the "wiring" of their brains.

While the knowledge of the similarity of all human brains should lead to inclusivism and give humanity cause to acknowledge its common condition and, in time, may even help eradicate human prejudices against those who "differ", it should also give anyone pause when considering the equally ubiquitous imprecision of this convoluted, gelatinous hodgepodge of cells.

> **I used to think that my brain was the most wonderful organ in my body. Then I realized what was telling me this.**
> — Emo Philips (Comedian)

It is only too human to admire and even be in love with your own brain. After all, it's the only thing you have to rely upon to get you through every moment of every day. Every decision you make, every action you take, every thought that enters your head, every feeling or belief that you've ever had is created and governed by this organ. If you don't have faith in your own brain, if you don't trust your own mind, upon what resource can you fall back? Are you willing to let someone else do the thinking for you, to come up with your opinions and to make all of your decisions for you?

14

If their brain is so similar to yours, do you really feel that they are going to come up with any better choices than you?

So, your usual position is to expect that your brain will always invariably work well and that it will not let you down, that it will always be reliable. And if you've successfully navigated life for a few decades, perhaps even prospered, it seems reasonable to think that your brain has done a reasonably good job enabling this abundance. With your present fortune, what possible reason would you have for changing how you think?

Indeed, there have been instances in human history where whole societies have asked this same question. For 1500 years during the Middle Ages in Europe and the Middle East, much of scientific inquiry was not only discouraged but outright punished for supposedly defying a divine plan or going against the natural order. For at least 3,000 years, the Ancient Egyptians discouraged innovation in many scientific and technical pursuits simply because the regular and predictable flooding of the Nile gave them all the food that they needed to free up their time to create an impressive culture; they didn't want to upset the perceived pattern of annual gifts that the gods had provided for millennia for their relatively comfortable lives. There are innumerable examples of this kind of intellectual stagnation throughout human history. Therefore, in conservative terms, for 4000 years, humanity's medical/scientific/technological advancement slowed to a crawl.

Now consider the medical/scientific/technological advancements made in just the last 100 years, and their continuing rapidly accelerating rate of progress. Imagine how much further along humanity could already be having been given back those lost millennia, and you will have the answer to your question, "What possible reason would you have for changing how you think?"

Your opinion of the reliability of your brain will likely grow in strength as you get older; if by your 40s, 50s or 60s you've maintained an occupation, raised happy children, built a comfortable home and look to have the potential to live to a ripe old age with your family and friends venerating you, your faith in the quality of your brain is probably close to unshakable.

Ironically, the purpose of this book is <u>to shake your faith in your own mind as much as possible</u>. If that underlined sentence doesn't appeal to you, or even makes you vaguely uneasy, take heart, you're quite likely normal, just all too human. Hopefully though, by the end of this book, that uneasiness will have abated somewhat, and it will be joined by a new-found appreciation of what your mind is capable of---when adequately disciplined. Instead of working harder, you can work smarter. And, when practiced by humanity on a large scale, the positive impact on the world as a whole could be considerable.

However, the above-underlined sentence may elicit a different response in you such as, "No, there's nothing wrong with my thinking processes, my brain has served me quite nicely, thank you very much...this book obviously doesn't apply to me..." If this is the case, please <u>at the very least</u> look in the chapter (in the center of this book, p.101) that lists cognitive biases and logical fallacies (CBLFs) and read the entries "Backfire Effect," "Confirmation Bias" and "Dunning-Kruger Effect." If the definitions for those entries elicit even a vague feeling of personal recognition, then hopefully your interest will have been aroused to read further.

If you read those CBLF definitions and their meanings are lost on you, so be it. Still, perhaps you could spare a little space in your long-term memory for those terms and their definitions. You will quite likely recognize them in yourself later in life.

Why is it that, after seeing earlier species of hominins and *Homo sapiens,* that humanity feels like the current version finally possesses a brain that can be considered the "perfect reasoning machine"? This would presume that the brain that existed one million years ago was fairly close to perfection. Then, by the time humankind began writing down history only a few thousand years ago, the final piece of the jigsaw puzzle of the brain had finally fallen into place. So that now, you've got the final, complete, ultimate model. As if no more improvements were necessary, no more fine tuning needed, the current human brain is as good as it

16

will ever get, as good as it will ever <u>need</u> to get. An impressive organ capable of creating computers, spaceflight and modern medicine.

And yet, the current, most updated model of this organ can still be instantly fooled by as little as ten straight lines:

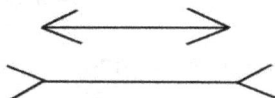

You can draw two parallel horizontal lines yourself, making certain that they are identical in length, and yet the moment that you add the arrowheads to one line and tails to the other line, your brain instantly makes a judgment...and an incorrect one at that: one horizontal line now appears shorter than the other. One part of your brain knows (in fact, it is absolutely <u>certain</u>) that the two horizontal lines are identical in length (after all, you just created them yourself); yet simultaneously, another part of your brain is telling you something that conflicts with your certainty. And it doesn't matter how long you look at it, hours, days, years. Part of your brain <u>won't learn</u>, even when another part of the same brain is pointing out where the first part is in error. What's more, it is quite likely that your brain will <u>never</u> learn!! Part of your brain continues to feed you incorrect information, constantly, and it probably will until your death. And yet, it is to this brain that is given the title of "the ultimate reasoning machine"? It can be very unsettling to realize that this example is only the tip of the iceberg when it comes to the ease with which your brain can be fooled. Even worse, <u>your brain is actually hard-wired to fool you, to continually feed you wrong information that on the surface, apparently seems correct</u>. This is an incredibly important point with which the reader must come to terms, and it will be returned to repeatedly in this book.

There are innumerable cases of amputees experiencing the sensation of a "phantom limb," i.e., sometimes, they still feel as if their amputated limb was still attached. Their brain's visual

17

center is telling them one thing (the limb is absent), while another part of the brain is telling them the opposite (the limb is present). These people aren't "crazy" or "delusional" or "ignorant" or "uneducated," they are simply slaves to their brain's hard-wiring, to what their brain is telling them is "true." It is all too simple and typical for the brain to be fooled as to what constitutes reality.

Now, imagine a more complicated scenario where many more areas of the brain are involved: You witness an accident, people are screaming, you are sent into a startled panic, and several people are hurt, including you. In the aftermath, the authorities are asking for eyewitness testimony from all those involved. When all eyewitness accounts are compared, there is surprising disagreement. You saw one Asian man collide with ten people (including yourself), while other victims (and also those not directly involved) noted it was one Latino man and two white women who collided with only seven people. These eyewitness account discrepancies are as common as the incidents that give rise to them, yet how are differing accounts possible? There can only be one truth, one utterly factual account. How can different people involved in the same incident produce different firsthand experiences? The answer is, because of each individual's built-in biases, and because of how adrenaline and other biological chemicals coursing through different bodies stimulate and alter different brains in different ways.

Think of your politics; you may belong to a family where every member is exposed to exactly the same news about what is happening in your country, yet different members of the same family have differing politics, different stances on the issues, different feelings about party members and their actions, but how? If the family members are all receiving substantially the same information, how can there be more than one opinion, more than one stance, more than one reality? Each person is convinced that they are the one that is correct; the others must be confused, less educated/intelligent, or perhaps they have their own agenda from which they may somehow profit by maintaining their own interpretation, or they may be outright deluded. Who can know which is the case? The short answer is, one cannot.

18

All one can do is put their beliefs under the withering glare of critical thinking (CT), to strip away as many biases and fallacies as possible and see with what one is left. Only at this point can constructive and meaningful dialogue occur between those of differing views. Until then, the discussion is very likely to be bogged down with the biases/fallacies of all parties involved.

If the human brain is such a wonder of nature, such a culmination of evolution, does it make sense that babies need so much protection and nurturing and children so much guidance and education before they can attain "an age of reason"? Does it make sense that adolescents seem to have to go through such a protracted phase of irrationality, questionable judgment or just "craziness"? Does it make sense that the prefrontal lobe of your brain (that is involved in higher reasoning) only seems to achieve "full development" by as late as 25 years of age? This could be years after earlier poor judgment resulted in significant negative circumstances for the individual. Does it make sense that so many human brains seem afflicted with different versions and levels of mental illness, anything from temporary sub-clinical depression to sociopathy and even psychopathy? How can someone who has had a brain injury suddenly have their personality fundamentally changed, to the extent that they are no longer even considered by their family and friends to be "the same person"?

Think of how susceptible the human brain is to something as normal as hormones (over long periods) and to something as natural as adrenaline, neurotransmitters and other chemicals (over short periods). How can a person be so angered by the words or actions of another that it impels them to physical violence? It's as if their brain translated its emotions into the actions of its subservient limbs and thus, into the resulting crimes.

When you consider those who oppose your views and beliefs, you may think, "The opposition must be idiots!! Are they really that stupid, that ignorant or that uneducated? Maybe they are suffering from a mass delusion, or are they all just crazy?"

But if the "opposition" number in the thousands or millions, does it seem reasonable to think that such a large subset of humanity actually possesses a substantially lower I.Q. than you? Or appreciably less education? Or that these millions all suffer from some form of mental illness en masse? How can so many people possessing the same incredible thinking machine as you suffer from mass delusion?

It's far easier to use this knee-jerk response, this kind of mental shortcut in response to undesirable views and leave it at that. After all, what's your alternative? You might have to admit that these millions of people weren't less intelligent, weren't less educated, or weren't suffering from mental instability or mass delusion. You might even come to the startling conclusion that the opposition came to their different beliefs and opinions using a very similar reasoning process to your own! This can be a monumental realization.

Ask fifty people, each from one of a dozen different cultures about 100 various issues that affect humankind. What are the odds that any two of them will have exactly the same 100 answers? Even if they were to agree on 75% of the answers (or even 99%), there is still that small percentage of answers that differ somewhat...but how can that be? Isn't there one truth that applies to all? How can each person have their own "version of truth," i.e., "what is true for them?" But it is this last phrase that demonstrates that they have fallen into solipsism, in which one's self is considered the ultimate or sole source and sum of all reality. Solipsism is often demonstrated with the question, "Am I the only person who actually exists and all others are simply illusions?" or "am I just a brain in a vat?" The likelihood is that you aren't the only person who exists and the world isn't just a simulation to see how you'll react. It's healthier to presume that you are only one person who has to share a world with billions of your kind, and that everyone needs to learn how to live with one another.

Considering those fifty people, the combinations of their 100 answers will likely be all over the map; coming from such varied backgrounds, with such varying influences and experiences, how could they all _not_ come up with different answers? Yet each is convinced that their answers are right and that anyone who disagrees with them is wrong. How can there be so many different realities? How can humanity ever hope to reach a consensus on any issue? On what commonality between all of these different people is to be the basis of reality, of truth? There is only one thing common to every single one of these people. Regardless of where these people live, where and how they were raised, what their experiences and education have been, they all possess a remarkably similar human brain. And the study of the thinking processes of how that organ comes to its beliefs, opinions and conclusions is where any hope for a speedy consensus of any kind must begin.

If humanity currently possesses the most advanced/evolved/ complex higher-reasoning brain with no need for improvement, why does almost every sizable country on the planet still have armed forces? Why would anyone worry that the inhabitants of another country were capable of attacking/invading their country if everyone possesses the same magnificent reasoning brain? Can't the politicians of the countries involved use their magnificent brains to come to some non-violent agreement? Shouldn't human reason be the final arbiter in trying to solve the admittedly complicated issues of international relations? Or is it that when the limits of human brain's ability to reason are reached, the brains involved on both sides switch to a more primitive level of brain activity that compels them to obtain the desired goal by force?

Think how common it is for the human brain to become deviated, distorted from the "norm": how often in your society do you hear of bogus science, alternative medicine, mass hysteria, ridiculous ideological movements, laws being broken, people maltreated, outright atrocities being committed? How often do you see people abusing inanimate objects---a machine stops working, and in their frustration, they begin to hit it as "punishment," as if the object possessed a form of agency and "consciously" did something wrong?

How often do you hear about people who committed some crime and said, "I was out of control...I wasn't thinking properly...I don't know why I did it...but I'm o.k. now, you don't have to worry about me anymore"? In fact, In many societies, the sentence and punishment of a crime can be modified depending on what mental state the perpetrator was deemed to be in when the crime was committed. If their victim was killed, the punishment wouldn't be meted out until it was determined 1) if the crime was pre-meditated (sometimes described as being committed "in cold blood"), 2) if the crime was merely a "crime of passion" (i.e., committed "in hot blood"), 3) if the crime was a crime of negligence (i.e., the perpetrator "wasn't thinking at all"), or perhaps 4) the crime was a result of "temporary insanity".

So the judge and jury are met with a choice of rather unwelcome thoughts about the human brain in general: 1) that a supposedly "advanced" higher reasoning brain is capable of ignoring laws of civilized society in favor of some warped personal gratification, 2) that a supposedly "advanced" higher reasoning brain can no longer be held fully responsible for its actions because the lower level, more "primitive" brain lurking underneath the "advanced" higher reasoning brain overcame the latter (but only temporarily of course), 3) that a supposedly "advanced higher reasoning brain was simply left on some inattentive "standby" mode while harm came to their victim, or 4) that the crime was committed during a mental interlude of "temporary insanity". In each of these cases, the "advanced" higher reasoning brain is abandoned or simply not brought to bear.

And consider how ironic that the laws involved were decided upon with the recognition, the outright admission that, yes, each person has it within themselves to be powerless to keep their passion from overriding their reason. Or that anyone can become "temporarily insane," and then somehow switch their brain back into sanity, or even "higher reasoning mode."

Consider an orderly crowd of people listening to a speaker who can incite them to violence with nothing more than rhetoric; in moments, a calm, docile orderly audience is transformed into an unruly mob, possibly becoming violent and destructive. And

22

then, after some time-frame, the madness seemingly evaporates, and the masses are somehow magically restored to calm, docile "order" once again. Perhaps you have been one of those whipped into a frenzy. How did you feel about the ease with which your brain had been influenced and manipulated, your actions virtually dictated by another as if you were a mere marionette on strings?

There has been an increase in the documentation of incidents of "road rage" where one moment, a seemingly normal, law-abiding, responsible driver is transformed into someone capable of threatening, violent, and even homicidal actions. Perhaps you have been incited to "vengeance" by intentionally cutting off someone in traffic because of a perceived slight of them against you. Would you have done such a thing if instead of driving, you had been walking and the other walker cut you off on a sidewalk? Is there something about the safety and particularly, the anonymity afforded by being surrounded by metal in a car? An anonymity that frees you from "normal behavior" to seek retribution and absolves your identity of your questionable behavior? One moment you're a calm, responsible, "normal" person, the next you perceive a "threat" to your personal space, and now an intimidating response on your part is warranted and justified. Always lurking underneath your facade of rationality is a dormant, lower-level, emotional reflex response created by your hard-wired brain.

Once harm has been caused by these underlying violent tendencies, and blood has been spilled, it is the rare individual indeed who can resist the typical response of vengeance (even when it is somehow deemed "justifiable" by society) and stop the cycle of violence in its tracks. It is so much easier (and sometimes even "expected" by society) to give in to the more typical pattern of revenge. This desire for vengeance, being a more base and primal emotion (like fear), is closer to the default setting of the brain. It takes far more mental effort and energy by the individual to supersede this baseline setting, to take the higher road and forgo revenge and instead seek to avoid or improve the conditions that lead to the initial transgression. It is far more natural and therefore more common for the individual to give in to the limitations of their brain.

But even if one discovers these limitations of their own brain, one does not have to be despondent about them, but the first step is to recognize them and be <u>aware</u> of them. Most people don't become despondent when they learn that the limitations of their legs make it impossible for them to outrun a car on the freeway; they just acknowledge this fact, and their awareness helps them avoid scenarios where harm could come to pass. In the same way, once the individual becomes aware of the limitations of their brain, they can avoid the situations where its limitations might cause harm.

Consider any totalitarian regime that has massacred thousands, millions perhaps, but is one day finally stopped. While its leadership may rightfully be brought to justice, many of the devout followers are somehow assimilated back into the "benign" society of the victims, and the society goes on. Did the followers suddenly turn from evil to benign? Or did the brains of the devout simply shift from following one set of patterns that seemed acceptable at the time to another set of patterns that seem acceptable now? Throughout all societies in history, there have always been these dominant ideologies that were basically deviations from the "norm." History repeats itself because the wiring of human brains and their resulting biases and fallacies repeat themselves.

> **Those who don't learn from history are doomed to repeat it.**
> —Edmund Burke (d. 1797 author, orator, political theorist, philosopher and statesman; George Santayana (d. 1952 philosopher, essayist, poet, and novelist) and others

Why do those who cheat people in politics or business or other endeavors think they'll get away with it? Read the news on any given day: these people get caught. You hear their victims say something to the effect, "We never thought that they were capable of this." And yet this has been happening throughout human history, for millennia. Why does the pattern keep repeating over and over? Partly, because the human brain is the same throughout history. And the human brain is very good at fooling its owner into thinking that they can get away with it, while at the same time the victims' brains keep them from thinking that it could ever happen.

The brain has evolved to become a <u>pattern-seeking machine</u>. As a result of the intricate connections between its various neurons and supporting cells, the human brain has the highest ability of all animals to assimilate the information fed into it from both the external world and from its own inner world. For this organ to begin the arduous process of reasoning and higher level thinking, it typically must start with some pattern that it detects within the incoming data. This pattern could be from any one of millions of possibilities; e.g. noticing over a period of time that the sky becomes brighter, and then after even more hours, the sky darkens; e.g. noticing a vibration that wasn't there a moment ago; e.g. noticing that after electing a political candidate, the economy gets worse; e.g. noticing a feeling of euphoria when viewing a beautiful vista.

But if a human brain senses a pattern, does it necessarily mean that the pattern is real or relevant? Once the brain has detected the sky brightening every day for several decades and that the bright disc that illuminates the sky always seems to travel from one side of the sky to the other, that brain may make a leap in logic that the bright disc is circling the planet. The pattern is detected, the inference is made, it seems reasonable and agrees with reality, yet the conclusion is still wrong. However, because that same brain has identified patterns before and it has made correct inferences about those patterns and been rewarded for it with positive consequences, that brain can still be fooled by future patterns. Because the hits outnumber the misses, the initial conclusion of the pattern-seeking is thereby automatically given the benefit of the doubt. These initial (and incorrect) conclusions can be extremely difficult to overcome.

While the structure of the human brain seems complex, its complexity seems to go hand in hand with the potential for poor thought processes. It is common for someone to sense some of the aforementioned distorted conclusions in another human's thinking. But because the distortions are enveloped in a recognizably human face, it seems reasonable to feel that one is still dealing with someone similar enough to one's self, simply based on their superficial appearance.

Yet, every single one of the infamous characters of history has had a human face. Perhaps earlier in their lives, their brains could operate much like the average moral person. But later, even if their face hadn't changed that much, their brain detected some "pattern" that seemed to make sense and the result was that the brain's thinking became deviated. That person later became capable of committing the heinous acts that led to their infamy. Ironically, as they were committing their crimes, their brain may very well have been convincing them that their behavior was acceptable, expected, mandated or sometimes divinely ordained. The "bad guy" rarely thinks of himself as a "bad guy." They tend to think that they are the "normal" one (or even the superior one) and that its the other people who haven't yet discovered the truth of the "bad guy's" line of thinking or "reality." The human brain is very good at convincing its host that it is always operating normally and rationally.

All of this is not to say that pattern-seeking is always a bad thing. It is this penchant for pattern-seeking that has enabled scientific researchers to identify different phenomena in nature through the scientific method. In most cases, engineers look for patterns that suggest ways to solve a problem. Even those in business, politics and sociology successfully use pattern-seeking to accomplish positive outcomes. Where things begin to deteriorate is the typical cognition of the average person in the day-to-day world. Once the average human has identified a supposed "pattern," the brain responds by attempting to explain that pattern with a hypothesis which is essentially made up on the spot, and more likely than not, the product of wishful thinking.

It is a human tendency to look on the peoples of other cultures and countries and feel that these cultures instill in their members a predilection for unreasonable behavior and sometimes violence. But consider: Germans are no more likely to be

26

inhuman than any other peoples just because of past Nazi atrocities. Russians are no more likely to be heartless than any other peoples because of previous Stalinist pogroms. Americans have no inborn tendency towards inhumanity because of the past slaughter, subjugation of and cruelty towards Native Americans. Nor the Japanese for their villainy during World War Two. Nor Ancient Romans toward the peoples they conquered or the Hebrews for butchering the Amalekites down to the last infant and pregnant mother. In each case, the leaders thought that they were doing the "right" thing. Their brains had detected a pattern where their ideology made sense. And very quickly, they amassed a following that either detected the same pattern, or trusted the leader of the ideology or at least decided that if they didn't necessarily agree with the ideology, they'd be better off following the ideology rather than be eliminated in its wake. But, in each case, when the ideology was at an end, and the atrocities ceased, did its previous followers simply become "normal" again?

There have been sociological experiments where two groups of "normal" people are arbitrarily separated into a group of "prisoners" and a group of "guards." Most tellingly, it didn't take long during this play-acting for the "guards" to begin abusing the "prisoners," without any suggestion or prompting to do so, as well as for the "prisoners" to feel like the abuse was "expected" or "normal." For no other reason than that a spontaneous, wholly arbitrary distinction was made between two groups, the brains involved settled on a pre-designated pattern of "acceptable" behavior. It's as if, lurking somewhere underneath a facade of "civilization" and "rationality," in any human brain, there is an undercurrent of subjugation, a potential for abuse and cruelty, just waiting to hatch out. And all that it needs to appear is the brain's recognition of some pattern to follow. If someone doesn't look like you or think like you, they are now labeled by your brain as part of the "out" group while the rest are part of the "in group."

The enemy is closer when you think.

Ask yourself: When you find yourself in an argument with someone, which of the following is closer to your initial mindset:

> A) "I know my opinion is right, and I've got to do everything I can to bolster my opinion, save face and get this other person to agree with the truth of my position."
>
> or
>
> B) "I can never be absolutely sure that my opinion is right, I need others to challenge me, and I need to challenge myself, and I will genuinely welcome being proven wrong if it will get me closer to the truth."

Your choice of A) or B) will shed considerable light on whether you genuinely seek truth or you merely want to remain comfortably complacent in your present way of thinking.

In future, you are likely to hear the names of various cognitive biases and logical fallacies (CBLFs) and other critical thinking (CT) terms more frequently as the discipline of CT is embraced by more and more people. These people are tired of the same debates being rehashed ad nauseum with no consensus, no reevaluation of positions, no real progress being made. Hopefully, you too yearn to throw off the shackles of your mind and unleash the staggering power and potential of your human brain. If you have the integrity to actively examine and test your own brain, you will be welcomed by others of true intellectual integrity with open arms....and open minds.

A percentage of the proceeds from the sales of this book will be donated to charities involved with spreading reason, logic, science and critical thinking as the necessary foundation for continued human existence.

Throughout this book, when not included in an author's quote, the term "god" is not referring to any specific monotheistic deity, but rather the specific god imagined by an individual. Since the concept of god tends to differ in details from person to person, the term "god" is a general one and written in lower case.

The quotes in the book are followed by the name of the person to whom it is most often attributed, or if the source is unknown, "anonymous" is used or the place for a name is left blank.

ACKNOWLEDGMENTS

If I have seen farther, it's because I have stood on the shoulders of giants.

—Isaac Newton (d. 1726/7 Co-creator of calculus, Astronomer, physicist, leader of the Scientific Revolution)

While this book contains original thought, no author exists in isolation. Each is educated, influenced and yes, biased by the information and ideas with which he/she has been exposed throughout their lifetime.

A full list of critical thinkers that have influenced this work and deserve mention in a tome like this would take another volume. Many of them are quoted throughout this work. In the interest of space, here is an especially abbreviated list (in no particular order) of the most immediately influential ideators:

Lucretius, Democritus, Epicurus, Socrates, Galileo, Bertrund Russell, Matt Dillahunty, Aaron Ra, David Silverman, Christopher Hitchens, Dan Barker, Neil Degrasse Tyson, Richard Dawkins, Daniel Dennett, Sam Harris, Mary Eisenmann, Catherine Noble, Ross Miller, Jessica Noble, Mighty Drake Christensen, Steven Pinker, George Bittner, Todd Krause, Lawrence Krauss, Peter Singer, Michael Shermer, PZ Myers, James Randi, Greta Christina, Victor Stenger, Jerry Coyne, Noam Chomsky, Richard Carrier, Michel Onfray, Peter Bhoghossian, Paul Kurtz, AC Grayling, Steven Weinberg, and Michael Martin.

For those who don't find themselves listed, may they find solace in the fact that it is the idea and not the person that is ultimately relevant.

PART I

THOUGHT EXPERIMENT

Imagine if, through advanced technology, one person can address all 7 billion humans on Earth simultaneously:

"Each of you has a choice to make...

1) You may emphatically hold a belief that you already have the answer of how and why you're on this planet and what your purpose is in life, and that after your Earthly form dies, you will be reborn in paradise and thereafter exist forever after in peace, love and happiness.

or

2) You may spend your entire life endlessly seeking to learn everything that you can, questioning your every belief with no guarantee that you will ever get to a point where you can be certain of any truth, always struggling to figure out your purpose in life. And then, when you die, you will be gone forever, never to exist again. You will, however, have the satisfaction of knowing that while alive, you tried to make as much of a positive difference in your world as possible. And that you were always striving for fact and truth, and that you were willing to accept any reality that you found, even when that the truth caused you to feel discord, disappointment, or even outright misery."

It is quite apparent which of the two choices above the vast majority of humans throughout history have chosen. But does the popularity of their choice make it a reasonable position?

HUMANS TEND TO BELIEVE TWO THINGS:

1) WHAT THEY WANT TO BELIEVE
2) WHAT THEY NEED TO BELIEVE

It seems sensible to assume that that which gives peace, love and happiness must automatically be moral, correct or true. After all, peace, love and happiness are what most humans long for and actively seek, no matter what method that they use to attain them.

Regardless of the likelihood that the following scenario will ever occur, imagining it via a thought experiment may prove illuminating.

In the last 100 years, humanity's rate of technological and sociological progress has increased faster than all of the millennia before it, almost exclusively due to the endeavors of science, logic, reason and CT. Advances in agriculture that feed an ever-increasing population; advances in medicine that extend life expectancy and perhaps, more importantly, quality of life; advances in science that inform humanity of its place in the universe with increasing clarity; advances in technology that have given humans reliable transportation (cars, jets, shipping), computer technology, and instantaneous communication with anyone else, regardless of their location. Ever larger numbers of people are being treated equally, regardless of skin color, ethnicity, culture, sexual orientation and gender identification.

During the history of man, there have been centuries, even millennia of technological, medical, scientific and sociological stagnation when CT, reason, logic and science were not only discouraged but actively dissuaded, attacked or punished. Considering the ever-accelerating progress of just the last 100 years, if human advancement during those millennia had grown at the same rate, how much further along could human civilization already be? If every single human on this planet actively practiced CT when making important decisions and creating their stances on contentious issues, then CBLFs would largely be erased and the major impediments to human progress, which have existed since the beginning of humanity, could fall away. The rate of human development would increase geometrically. It staggers the imagination.

If every person put aside their wishes and desires of what they wanted to be true, and instead accepted as many proven things as possible and discounted as many unproven things as possible, progress would accelerate faster and faster. All of humanity, as well as the planet and all of its living inhabitants, would benefit.

Imagine a scene in the future when someone speaks at a press conference, and every person reporting, indeed, every viewer listening, can spot every cognitive bias and logical fallacy used by the speaker. They hear something recognizable and think to themselves, "You didn't just employ that tired old fallacy, did you? We learned these biases/fallacies throughout grade school, secondary school and college! You didn't really think that we wouldn't notice, did you?" Listeners could speak up during the question/answer phase of the conference, "Excuse me, but when you said 'such-and-such,' it was quite evident that you were employing the 'straw man' argument of your opposition's stance.

34

Would you like another opportunity to respond to a more accurate portrayal of their position?"

It would also be most illuminating if, during the conference, a judge controlled a large display behind the participants listing each of the speaker's CBLFs so that those who hadn't caught all of them could benefit from this measurement of the speaker's reasoning ability and integrity. Perhaps, a "referee" would call "penalties" on participants when they broke a rule of critical thinking: "Participant A committed the 'communal reinforcement' bias penalty: she will sit out of the discussion for 10 minutes so that the others may continue the conversation constructively." Once a participant committed a certain number of penalties, judges would permanently eject them so that only those who followed the rules of mature discussion would remain. Participants would quickly realize that the only way for them to stay relevant and integral to a discussion would be to employ CT.

Another frequent tactic speakers employ when confronted with a challenge from someone who recognizes their questionable rhetoric is to change the subject quickly. They may voice it with a convincing inflection as if they are responding to the challenge, but instead go on to some other non-related, less contentious aspect of their agenda. The speaker depends on the likelihood that other questioners would like a turn with their own questions. So if the speaker diverts to another questioner (who isn't likely to follow-up on their colleague's challenge but more likely to favor asking their own question), the speaker may just well dodge the original challenge while also looking "fair," by giving other questioners a chance.

But if all present could work together in a kind of non-voiced solidarity, to hold the speaker accountable for all of the weaknesses of their rhetoric and get to the truth of the matter, speakers would quickly learn that by continuing to employ these deceptive tactics, they would be commanding a sinking ship. The only "ships" that were eventually left (i.e., well-reasoned, critically thought out arguments) could work towards progress.

After several of these press conferences, speakers would realize that anyone in their audience could see through their weak arguments and their attempts at deception and they would have no choice but to give up their tactics and present something much closer to reality. After several months, far less time would be wasted by speakers spouting untruths, half-truths, distortions, distractions or by using other standard tricks with which their audiences were now well aware. Think of the time saved and the speed of progress made. Think of the relative ease of holding speakers accountable by preparing their audience with the knowledge of these CBLFs.

Here again is another positive example of pattern-recognition. If children learn CBLFs from an early age and all throughout their education (continually reinforcing this specific knowledge base) then any student, and eventually any person could recognize the pattern of these fallacies/biases whenever confronted by them with the same ease as they recognize common grammar errors and errors in math. "You shouldn't employ a double negative in grammar," "Sorry, 2+2 does not equal 5", "You shouldn't let your confirmation bias influence your stance on immigration."

Beyond press conferences, anyone could recognize these CBLFs in any conversation with any other human at any time, or while reading any book or magazine or website. It would be as natural as drawing breath for any person to employ CT whether informally, with a friend or family member, or formally when the stakes were possibly higher, like deciding if a political candidate maintained integrity while relaying information and making arguments, rather than merely trying to convince their audience, mislead them or simply tell them what they always want to hear.

36

A great irony is that sometimes, even the speaker doesn't realize that their speech is erroneous or misleading. There is always the possibility that they have merely misled themselves (or been misled) or have been so comfortable hearing a familiar (though erroneous) pattern, that they feel comfortable repeating it. They haven't employed CT to check their own story and their own thinking process. Or perhaps in order to be elected or remain in power, they merely repeat the pattern that they know their audiences want to believe or need to believe.

It's a common occurrence because the human brain has always been common to all. *Homo sapiens sapiens* is just "the latest model" of a long line of primate brains. Humanity's arguably "higher-reasoning" brain has evolved directly on top of a more primitive primate brain, which evolved on top of a more primitive mammalian brain, on top of a more primitive reptilian brain, etc. While modern humans have the advantage of calling upon this "higher-reasoning brain" when desired, they don't necessarily avail themselves of the opportunity all of the time. The default position of the brain is not the higher-reasoning mode. The more primitive areas of the brain, working with their comfortably familiar patterns, are still the foundation of many of the individual's thoughts and actions.

The sooner people realize and accept that humanity is merely another primate species (albeit an arguably more intelligent one) and that there is still plenty of potential for improvement in their reasoning centers, the sooner people can work to advance human society in spite of the brain's limitations. And when all of the effort and energy that is currently put into attempts to rationalize an individual's beliefs is instead channeled into critical thought processes such as skepticism, reason, logic and science, all of the planet will benefit.

CRITICAL THINKING

While this book does deal primarily with the <u>need</u> for critical thinking (CT) in everyday life, it is not a formal course in CT. There are many excellent websites and even entire courses available online (many that are free) that can help you acquire that "skill set." However, a formal curriculum in CT isn't even necessary to begin the practice of CT. Thus the following distinction:

> **Critical Thinking consists of 1) a skill set, and 2) an attitude.**
> —Peter Bhogohossian (Philosophy Professor, Writer, CT Researcher)

Formal courses in CT teach the skill set. It is the latter attribute, the attitude which, in the long run, is far more important. This book takes the position that the first person that you have to watch for non-critical thinking is yourself. You must come to terms with the fact that your brain is likely fooling you at any given moment about any given topic. You must hold your thinking to the highest accountability possible before you can begin to hold others accountable for theirs. And if your highest goal is to come to truth, your critical, skeptical attitude must also contain a <u>genuine desire to be proven wrong</u>, when you are, in fact, wrong. This specific desire is the fastest way to make progress in any cognitive endeavor. You must begin your pursuit of truth prepared to cast away your long-held comforting beliefs, your dear, deeply-loved "truths" of a lifetime, even when they have brought you much contentment, joy, success and fulfillment; if your beliefs are eventually shown to be unjustifiable or proven wrong, you <u>must</u> discard them. If you don't, you are no longer operating with intellectual integrity.

The benefit of this attitude is that, in a given area where your beliefs have been proven wrong, your intellectual progress will no longer be slowed by following blind alleys nor by being bogged down or distracted by any related inaccuracies. Your attention can be focused solely on valid arguments, reasoning, logic as well as the benefits of the scientific method. If you can honestly get to that position, the attitude that truth is the ultimate goal, regardless of where it leaves your former opinion, the rest is just details. Still, for most humans, getting to that mindset is a massive paradigm shift. It's just not the way most people have operated throughout their lifetimes. They've used mental shortcuts for most of their lives and after having attained some success through them, they feel validated in continuing to use them. At some point, they may begin to think their thinking process is nearly infallible. Or at the very least, their default position is to always give their initial conclusions the benefit of the doubt; and they are likely to keep to that initial position until someone proves them wrong (although sometimes they'll hold their position even after having been proven wrong).

There are even particular vocations whose practitioners are well aware that most humans operate with mental shortcuts. These practitioners are so aware of the blind spots in cognition possessed by each human that they can base their livelihood on it; they are the marketers, the politicians, the magicians, astrologers, fakirs, and palm-readers (not to mention those that are combinations of these). These are the students of the human condition that know the buttons to push that will have a significant percentage of their audience fooled by their presentation. And when their performance is over, these showmen may think to themselves how pathetically easy it was to lead the sheep to the slaughter.

**You can sway a thousand men by appealing to
their prejudices quicker than you can convince
one man by logic.**
—Robert A. Heinlein (d. 1988 Dean of Science
Fiction Writers)

Magicians know how to misdirect the attention of their audience:
"Look over <u>here</u> so that you don't see what I'm doing <u>there</u>...."
and a miracle seems to occur. When the magician fools your
brain, they entertain you. And when you applaud the magician
you are in essence saying, "Please, exploit more of my brain's
blind spots and my faulty interpretation of reality!"

The marketer knows to avoid focusing on the negatives of their
product while dwelling on those aspects that she knows you will
like. And once their company gives you what your biases wanted
in the first place, you get a twinge of positive feedback in your
brain, and you're more likely to buy more of that product or
service offered by that company. The astrologer/palm-
reader/faith-healer knows that you <u>want</u> to experience something
unusual, inexplicable, transcendental or paranormal, so they're
going to give you the experience that you already want or
expect--- the definition of a ready audience. While the results of
these performances may seem harmless or have no lasting
effect, you should at least recognize them as everyday examples
of your brain fooling itself (and in some cases, of your brain
<u>wanting</u> to fool itself).

When it comes to a debater using these tactics though, they may
lead to real lasting harm. After listening to a debate, you are
likely to agree more with one side than the other and thereafter
act in response to your consensus. But if the team that you
agreed with based the attractiveness of their arguments on
CBLFs, again, they have gotten you to agree with them based on

40

nothing more than the errors and biases of your own brain. And this is an example of when real harm can happen: if you are using weak reasoning skills in one facet of your life, you're very likely using them in many areas of your life.

If you did no more than read through the list of CBLFs included in the center of this volume (p. 101) and familiarized yourself with their definitions and examples, you could make much progress in CT even without a formal course in it. You would at least be prepared to recognize in your own thinking process these biases/fallacies and after practice, identify them in every other human being to which you listen or interact. And of course, maintaining the proper attitude is all-important: The epitome of CT is to reach the point where you genuinely look forward to being proven wrong, or to proving yourself wrong, to accelerate the progress and accuracy of your perception of the world.

But always keep in mind: the goal of CT isn't necessarily to lead you to discover ultimate truths. That is a process that may take a lifetime, and there is still no guarantee that you will ultimately find any truths. While that may sound discouraging, it by no means implies that CT is a waste of time; discounting the biases/fallacies in your own thinking will streamline any process of discovery, and you will simultaneously decrease the chance of being misled in any cognitive area. A formal course in CT (while not necessary) can accelerate the process even faster. In addition to a memorized list of biases and fallacies, you can add a detached, healthy skepticism as the initial reaction to ALL claims (whether they be natural, supernatural, scientific, paranormal, metaphysical, faith-based, etc.). And it will be much more difficult to be fooled or misled, by anyone else, let alone your own brain.

As can be seen by the collection of irrational nonsense (p. 174), the human capacity to sense false patterns in the world and subsequently to invent phenomena in an attempt to explain these patterns has been limitless for time immemorial. Because there are thousands if not millions of these topics that have been created by the human mind, it is far too overwhelming and impractical to investigate each one of them to conclude whether each one is of worthy of acceptance.

This human propensity for creating irrational ideologies and phenomena is one vast area where CT can show it's usefulness. By approaching each "fact," each "truth," each "ideology" and each "phenomenon" with the same skepticism, it is a simple process to discard the topics that show no evidence. When you begin this process of inquiry with the presumption that you're are as easy to fool as anyone else (and that your brain is likely fooling you at any moment), it is much easier to be on your guard and to insist on the rigor and personal integrity afforded by the CT process.

While there is no ultimate list of CT questions, just to give the reader an example, the following is a very generic list of critical thinking questions to apply to almost any area of human inquiry, utilizing the question categories of "Who?", "What?", "Where?", When?", "Why?" and "How?":

Who:...will this benefit?...could this harm?...is most directly affected?...would be the best person to consult?...will be the most salient people involved in this?...deserves recognition for this?

What:...are the strengths and weaknesses of this proposal?...could be another way to look at this? ...might be another alternative?...might be a counter-argument?...might be the best/worse case outcome scenario?...might be some confusing tangents to avoid?

Where:..does this occur in the actual world?...is there the most need for this idea?...could this idea become a problem?...can we research this more?...do we go for help with this?..are potential areas of improvement with this proposal?

When:....is this proposal acceptable or unacceptable?...will we know if the proposal has been proven as valid or invalid?...would this proposal benefit our society?...would this proposal cause a problem?...would be the best time to take action (if any) on this proposal?...will it be known that action on the proposal has succeeded?...has this proposal caused advantage/disadvantage in our history?...can we expect another implementation of the proposal to cause the same advantages or disadvantages?

Why:...would this be a problem/challenge?...how relevant is it to me/others?...are people influenced by this?...should people be informed about this?...has this situation come about?...is there a genuine need for this today?

How:....does this change or disrupt things?...do we know the entire truth about this?...do we know that we have adequate information to make a decision about this proposal?...can we approach this

possibility safely?...does this benefit
us/others?...does this harm us/others?

Each category of questions above is hardly exhaustive, and not every inquiry listed above necessarily applies to every area of investigation. But the benefit of asking so many questions about any topic helps overcome the limitations of an individual's imagination and experience. Again, few people are formally taught in school or by their parents to memorize a handy list of every question necessary to ask in a given situation. It is wiser to presume that every human has their biases and that it's critical to accumulate as much data and evidence as possible (especially when it seems to argue against your point), and to be prepared for (and eventually look forward to) being proved wrong.

Most humans like being able to cling to a "truth" or "truths" as they live out their lives. As they grow and mature, increasing the level of their experience and hopefully their wisdom, they naturally like to encapsulate this hard-won knowledge in the truths that they hold dear. The following is one possible representation of the stages of truth-seeking that the individual may progress through with the aid of CT:

STAGES OF TRUTH-SEEKING

I. I'M ALWAYS RIGHT, THOSE WHO DISAGREE ARE ALWAYS WRONG

II. I'M USUALLY RIGHT, THOSE WHO DISAGREE ARE USUALLY WRONG

III. I COULD BE WRONG, BUT IN THIS INSTANCE, I'M RIGHT AND THOSE WHO DISAGREE ARE WRONG

IV. I'M SOMETIMES WRONG, BUT I'M LOATHE TO ADMIT IT

V. I'M SOMETIMES WRONG, BUT I'M MATURE ENOUGH TO ADMIT IT

VI. I'M FINE WITH BEING WRONG BECAUSE IT INCREASES THE ACCURACY OF MY MODEL OF THE UNIVERSE.

VII. I WANT TO ACTIVELY SEEK OUT WHERE I AM WRONG, TO INCREASE THE ACCURACY OF MY MODEL OF THE UNIVERSE!

If you prove me right, I have learned nothing. But if you prove me wrong, I will have learned something.
—Socrates (d.399 BCE Philosopher)

So many discussions and debates get bogged down or side-tracked by CBLFs, participants on both sides of the debate simply don't notice them. It isn't unusual for a debater to recognize one of their opponent's biases or fallacies, but it is rare indeed for an individual to begin creating their own arguments only after extended self-examination. It is the contention of this book that the best use of CT should be that each person should start by being critical of their <u>own</u> thinking, their own thought processes, long before the debate starts. Think how rare it is for a debater to back down from their position just because their opponent pointed out the original debater's fallacies/biases. If the debater won't back down from their position when their reasoning is demonstrated to be wrong, does anything change? Is any progress made? Sadly, if the successful debater thinks he has his challenger on the ropes, there would be minimal incentive to alter his <u>own</u> thinking. The losing debater isn't likely to change their own thinking because they want to save face. However, before the debate even began, if both individuals were to run their <u>own</u> opinions through the filter of CT, recognizing their <u>own</u> biases/fallacies, much time would be saved and any remaining points that survived this self-evaluation might lead to a constructive debate.

To have as much intellectual integrity as possible, one should desire to accept as many true things as they can and deny as many false things as they can. Progress in any endeavor is thereby made more likely, and regress less likely.

Whenever an ideological demagogue was asked to give an invocation or a speech in consolation or explanation after some calamity (natural disaster, war, terrorist attack), it would be even more productive if a teacher of CT were to speak afterward. They could point out, yet again, the need to avoid employing CBLFs as explanations of events and the importance of using the best possible cogitations to find truth.

46

CERTAINTY

Uncertainty is an uncomfortable position. But certainty is an absurd one.
—Voltaire (d.1778 Writer, Historian, and Philosopher)

It might seem obvious that feeling certain about one's beliefs would be the most comfortable and desirable position. Would you feel better going through life always being able to state, "I am already certain that I am right about this" rather than saying, "I'm not sure what my stance should be on this issue, I see valid points on both sides? There is no black and white position here; there is instead a vast area of gray?" There are those who would admonish this latter position, proclaiming, "Why are you so indecisive? Quit equivocating and take a stand, take a solid position on this issue and remain resolute and adamant!"

They may feel that appearing resolute shows more strength, that this supposed certainty lends more weight, more validity to their position. That the more certain they are of their position, the truer that it must be. But do they really think that being unmovable on a position is the way to solve an issue? This inflexible position is the essence of close-mindedness. If people on both sides of an issue are unmovable and resolute in their stance, by definition this means that there will never be any compromise, no progress, no solution; they have damned themselves to an eternity of frustration and futility as well as contention and animosity.

Suicide bombers are certain that their beliefs and their causes are true. Patients that use homeopathic remedies are certain that they're doing something for their health. Those who believe in ghosts are certain that the paranormal realm exists. Throughout history, the religious faithful have often been certain of their beliefs, no matter what religion it was: Hinduism, Judaism, the Olympic pantheon, the Canaanite pantheon, Zoroastrianism, Catholicism, Shiite Islam, Sunni Islam, Mormonism, Protestantism. If you were ever one of the religious faithful, at some point you were likely certain that every other person who had ever lived on the planet that didn't share your beliefs was wrong; at the same time, those other persons would have been certain that you were the one who was wrong. Does your certainty make your beliefs true? Does their certainty make their differing beliefs a different kind of true?" You are both certain of your beliefs, but both beliefs can't be true; so how do you figure out whose belief is actually true? How in fact do you determine if either belief is true? Do you really think that your certainty is somehow better than the other's certainty? To be certain is to declare something absolute. How can one truth be "more absolute" than another?

The brain is exceedingly good at pointing its owner to certainty, again, because certainty is a comfortable and seemingly desirable position. This knee-jerk, rule-of-thumb position of seeking comfort and avoiding discomfort is extremely attractive. If one doesn't bother to think any further, they will likely go with the default position that their brain is feeding them, in this case, the relative comfort of certainty. And this is yet another example showing where CT is so necessary. The critical thinker should stop at this point and ask themselves, "I'm comfortable with this position, and I even have a "feeling" of certainty about it, but have I rigorously tested my position to see if it's actually valid or not? For that matter, can I ever be certain that I've tested my position enough? Will I be able to assume after some amount of testing that I will finally have perfect, complete knowledge about my position? Can I ever be certain that there will never be a future discovery that could call into question my certainty?

Someone once said, "A lead weight doesn't float. It doesn't float even if you <u>want</u> it to very, very badly...!" It's the latter part of this sentence that is the most salient: the <u>strength</u> of your desires does not determine what is true or even what is possible. What most people mean when they speak of the <u>certainty</u> of their beliefs, is in fact how strongly they are <u>convinced</u> of something. Both words have nine letters and begin with the letter C, but beyond that, all similarity disappears. Once more, the human brain seems to have the default position of "I am ready to be fooled," and by making the mistake of employing CBLFs, the brain can easily become convinced, to the point of feeling certain. The brain can indeed become convinced despite compelling scientific evidence, logic and reasoning that disproves this same certainty. Ironically, the convinced person then looks on all others holding a conflicting or unsettled viewpoint as the close-minded, the deluded, the irrational; they are the ones that need convincing.

To take a practical case in the real world, suppose that a trusted friend of yours is an incredibly successful engineer. She is <u>certain</u> that she has created a mechanism that, when you wear it, would allow you to hover in the air after stepping off of a cliff, rather than let you plummet to your death. She is ready to strap it onto you at this very moment and lead you to the cliff outside. Remember, you trust her, and she is an engineer with many past successes and besides, she isn't making this claim lightly, she is <u>certain</u> that she is right.

Is your first reaction to think, "Well sure, let's do this!"? If the result of a failure is an untimely death, chances are, your reaction will be, "Maybe we could test it on a mannequin first?" In other words, despite your trust in her, despite her superior qualifications and her track record of past successes and the fact that she is <u>certain</u> that she is right about this mechanism, you still hesitate, you don't automatically accept her certainty as proof of future success. You seem to have doubts; you seem to be exercising a healthy skepticism, desiring actual evidence rather than just another person's reassurances of certainty.

So what is the difference between an expert's certainty about their beliefs and anyone else's certainty about their beliefs? Just because someone else is convinced or certain doesn't seem to mean that you must also be convinced. But <u>should</u> you be convinced? If someone says, "Look, I feel to the depth of my soul, to the very core and fiber of my being that I'm right...and that's enough for me, shouldn't that be enough for you?" Your answer is likely still, "well...no, it isn't enough....perhaps your past successes have <u>convinced</u> you that anything that you create will be successful. Perhaps, you've made an unknown error in your calculations and won't realize it until your mechanism fails in one of its first tests. But before I put my life on the line, I'd actually like some evidence please". The engineer hath said, "I'm certain (i.e., I am strongly convinced) that this will work", in essence, "I really, really, <u>really</u> want this mechanism to be successful!" In answer, you hath said, "Your certainty and desires mean <u>nothing</u> when it comes to my <u>reality</u>."

One may read this and ponder, "But with critical thinking, I might never come to a final position on any issue ever! I could be wallowing in second-guessing and uncertainty for my entire lifetime!" Indeed...welcome to the double-edged sword of CT. As stated earlier, CT doesn't guarantee some direct path to truth; it merely serves to help you avoid as many fallacious and biased paths as possible. Yes, even after years of CT on a subject, you may still be left with unanswered questions, lingering doubts and uncertainty on any given issue. The positive aspect of this uncertainty is that you are left with an open mind, you are always ready to modify your world-view with the benefit of increased

50

knowledge and evidence. And you won't have made mistakes due to your biases.

Your admission of uncertainty does not mean that you can't ever make decisions or choices to get through your daily life. Your admission doesn't mean that you can't take stands on issues. It is just an honest way of saying, "I will do the best that I can for the time being with the knowledge that I currently have. But because I know that I have biases, I will always be open to new evidence, new ways of looking at an argument. And I will have enough integrity to admit when I'm wrong or need to have my world-view modified, even when the modification doesn't necessarily bring me happiness." In retrospect, this conditional position is still preferable to having to say, "Well sure, I was wrong about my position, but at least I was certain about it...."

THE DANGER OF FOLLOWING HAPPINESS

That title may strike you initially as rather odd. How could following a path to happiness be dangerous? You may think, "Don't I want to do things and think things that make me happy? Isn't the pursuit of happiness the ultimate goal of every person?" You may have heard someone say, "I know there's no evidence for it, but I believe such-and-such because it makes me happy. It makes me content, it gives me <u>some</u> answer to a soul-searching question or it gives some ultimate meaning or purpose to my life." You may have even thought it yourself. However, if your ultimate goal in life is to find truth (no matter how the truth makes you feel), then it is far better to accept any disappointment, sadness, misery, or helplessness as a consequence as long as it means that you are accepting the truth.

There is no law stating that the truth necessarily has to be a pleasant thing or even a pleasant thing to all people.

HUMANS TEND TO BELIEVE TWO THINGS:

1) WHAT THEY WANT TO BELIEVE

2) WHAT THEY NEED TO BELIEVE

Most people don't really want the truth. They just want the constant reassurance that what they believe in is the truth.
—Anonymous

Once you've acknowledged what you want to believe or what you need to believe, your pattern-seeking brain (PSB) is going to search for and give more weight to anything that bolsters that belief, and it's going to avoid or give less weight to anything that argues against that belief. That is, it will if you let your brain remain on its default setting.

If you had a conversation with someone who believed in something that you didn't and they gave as a significant reason for that belief that it made them happy, or that the absence of that belief made them sad, how would you rate their thinking process? Does your happiness with your belief system necessarily refute their different belief or vice versa? Are personal emotions and feelings of happiness to be the final judge of what is true?

There are billions of different people in the world, with various emotional responses to myriad issues; and they hold mutually contradictory belief systems, which by definition means that not everyone can be right about their beliefs. How will an individual go about determining what is true? Even for those that happen to be right about a given issue, should they be basing their belief on their <u>feelings</u>? If one is frightened or depressed at the thought of their eventual death, they may be more likely to believe that after death, they will have an afterlife in paradise just because it makes them feel better; but is this a valid way of seeking truth, to take the path of least fear or discomfort? Or to merely take an irrational path towards happiness?

> **Reality is the stuff that remains after you stop believing it.**
> —Anonymous

Facts do not cease to exist simply because they are ignored.
—Aldous Huxley (d. 1963 Writer and Philosopher)

The early pioneers of human flight felt very enthusiastic and confident that their designs for early gliders and powered aircraft would take them into the sky. But those that based their designs on what they wanted, or what made them feel good (rather than on solid physics, engineering and aerodynamic theory) were the ones that either never got off the ground, or accelerated toward the ground to their untimely demise.

The Wright Brothers were ultimately successful, but not because they thought, "our machine must resemble a bird as closely as possible." They may have indeed enjoyed watching the beauty and wonder of birds on the wing, but they likely didn't begin by assuming that a stabilizer must be forward and the rudder aft and wings should warp merely because they thought this setup was aesthetically pleasing. Instead, after experimentation, hypothesizing, researching and trials (including many, many failures), they determined that, regardless of what the eventual design would look like, the pilot must have the ability to control the flight in the three axes of pitch, roll and yaw. That was how physical forces operated, and they had to deal with the actual way that the world worked. And so they became the most successful at creating a line of successful flying machines because their designs took into account what nature required. No one can make a machine fly by ignoring the world's natural properties, even if they really, really want it to fly.

And with any belief, if you can forgo evidence to the contrary just because your own wishes give you a positive feeling, this mindset is very likely to creep into your daily thinking. You may find yourself denying some discovery of science because the new information makes you feel uncomfortable or it doesn't bring you as much pleasure or satisfaction as your own belief; you may dismiss the safety of vaccines because an alternative view gives you an explanation for your child's behavior; you may find yourself accepting that the sun and the stars revolve around the Earth, because it makes you feel better that you and your world appear to be the center of the universe. But your personal happiness and your emotions don't determine truth.

It does seem strange to embrace a truth that has some negative connotation, such as anger, sadness, or depression. Why would someone want to think of themselves as merely one of billions of humans on a tiny planet in an average solar system in a mundane neighborhood of a run-of-the-mill galaxy which itself is only one of hundreds of billions of galaxies? The realization may not make you feel very special, that you are so unimaginably small compared to the whole of the universe; it can also be unsettling to think that the vast majority of the cosmos may not even be aware of your existence.

Taking a different tack, wouldn't it make you feel much more relevant and important if you and your planet were the center of everything and that all the stars and galaxies revolved around you? Isn't it infinitely more pleasant to feel special? Don't you want your existence to be significant? Isn't it more desirable to believe that you were created with a unique purpose within the vastness of these dimensions? It may all depend on which you value more: happiness or truth. But if you set out in your life with an underlying desire that every truth that you accept must end up making you happy or content, your brain is quite capable of rationalizing everything to that end. Humans are exceedingly good at convincing themselves of what they want to believe, or what they need to believe.

There is no law stating that the universe owes you recognition or relevance, or even a purpose to your life. To avoid this grim possibility, the vast majority of people have been much more comfortable imagining some outside agent or phenomenon (i.e. a pattern) that will specify or <u>give</u> them their purpose in life. A specific purpose, already spelled out by an ultimate authority, one that the individual can always point to and use as a foundation for their existence and relevance. The individual imbues this deity with omnipotence and omniscience; the god is assumed to have done all the thinking and the work up front so that the individual doesn't have to do any thinking, or take responsibility for their decisions. All the individual has to do from then on is to profess faith in the "royal decree" and follow it. If something in their life goes as they wish, they can credit the agent; if something doesn't go as they wish, they can raise up their palms, "It is as the gods/fate wills." They can be satisfied that the situation is "out of their hands"; "it's not my fault anymore", "I don't have to keep trying, I don't even have to think about it anymore". The mental and emotional relief gained from this resignation to something deemed "incomprehensible and uncontrollable" can be attractive, but the willful surrendering of one's reason and responsibility doesn't befit a mature individual.

If something does go wrong in their life, many individuals have desired some answer or even a scapegoat on which to place the culpability, "I didn't follow the commandments faithfully enough, it's my fault", or "There is a demon who is doing this to me" or "This calamity is part of the divine plan, I can't make sense of why I have to go through this, but the designer of the plan <u>must</u> know, and I am bound to comply unquestioningly". Similarly, it is common for children to label an inanimate object with agency to explain why events occur; when their finger gets slammed in a door, they immediately construct an understandable answer, "The door bit me!" At least in the short term, having an "answer" as to why things happen is more satisfying than having no answer at all.

But at some point, the "child" must mature into an adult and begin to take on the responsibility for their own thinking and decisions and actions and formulate their own direction in life. It takes much more mental effort to do this and it can be overwhelming and even scary to take on full responsibility for one's self. That's what it means to be a true adult:

It's ultimately up to the individual to take responsibility and give purpose to their own life, and thus create for themselves the potential for recognition and relevance.

It's an intimidating but ultimately satisfying and rewarding responsibility. And it may take years or even decades for each individual to decide for themselves what their purpose in life is; they may also decide they have several purposes in life or that their purpose changes and evolves over their lifetime. Regardless, they have the potential to attain the satisfaction, the self-esteem and perhaps even the pride by being under their own direction, rather than being the pawn of something imagined, supernatural, inexplicable and/or unquestionable.

Even so, in an attempt to validate a particular opinion or belief, people will often point to examples of famous or very intelligent people believing in the same things that they do. It's comforting to be able to point to someone "more important" or "more famous" than you, an "authority" that shares your worldview. But it turns out that "very intelligent people" are simply more capable of rationalizing their unproven beliefs. The fact that some people are "very intelligent" about certain subjects does not mean that everything that they believe is, by default, an intelligent viewpoint. Sir Isaac Newton is argued to have possessed one of the highest I.Q.s ever known, yet he considered himself one of the religious faithful, while simultaneously dabbling in the preposterous pursuit known as alchemy. But his relevance and importance to humanity stem from his mathematical and scientific exercises, not his time on his knees praying or his attempts to turn lead into gold. In essence, the usefulness and value of his contributions to humanity were due to his CT in science and mathematics, rather than his beliefs or wishful thinking.

Some modern scientists still have some measure of religious faith or superstition even after their scientific investigations have made these concepts superfluous. Humans are good at compartmentalizing different areas of their knowledge and beliefs. They can switch to the CT portion of their brain in order to do valid science, but the next moment, seeking the old comfortable pattern of belief, they allow their brain to resume the default setting of "I am ready once again to be fooled."

As more and more areas of human ignorance and imaginary phenomena are evaporated by the knowledge gained through science and the use of other forms of CT, the provinces of the paranormal, pseudoscience, superstition and religion continue to shrink. Yet, many of the followers and the faithful still doggedly grasp at any straw of unanswered questions in an increasingly desperate attempt to keep their belief in the picture somewhere, somehow. Their faith has kept them happy for so many years that they aren't quite ready to give up on it just yet. Their brains are still too used to the comfortable pattern.

There have been animal experiments where the subject is given a choice: receive food or press a lever that delivers stimulation to the pleasure center of their brain. Many of the animals continued pressing the lever, over and over, even to the exclusion of eating, until they finally starved to death. They became so enamored of the repetition of the pattern "press-the-lever-receive-pleasure" that nothing else mattered, not even bodily sustenance, and they very possibly died with a smile on their maw. This is very similar

58

to the case of the human animal that prefers the pleasure received from repeating the familiar patterns of their thinking process; each repetition of the well-rehearsed opinions resulting in a release of endorphin or other chemical to the pleasure center of the brain, sometimes to the exclusion of benefit from new, proven, more accurate and useful information. And just so, billions of people have died (many far too young) by clinging to their cherished but still erroneous beliefs; and they very possibly expired with a smile on their face.

It is vital to start all contemplation by doubting your own thinking process from the outset. Once you realize that different humans have come to their conflicting belief systems because of their faulty thinking processes, you will accept that true progress can only be achieved once one discards the idea that their "truth" must by definition, be correct. If you ever utter (or even think of) the phrase, "well, it may not be true for you, but it is true for me...", you are quite likely wrong. If you have by sheer chance, actually attained a truth, it may be for a very bad reason. And chancing upon the truth for the wrong reason can be rather unfortunate in the long run. You may indeed gain an immediate benefit from a single success achieved by a faulty thinking process; the danger is that the gratification and happiness that you receive from that benefit may lead you to think that you can come up with other "truths" by the same faulty thinking process. That is potentially dangerous.

The first step to demonstrating that truth is your ultimate goal is thinking to yourself, "When it's based on evidence, I am going to accept any fact as being true, even if it doesn't make me happy—I will accept it even if it makes me angry, disappointed, sad or depressed." This way of thinking doesn't ensure that your life will always be a happy one, an endlessly comfortable journey, but at least you can take satisfaction in the knowledge that your "truths" weren't simply based on illusions that made you happy.

FOOL ME ONCE, SHAME ON YOU;

FOOL ME TWICE, SHAME ON ME

> **It's easier to fool people than to convince them that they have been fooled.**
> —Samuel Clemens/Mark Twain (d. 1910 Writer, Humorist, Entrepreneur, Publisher, and Lecturer)

> **One of the saddest lessons of history is this: If you've been (fooled) long enough, people tend to reject any evidence of (being fooled). You're no longer interested in finding out the truth. It's just too painful to acknowledge, even to your self, that you've been (fooled). Once you give a charlatan power over you, you almost never get it back.**
> —Carl Sagan (d. 1996 Astronomer, Cosmologist, Astrophysicist, Astrobiologist, Author, Science Popularizer and Communicator)

It may be a painful experience to discover that one has been scammed, but the experience may be worthwhile if it makes the individual forever after skeptical of any and all claims.

Trust can be a huge issue when it comes to your cherished beliefs. Consider the following scenario: unbeknownst to you, you were kidnapped shortly after birth and raised as the child of

60

your kidnappers. The kidnappers may have even been exemplary, loving parents and you've grown to be a respectable, contributing member of society. Then one day, the authorities contact you and tell you the truth: the people that you've always held as your parents, that you have loved and trusted your entire life, committed a heinous crime: kidnapping you as a baby. They are led away in handcuffs, imploring you, their "child," to intercede on their behalf.

Shortly after, you are introduced to your birth parents that have never stopped looking for you. They tell you that they have always loved you and that having you taken from them was an agonizing loss; they have had their lives turned upside down, for years of misery and uncertainty. Your birth mother shows you a picture of you as a newborn in her arms taken the day of your birth, and it shows the unmistakable birthmark on your shoulder that you still possess. In the background is your birth father holding up a sign that says, "Proud Daddy." They show you the scrapbooks that they have crammed with every newspaper and magazine clipping that concerns this nationally known kidnapping case as well as the police reports. And of course, a blood sample is taken of all parties concerned showing that you are in no way related to your kidnappers and are a spot-on match with the "birth parents."

You are stunned. Your entire life as you have known it has been turned upside down. The trust that you have placed in your supposed parents has been torn to shreds. Your psyche is twisted into a confused mass. Now, you don't know who you can trust. What is reality now? Is it what makes living life more comfortable for you? How do you go about the daily business of figuring out "truth" in the world? What constitutes truth? Is it merely what other people tell you?

But the evidence of the crime is too complete and perfect to deny. Your rational mind may accept it readily, but your emotions cannot be turned off and on by mere facts. Your brain's first reaction is to go into defense mode: "No, I don't <u>want</u> to believe this, it's not the familiar pattern that I'm used to, this is not what has always been true for me." You have an entire life of experiences, memories as well as an emotional attachment to these people, they are intertwined with your entire psyche. They have helped form the person you are and the "truths" to which you cling. You cannot just dismiss your experiences of a lifetime; what is your life after all, if not the sum total of your experiences?

While it may seem understandable and even reasonable to cling to your experiences and feelings and use them as the crux of your beliefs, here is an example that shows that they may not always be reliable. Sometimes, people have to compare their experiences with those of others, and if the two are mutually exclusive, one must find more reliable disciplines on which to base their truths. These disciplines are logic, reason and CT and science. Agreed, none of these mental disciplines would have likely prevented the original kidnapping or the damage done to the victim's psyche; but at least when the victim knows the truth and asks for a reliable path forward, these practices are the most reliable starting points.

But it doesn't have to take being kidnapped as a newborn to elicit the uncomfortable feeling of a newly realized truth turning one's world upside down. Throughout your life, you may have invested a great deal of time, effort, thought and struggle in coming to your positions on various contentious subjects. These positions, your "truths" are important to you, dear to you, vital bricks in the foundation of the building entitled, "your understanding of the world," i.e., your world-view. And whenever incontrovertible evidence is presented to you that refutes your idea, your initial reaction is likely a negative one, a defensive one. You don't wish for any of your bricks to be threatened with damage, let alone outright removed from your foundation. Who knows how many disrupted bricks it will take to have the foundation of your worldview come crashing down? Ten bricks? As little as five bricks? Perhaps, just this one foundational brick?

When faced with an unpleasant fact, your brain automatically goes into defense mode: protect that brick at all costs, nothing must happen to the brick (or at least no outsider should witness the brick compromised). When it is pointed out to people how silly their beliefs seem to others, they often get furious. They don't like it when someone implies, "You do realize that you've been fooled by this idea for a great deal of your life, don't you?" And no one wants to believe that they could have been mistaken about anything so important for so long.

As you read through the chapter of CBLFs (p.101), you will spot numerous entries (backfire effect, file drawer effect, cognitive dissonance, the illusion of understanding, etc.) that help the human brain do just that, transition to defense mode. This defensive mindset allows one to maintain an incorrect conclusion in the face of undeniable evidence.

All humans do this to varying degrees, even without intending to do it; it's just how the human brain is wired, it's the default position. But it doesn't mean that the mind has to remain <u>stuck</u> on that setting. When one is armed with CT and can spot their biases and fallacies, eventually the misinformation that results from them can be dismissed, and the person can progress in their life, forearmed for the next inevitable onslaught of their brain's fallacies and biases.

For most humans, it is very uncomfortable, even painful to use the phrase, "I was wrong." They are in essence saying that they were mistaken, perhaps deluded about some assumed truth. They're admitting that they wasted their own time and may have also wasted other people's time with their error. But by merely making this admission, they now have the potential to avoid more wasted time. Their worldview may be a little more accurate for the future, and they may make more progress.

If you had to walk to the next village carrying a sack of grain on your back and upon your arrival, you find the sack empty because it had a small hole that allowed the grain to slowly leak out along the path, you might feel rightly abashed, your efforts wasted, your task unfulfilled. But your experience would likely forearm you for the future ensuring that any sack that you used for such a labor was stout and reinforced for the future. So it is with discovering that your thinking process contains the holes of these CBLFs. It can be painful and even alarming to find out how you've been wrong in the past, misguided, your efforts wasted, sometimes for years.   But the experience can forearm you for the future by ensuring that there are no holes in your thinking, that by employing the methods of CT, you are reinforcing your thinking process for the future.

SHOULD THE TRUTH REQUIRE REPETITION?

When you think about political, moral or ideological subjects, do you repeatedly dwell on the same examples, the same arguments every time? Do you even attempt to approach the topic from a different direction, a different worldview, perhaps even that of your opposition? If you feel your beliefs hold some truth, why should they require endless repetition?   To prove your devotion to your faith, you may pray five times a day, or go to your place of worship weekly, perform the rituals regularly or observe the holy days. Are your beliefs so tenuous that the best way for you continue in your faith is to repeat a rite or mantra so often that the pattern merely becomes familiar and comfortable, expected, even joyful? Does repetition make your beliefs stronger, like the repetition of exercise makes a body stronger?

> **Truth does not demand belief. Scientists do not join hands every week singing, "Yes, gravity is real! I will have faith! I will be strong! I believe in my heart that what goes up, must come down, Amen!" If they did, we would think they were pretty insecure about it.**
> —Dan Barker (Musician and Former Preacher)

You seem to know that those who hold different beliefs from you are wrong and you pity them as they bow their heads, hands clasped repeating their mantras as they further delude themselves—so how do you know that by the repetitions of your mantras that your belief is the valid one? Is it possible that one of the reasons that you feel your beliefs are true is that you keep

65

repeating them over and over, possibly as part of some daily rite until they become a familiar, even comforting daily pattern? Even if you deny it, why should the truth require this repetition? Does your self-confidence on these subjects need constant, repetitive reaffirmation and reassurance?

Does a deity have such low self-esteem that they need constant reverence from a fallible primate to feel venerated and relevant? When you finally die and join your god in some paradise, will they require you to repeatedly honor them, respect them, pray to them for billions if not trillions of years? What is it about this deity that needs billions of lower beings to go on and on praising it? Will there ever be a point where the god thinks, "It's been a few billion years, that's enough of the reverence and worship, I've got all that I need"? Or will they just sit on their throne 24 hours a day, 365 days a year, forever scanning the vast multitude as they kneel with heads lowered and hands raised?

After 10 million years of continuous, repeated worship of your deity, suppose you were to ask the individual next to you, "Say, do you want to skip the worship for a few hours and go sight-seeing? I've always been kind of curious what the rest of this place looks like." They look at you aghast. "Are you kidding? We can't! This is what we signed up for! For our entire lives on earth, we kept praying for this; we kept trying to convince non-believers to convert to our belief. We hoped for this: living forever only to praise our deity forever and ever! Even with the billions of us already here in the amphitheater, there are thousands being added every day! Sure, our deity is all-powerful and perfect, but he still seems to have this peculiar need and expectation of worship that, for some unfathomable reason, only the imperfect can provide. Our brethren even killed those that didn't believe as we do, just to make it possible for us to arrive at this point! You'd better get used to it; we will never be able to stop worshiping. Our deity's demand for it is insatiable!"

66

SHOULD GOD REQUIRE COMPLEXITY?

When asked for proof of a god, one of the most common responses from the faithful is along the lines of, "Just look around you! Look at the grandeur and magnificence of nature and the complexity of the human body! Look at the incredibly complex information contained in DNA!" But should an all-powerful being require complexity to accomplish a task? It is tempting and common to assume that any process in nature which appears to a human level of intelligence as "complex" or "complicated" required a "designer."

Look at any snowflake under a microscope and the observer sees a seemingly beautiful, elegant and symmetrical hexagonal form, each of the six sides a nearly perfect duplication of the other five. It would seem that such an ideal design would require a designer. But it has long been known by scientists that physics and chemistry make spontaneous snowflake formation and symmetry unavoidable. The angles of the bonds between the hydrogen and oxygen atoms in the water molecules, coupled with the changes in physical phase brought on by a drop in temperature at a known rate combined with various convection currents in the sky (plus other measurable natural factors) make the formation of such beautiful structures in countless different designs inevitable; all without any supernatural intervention.

The genes of a given species are regarded as the "information" or "blueprint" for building the organism, a "code" that some consider literally "written" into the nucleus of each cell. Following this supposition, one could compare different species to decide which genome is more complex and therefore which shows even more "design" by a designer. A simple starting point would be counting the number of genes "written" in each genome. Of the animals that have had their entire genome sequenced, so far, the animal with the most genes (about 31,000) is the freshwater crustacean *Daphnia pulex* or water flea. Humans have only 23,000 genes. *Daphnia* is a relatively simple, microscopic creature compared to a human, but its genetic makeup appears more complex by sheer size alone. Why would a god spend so much more time on putting together the genome of the water flea?

Assuming that complexity indicates design is assuming too much. When comparing the genome of humans and chimpanzees, there is an approximate match of 98.8% of their genes, can a difference of 1.2% make such a difference between a "lowly" ape and the "naked" ape? Of course, with all living things, it isn't just the size or "complexity" of its genome that determines their form, it's also how and which parts of the genome are expressed. When all is said and done, *Homo sapiens sapiens* is just another ape that has evolved a bit differently.

The labels of "complex" and "designed" are merely the result of a bias of a human brain assigning the labels unnecessarily, due to wishful thinking and a lack of knowledge or imagination.

For example, the process of human blood clotting is often cited as an example of "irreducible complexity" due to the numerous steps involved and the network of complicated chemical reactions needed for its success. Surely only an intelligent designer could have come up with a phenomenon so amazingly intricate and complex. However, those familiar with the work of the cartoonist Rube Goldberg may detect an interesting parallel. Goldberg was famous for devising complex schemes to achieve relatively simplistic ends. In essence, the subject of each comic panel would make do with what was already immediately available to accomplish a goal, rather than engineering something more straightforward and novel from scratch--

--but all for a good laugh.

A typical example: In order to switch on a reading light in a room, the reader opens a book...the rush of air from the opening pages blows a toy windmill's blades whose rotation is translated through the windmill's axle to pulleys running a belt that pulls up the door of a cage, allowing the rabbit inside to escape onto a treadmill...where a waiting dog chases said rabbit...the rotation of the treadmill is linked to a lever with a fake hand on the end whose raised finger pushes up on the light switch resulting in the desired action of the light being turned on. Each step in the process is simple, successful, useful and achieves the necessary action/step to further the desired process, and all with materials already on hand-- but taken as a whole, it is a ludicrously complicated and complex process. The reader considers this for a moment and justifiably concludes, "Well, there's certainly no denying that it works, but there are much simpler and far more efficient ways of doing this...."

So why is it that when shown the intricately complicated and complex diagram of blood clotting does the same reader consider it for a moment and somehow conclude, "Wow, so many incredible steps, what an amazing process! I see the hand of god!" There seems to be an inconsistency with the viewer's judgment. It seems that in the everyday life of humans, when it comes to the issue of the mechanical, needless complexity deserves derision. But when it comes to something biological, needless complexity is presumed "made by God." No matter how inefficient the biological system looks, no matter how fraught with breakdowns, it will be viewed through the bias filter of the believer as beautiful and amazing. Is it possible one is employing a double standard?

If a god is all-wise and all-powerful (or at least vastly more powerful than a human), why the need for all the complexity?

Why so many complicated steps where an error in any single one of them can dangerously decrease the effectiveness of blood clotting? Instead of 20+ steps, couldn't a god have figured a way to have done it in 10 steps? Or 3? Or even one step? Come to think of it, couldn't a god have designed creatures so that they couldn't bleed in the first place? By the same point, why all the separate organs, circulatory systems, nervous systems and digestive systems, each prone to age, inefficiency and disease at any one of a hundred areas or processes? Couldn't a god have designed creatures as hollow bags of skin that are still fully functional?

And if a god's ultimate need or desire from humans is faith, reverence and obeisance, why bother with bodies in the first place? Why not just create their brains, making sure that they can survive and function without the need for blood, oxygen, nutrition, protection, etc.? Furthermore, isn't there a way to merely create human minds, without the need for a physical brain? Is this beyond the power of an "all-powerful" deity? This skeptical questioning can be carried on and on and on resulting in an infinite regress into ever more fundamental questions, yet never yielding any satisfying answers.

It seems ridiculously complicated to have to create and "design" all of these complex structures, steps and functions for some ultimate purpose. However, in the light of evolution (which can never create something from scratch but instead modifies existing structures and functions into different structures and functions) this kind of patchwork, "modify-something-that-you've-already-got," Rube Goldberg-style complication makes total sense. What's more, the history of evolution and its effects on the structures and functions of organisms is ultimately traceable to that same aforementioned, genome and its constituent, the amazing DNA.

70

Unfortunately, some have given DNA (deoxyribonucleic acid) the troublesome moniker, the "blueprint of life." On one level, this label has some limited accuracy in that DNA does act as a "template" for the structure and function of a given organism. An alteration (e.g., a mutation) in any part of the "template" or the "blueprint" has the potential for altering the resulting structure/function of the organism. The troublesome aspect arises when humans seize on this idea that a blueprint/template requires a designer. A "code" like DNA, which contains "instructions" or "information" seemingly must therefore have an intelligence behind it. And often, DNA is literally written as a code: a nearly endless line of As, Gs, Cs and Ts (abbreviations of Adenine, Guanine, Cytosine and Thymine, the nitrogenous bases of each nucleotide). It seems reasonable to look at these letters and think that one is looking at a "code," i.e. "information" literally "written" into an organism's genome.

But one must keep in mind that these As, Gs, Cs and Ts are merely a human-made shorthand that simplifies the study of the genome by the limitations of the human intellect. Once the viewer is presented with the actual three-dimensional structure of DNA as a double-helix studded with different sized "spheres" representing the atomic structures of the As, Gs, Cs and Ts, any resemblance to a human "code" evaporates. And while it may closely resemble something cobbled together by a child using their building set, like the snowflake, the amazing structure of DNA results from unstoppable physical forces and the chemical bonds of the atoms involved.

It is the chemical interaction of these sphere-studded double helices "rubbing up against" other chemical structures studded with differently-arranged spheres that result in the life processes at which humans marvel. The same scientists who, over decades of unceasing inquiry, testing and research, have teased the details and intricacies of these chemical structures and interactions have also created three-dimensional movies showing these complex interactions. And just like viewing a Rube Goldberg contraption, the skeptic will likely conclude that, while complex and amazing to watch, these processes are ridiculously complicated and fraught with the inevitability of translation error and mutation. Shouldn't an omnipotent god be able to wave their hand and have the creation of newer superior organisms happen instantaneously without the complexity and the chance of error?

Picture a vast forest of trees viewed from the sky; there is a combination of Dogwoods (D), Oaks (O), Elms (E), Maples (M) and Pecans (P). If you take a photograph from several hundred feet high, your image resembles a mass of green foliage where it is challenging to separate the different kinds of trees. If you descended closer to the ground, you'd have a slightly simpler time differentiating each type of tree, but at the expense of not being able to see the structure of the entire forest all at once. The fact is, each separate level of investigation is limited and susceptible to a human level of bias as to its analysis and interpretation, and ultimately its usefulness and value. So only by investigating the environment from different distances and different levels (and preferably, by multiple viewers to come to a consensus and filter out the biases of all) is it possible to get as complete and accurate a picture of the forest as possible.

So, to simplify things for the limitations of human intellect, you create a birds-eye-view diagram that shows each type of tree in its given location, using only the above abbreviations. Your chart is now a scattered pattern of Ps, Ds, Os, Es and Ms. In one corner of the diagram, you happen to note that a short span of the letters spells out "Moped." This collection of letters in English just happens to have a human significance: a word meaning either "a motorized bike," or the past tense of a verb meaning "to have appeared sad." Your brain seizes on an instantly recognizable pattern and even assigns a significance to it, regardless of the fact that it was a totally chance occurrence made possible (and virtually inevitable) by the wholly arbitrary assigning of letter abbreviations to the English names of a relatively limited set of tree species. But you were helpless; your brain sensed the pattern even when you weren't looking for it. And only by using some rudimentary CT skills, were you able to filter out this distracting "finding." In hindsight, assigning importance to this "pattern" seems superfluous if not ridiculous.

Yet, those with less education in the sciences (or those with too much bias) are all-too-ready to see "information," a "code" or some "instructions," written by the hand of a deity. If you approach a given phenomenon with a pre-existing mindset, a bias of wanting to see divine influence, you are much more likely to interpret any anomaly found as further proof.

Seek and ye shall find.

THE DESIRE TO FEEL SUPERIOR

Most people would probably admit that it's much more attractive to feel informed than ignorant, "At least I have an answer, I don't have to say, 'I don't know.'" If there is one primary position that has gotten humanity into more trouble than any other, it may be belittling those who make mistakes or who simply admit ignorance in some area. The fact is, there has never been a human in history that has never made a mistake, or an honest individual that never had to answer a question with, "I don't know."

> **Uncertainty is an uncomfortable position. But certainty is an absurd one.**
> —Voltaire (d.1778 Writer, Historian, and Philosopher)

In an argument, where one person is trying to convince the other person, the last phrase that they probably would want to use is "I don't know." It may make one sound less convincing, they may feel less empowered, less able to contribute to a discussion, or lacking the required knowledge, they have less control over a given situation. Current society even seems to look down on someone professing ignorance; "If you don't have some answer, why should anyone listen to anything that you've got to say?"

And at some point, if you are shown to be wrong about your position on an issue, then you may very well be ignored or ridiculed, if not outright vilified. But this mindset/bias works against a society that values honesty, integrity and progress.

74

Frequently, more progress is made in science and innovation by studying the failures rather than the successes; but this openness to so-called "negative outcomes" can also be applied to many if not most other human endeavors.

Ignorance is nothing shameful; imposing ignorance is shameful. Most people are not to blame for their own ignorance, but if they willfully pass it on, they are to blame.
—Daniel Dennett (Cognitive Scientist and Philosopher)

If human society can progress to the point where each individual is comfortable with professing their ignorance on a given subject, and where others will think more highly of them for their admission, as well as their honesty and integrity, progress will occur all the more quickly. After all, if the individual just wishes to avoid appearing ignorant, and subsequently parrots some related nonsense that they've heard before, or even makes up something on the spot, how will that speed up or advance the search for truth?

The wiser you are, the more you believe in equality, because the difference between what the most and least learned people know is inexpressibly trivial in relation to all that is unknown.
—Albert Einstein (d.1955 Nobel Laureate Theoretical Physicist)

Recall the medieval barber (forerunners of modern physicians), who when confronted with a patient with dire symptoms offers the patient's parent an honest and open admission: fifty years ago, his colleagues would have thought their child's disease was caused by demonic possession or witchcraft. But with the advantage of an additional five decades of study, the new view is that the patient is suffering from an imbalance of bodily humors, caused by a small toad or dwarf living in her stomach. So the barber proceeds to bleed the patient in an attempt to restore this balance of humors.

The parent is initially grateful to this "authority" for possessing this new supposed "knowledge." Because otherwise, the parent would have to profess total powerlessness to help their child. Having some answer is better than having to admit ignorance of the cause of this condition; any intervention has to be better than no intervention. Inevitably, the patient swiftly dies. In her grief and rage, the parent tries to get the barber to admit that he's just as ignorant as anyone else as to what caused their child's death.

The barber briefly considers that it may have been wrong to blindly follow the medical traditions and superstitions of past centuries. Perhaps medical hypotheses should be tested analytically, through experimentation and a "scientific method." Maybe this scientific method could be extended to other fields of learning: the natural sciences, architecture, navigation. It might even lead the way to a new sociological movement, an age of reason, a Renaissance! But almost immediately, the barber realizes all the work that would be involved in attaining such advances and persuading his patients of their efficacy. He then cheerfully abandons the possibility of this advancement in favor of the established procedures, the routine, the currently accepted pattern. After all, doesn't this "authority" already have an "answer"? Isn't the fact that he has some answer good enough for you? Why is any questioning required or any additional thinking necessary?

Another common human tendency is accepting only the "answers" that already agree with your preconceived biases. In the long run, it is much better to admit one's ignorance, one's uncertainty and especially, one's biases before settling on any "answer." Honesty, integrity and skepticism in one's ignorance lead to much faster progress than accepting the unexamined "answers."

One can't expect rapid progress in any human endeavor when one isn't willing to admit the limitations of their knowledge; they are likely to continue to blunder on making mistakes, even with the best of intentions. Nor is progress likely while others are willing to accept any "answer" rather than no "answer" at all. No one has all of the answers; everyone is ignorant in some areas. And ignorance and the willingness to admit it is a good thing; it shows honesty and humility, and an open mind. And it allows correction of past mistakes in reason, which in turn leads to the potential for additional learning and growth.

PERSONAL EXPERIENCE

By its very definition, any experience is personal, something only the individual will perceive in precisely that way. Even others who were in the same place and time can have a personal experience different than the person next to them. Several people witnessing the same accident will experience it in different ways and give slightly varying accounts. Whose is the correct interpretation? If all of the separate experiences are reported differently in some way, whose experience is the "truth"?

A core problem of the personal experience is that the outsider cannot deny that the observer felt, acknowledged and remembered it the way that they report; it would be silly to say, "You couldn't possibly have been that happy about seeing your new nephew..." One is left either having to take the observer's word for it or putting that personal experience to the test.

It is also pertinent to note that the same person's report of their personal experience often changes subtly over time; the size of the crowd that witnessed them scoring the goal grows over the years from a handful to scores to hundreds, eventually maybe into thousands. They may not be consciously changing their experience, but their brain's subconscious may be allowing it to change nonetheless. Regardless of its current state, the memory of their experience is just as real and accurate to them today as it ever was in the past, even when their brain has permanently changed the experience. In other words, their "reality" 30 years ago was scoring a goal in front of 20 people; their "reality" now 30 years later is scoring a goal in front of 200. They have had multiple realities, which one is "real"? Is the truth merely the memory that their brain convinces them of at any given time?

It has been shown in experiments that external stimulation of certain areas of the brain can elicit personal experiences in the

78

subject that seem very "real": feelings of pleasure or spirituality, recall of childhood memories, "out-of-body" and "near-death" experiences, as well as "psychedelic trips." Virtual reality technology enables the subject to have personal experiences artificially. The definition of one's reality becomes very blurry. These results show yet another reason why a personal experience may not necessarily be factual, meaningful or particularly useful.

It is instructive to compare the definitions and synonyms of "evidence" and "experience": for "evidence," you get affirmation, attestation, confirmation, corroboration, demonstration, documentation, proof, substantiation, verification; for experience, you get feel, sense, intimacy, involvement.

Experience does not equal evidence.

Another of the main problems with personal experience is that it doesn't benefit anyone else--unless the unquestioning acceptance of someone else's personal experience somehow benefits the outsider somehow. And if that is so, one would do well to define what is meant by "benefit." If it's an emotional or "spiritual" experience, it can't be tested in detail; it can't be verified for the use and benefit of others showing a natural, healthy skepticism. Personal experience isn't a reliable basis on which to base any action or thought or belief in the future, either for the observer or the outsider.

For this and other reasons, humans developed the discipline of science with the deliberate goal that it would discount personal experience and human bias as not being reliable enough on which to base knowledge and fact.

Two scientists seemed to experience the production of an excess of energy as the byproduct of a simple experiment, which they thought implied the creation of "cold fusion" (a possible source of cheap, clean energy). The remainder of the scientific community began with the usual, expected and necessary skepticism stating, "That would be interesting and exciting if true; but we wonder if other investigators do the same experiment, will they necessarily experience the same phenomenon?"

And sure enough, over time, the vast majority of labs couldn't replicate the scientists' experience. The personal experience of the original scientists didn't withstand the rigorous scientific tests of reproducibility, or reliability; the experience of two respected, experienced investigators couldn't be verified, it wasn't reliable, and therefore, it wasn't useful for humanity as a whole. And this refutation was good because future research wouldn't be based on such an unproven foundation; time and resources wouldn't be diverted to unproductive avenues. The researchers' personal experiences, biases and hypothesis could be swept to the rubbish heap as a waste of time, along with other such "personal experiences" as homeopathy, astrology, reiki and Ouija boards. By holding these experienced and previously successful scientists to the highest standards of inquisitive integrity possible, the scientific method triumphed again. It may not have produced new science, but at least it didn't enable pseudoscience.

The reason most people put so much emphasis on personal experience is that it is so immediate, and it can be very intense, overwhelming and seemingly undeniable. Additionally, most people would feel better thinking that their experiences were reliable, that they mattered, that they helped to explain some part of their universe. They would prefer to feel empowered by their experiences, so that they could be, to at least some extent, self-reliant; they wouldn't have to rely on someone else's knowledge and experiences for their own worldview. After all, it is much easier to trust yourself than to put trust in someone else. There is always some chance that another person might be trying to convince you (or fool you) for some reason of their own. But why on Earth would you try to fool yourself? Of course, the answer is: you may not be <u>trying</u> to fool yourself, but your brain is quite capable of misleading you nonetheless.

Often when questioned on how they know that a god exists, the believer uses phrases like, "I've had personal experiences that

1) ...felt like god talking to me,"

    or

2) "...felt like god steering me in this direction"

    or

3) "...felt like god enveloping me in his loving arms"

But how does one differentiate between genuine communication with one's deity and an instances of vivid imagination? Inspired wishful thinking? Biased interpretation? Hallucination? Delusion? It seems unlikely that any of these alternatives will even be considered if the believer automatically gives a biased credence to any experience that they have had. This will be explored further in the ensuing chapter "The Extremist vs. The Moderate." Such interpretations of hearing god can lead to anything as seemingly benign as simple blind faith to a parent killing their children and religious terrorists blowing up scores of innocent people.

When faced with this line of reasoning, the brain of the believer often defends its interpretation of its experience with, "Well, my god would never ask me to do anything like that." This kind of "No true Scotsman" fallacy (see) is often integral to the believer maintaining their position. Forgotten are the parts of their holy scriptures that are rife with instances where the prophets believed that the deity commanded such wholesale destruction.

Think about all of the times others have tried to convince you of their mindset based on their own experiences. What you'll notice is that 99% of the time, what they are saying boils down to: "Look, this is the way I experienced it, so you should too..." They are asking you to give them and their experience validation. What they are also tacitly suggesting is, "If you don't experience this the same way that I did, you are in essence saying that I'm deluded, or hallucinating or just crazy or maybe stupid. You're implying that my personal experience is less accurate, has less value, less benefit and less importance than your own." They may get very defensive and even say that you are insulting them if you don't agree with the validity of their experience.

Again, the vast majority of humans want an answer, sometimes any answer, they are attracted to certainty, and they want that positive feeling as fast as possible; any lingering doubt or uncertainty does not imbue them with positive feelings. Admittedly, the immediate self-questioning of each one of your experiences and the reliability of your resulting conclusions bogs things down considerably and slows up the instant gratification that appeals to most people. As people go through their daily lives, they want the comfort of relying on the assumed legitimacy of the unrelenting wave of personal experiences continually happening to them, as well as relying on the validity of the resulting conclusions they make about their reality.   People don't typically desire to feel like a visitor in an alien world, where they would never be absolutely certain of anything.

What happens the other 1% of the time is that a person that describes an experience of theirs (that perhaps you've never had) and asks, "Do you think that I could be imagining this? Is it possible my brain is playing tricks on me? Am I making some error in logic or reason? Is there some way that I could test this so that if I'm wrong, I won't be wasting my time with this supposed phenomenon anymore?" This scenario happens so rarely in day-to-day life because it isn't typical for a human to begin with the supposition that they can always be fooled. It isn't typical for a human to withhold their judgment of the validity of their own experience, they readily accept their immediate interpretation of their experiences as reality. But withholding final judgment is the superior approach; better to hold a position of uncertainty, of self-doubt, or at least of self-skepticism than to always assume that you've got it right every time.

> **Everything happens for a reason...except when it doesn't. But even then, with hindsight, you can come up with an explanation that satisfies your belief system.**
> —Anonymous

With humans, first comes the experience, then comes the explanation. The latter typically falls under one of three general categories: 1) desirable explanations 2) undesirable explanations and 3) ambivalent or non-explanations. While it is possible to attribute events to non-sentient causes (e.g., chance, nature or the laws of the universe itself), the influence of human bias often attempts to explain the experience as the will or action of some kind of agent. That is, something or some being that possesses sentience as well as the ability to affect the world, thereby enabling the experience.

Again, most people want an answer, an explanation; they're usually not satisfied with either no explanation (continued

83

ignorance) or even an explanation that leaves them ambivalent, unsatisfied or without any emotional response. They aren't likely to be satisfied with an undesirable explanation since as was asserted earlier, it's more common to ascribe events to causes and answers that create happiness and good feelings. Most people aren't happy thinking that negative events happened because there is an evil agent that made them happen, but they may believe it anyway if it means having some answer. It even leaves open the door that they may be able to influence the evil agent by modifying their behavior. But it's even less desirable to conclude that a major catastrophe (such as an Earthquake, a hurricane or perhaps the death of their child) occurred by causes beyond their control; after all, that might leave them with a feeling of helplessness or impotence. They unconsciously feel that it's more desirable to attribute the negative events to a desired explanation, something that is in control, such as a god with a divine plan, even when both the god and the plan are themselves inexplicable. The human brain is most adept at maximizing the convenience of its beliefs.

A PERSONAL GOD/ A PERSONAL TRUTH

I distrust those people who know so well what God wants them to do because I notice it always coincides with their own desires.
—Susan B Anthony (d.1906 Abolitionist, Social reformer and Women's Rights Activist)

Many monotheists like to refer to their own deity as a "personal god." In other words, theirs is not an impersonal god who created the universe and then faded into obscurity, never again to influence his creation. Theirs is not a god that started evolution and merely let it take its course. Their god does not merely take care of global matters or even the issues of a small community. Their god thinks about them underlined, all day every day, and also listens to their prayers and often intervenes because of those prayers (even when it changes the god's original "perfect" plan). This focus is an understandably comforting thought; after all, no one wants to think that their parent only thinks about the family as a whole rather than their own individual wants and needs.

If you are a human that has just imagined an explanation for your experience that relies on some all-powerful agent, you are also more likely to conveniently describe that agent as a pattern relatable to a human, such as a god that has created you in their own image. It would seem strange for a human to imagine a multi-tentacled green alien with horns and seven eyes as being their personal god. It's more comforting and empathetic to imagine a loving human-like deity who reminds you of an elderly, wise relative.

But even for the believer, it is advisable to avoid imagining this personal deity as too personal or too relatable; the more relatable, the more human, and a god can't be human. A god has to be something above mere humanity: supernatural, all-powerful, all-knowing and infallible. And difficult future situations might be more workable if it was agreed from the outset that mere humans weren't intended to understand or weren't even capable of understanding why this god would, for example, allow your home to be destroyed by a hurricane or require the death of your child for his plan. But not to worry, your brain has also conveniently bypassed your lack of comprehension of your god's plan by convincing you that as long as your god does understand, your brain is off the hook. It definitely helps that you imagined him as all-wise and omniscient from the start. To make existence more bearable going forward, you can just file any inexplicable episode of life in your choice of several sections in your brain: the "Not allowed to know" niche, the "You wouldn't understand anyway" area, or the "Because I said so" zone.

It is ironic and somewhat paradoxical that humans would first create a god that was on one level relatable (appearance), but not entirely relatable on all levels (e.g., comprehensibility). That is, within the limits of human intellect and human knowledge, mankind's creation of a god may give some explanatory power about how things happen, but not always why. It seems that humans still want some answer to fill a void, but they don't necessarily want to delve too deeply into the reasons behind the answer.

Then there are those monotheists who not-so-surprisingly find a comfortable middle ground to relate to their god. They don't like the baggage that comes with being the member of a "religion," especially since virtually all religions have had such questionable moral histories (persecutions, inquisitions, heresy trials, sacrifices, executions, crusades, jihads, wars, etc.). These nonconformists announce that they have risen above a mere set of doctrines and dogmas, rituals and mantras into which "organized religion" has devolved; these believers imagine they have a personal relationship with their personal god. As Ms. Anthony implied earlier, the amazing frequency with which these people's wishes and beliefs coincide with their personal deity's commandments is sure to strengthen that relationship. This coincidence also lends the believer the additional convenience of a perfect record of devoutness and piety. In essence, the individual has imagined a deity who is a perfect reflection of their own biases, point for point. Only this particular reflection just happens to be omnipotent and in charge. Therefore, their personal god makes the rules, which must be obeyed by all...and this means you.

However, despite the shortcomings mentioned above of organized religion, some believers will still seek out a conventional place of worship, perhaps for the social aspects, or the sense of community and fraternity, plus a ready-made source of playmates and friends for their children, not to mention additional child care when needed. You may have heard of people who "shop around" for a house of worship..."Yes, we've been trying several congregations but haven't found quite the right fit yet." Here is an instance of someone saying that they need to keep looking until they find a group that believes essentially the same way that they already believe. On the surface, that may seem obvious and even expected. But contemplate it a bit further; they are in essence saying, "The other congregations that I've rejected have got it wrong...only my version of belief is correct in its entirety. I am the ultimate authority on how to interpret the sacred texts, which doctrine is right, what is moral, what is true. Once I've found the congregation that matches my doctrine the most closely, not only will I feel the most comfortable, but I will have my own beliefs validated and reinforced; they will be reflected/repeated back to me over and over again. And because this denomination falls in line with my specific beliefs, I can appear totally pious, following the doctrine to the letter because I took the trouble initially of ensuring their doctrine agreed with my beliefs in the first place!"

Now, consider that every one of the rejected houses of worship included some authority figure: a priest, a pastor, a rabbi, an imam or guru. This authority had studied in genuine earnestness and in depth, for <u>years</u> at a seminary or the equivalent. They had access to not only the "purest" versions of the holy writ but also commiseration with noted professors and scholars, and access to a large library of argumentation and commentary on all possible religious tenets.   Each of these religious authorities feels that, above all of their congregants, they know best how to interpret and disperse the word of god(s). Consider if the "House-of-worship-shopper" dismissed the personal doctrines of each of these congregant leaders. The shopper is saying, "Despite your years of religious education, study, deep contemplation and experience, you obviously still have got some things wrong, and I don't have the time to set you straight. I'm off to find the religious authority who, despite studying the same texts for just as long as you, already agrees with <u>my</u> interpretation". Why would someone seek an outside authority when they've already determined that their own mind is the ultimate authority?

Freedom of religion allows me to interpret religious texts exactly how it fits my worldview already.
—Stephen Colbert (Comedian, Television Host, and Author)

Additionally, you may further fine-tune your choice of house of worship to encompass other biases that you possess. If you've decided that certain aspects of human sexuality are immoral or an abomination, it's a simple matter to find a denomination that already agrees with you. If you espouse living frugally and giving a substantial percentage of your income to this institution, there are a multitude of congregations with open arms; if you believe your faith should lead to your personal financial prosperity, you will find plenty of the like-minded. If you identify as female and feel that women should be subservient to men, denied equal opportunities in life and denied equal representation in civic matters, you will have no problem finding the faithful who can cite chapter and verse to that assertion. With so many biases with which humans have approached their world, it is small wonder then that there are thousands of faiths, denominations, sects and cults tailored to those biases.

Once you've found the pattern of biases that most closely matches your own, the next question might be: why do you need to have your personal beliefs repeated back at you on a regular basis? Is it possible that the consistent repetition of this doctrine, this pattern, continually reinforces your own beliefs in your mind, increasing your level of certainty? Is it possible that without the repetition of the pattern that your mind might have more opportunity to wander, to pose challenging questions to itself about what you believe and why you believe it?

And of course, seeking conformity doesn't stop at one's religious beliefs; this mindset of seeking out those that are like-minded extends to many other thought processes and ideologies, such as one's politics, one's child-rearing rules, one's circle of friends, etc. Who do you tend to associate with the most, those whose politics and parenting style and worldview is similar to yours, or do you actively seek out the company of those whose outlooks differ? If you extol the virtues of diversity, do you engage daily with it, or do you merely approve of it on an intellectual level, but as a daily course, continue to practice your own relatively narrow worldview with others whose worldview conforms with yours?

Being a species with a propensity for communal cooperation, most people prefer to avoid contentious confrontations in social settings whenever possible. They avoid bringing up potentially sensitive subjects such as politics, religion, and parenting styles. If they did, it might entail the extra effort of having to explain their reasoning for their views to others, sometimes repeatedly over many different occasions and with many different people; the repetition can be exhausting and frustrating.

Therefore, when given a choice, most people tend to seek out a group where they know they will be welcomed and accepted unquestioningly because the majority of their views fall in line with the rest of the group. It is very comforting to have your personal opinions and beliefs repeated back to you, seemingly validated by others, and further reinforcing your own mindset. This repetition can be especially gratifying if others of the group have had a different life experience than you, yet still come to the same conclusions. Could so many diverse people possibly be wrong about the same subject or belief?

The unexamined life is not worth living.
—Socrates (d.399 BCE Philosopher)

But how reliable are your views and opinions when you are now actively avoiding having them questioned by others or yourself? Will you ever arrive at a point in life where you can honestly say to yourself, "I have thought about this subject enough, and I have made up my mind that I am right about it. Further contemplation, further questioning, further challenging of it are unnecessary and time-consuming if not outright ridiculous"? Think of those people with whom you have disagreed in the past; if you labeled them "close-minded" because they listened to your arguments, yet refused even to question their own opinion, you could now empathize with their closed-mindedness. Ironic.

No opinion, no viewpoint, no fact, no truth should <u>ever</u> be immune to future challenge and testing. There should never be any thought or idea considered so sacred and sacrosanct that it is beyond questioning. Even if the sacred has withstood repeated challenges for centuries, it must always be open to future questioning. Because once you have closed the door to free inquiry, once you have closed your mind, effectively turning it off, you have just given up the only part of yourself that differentiates you from the other animals.

The only way that humanity has ever progressed is by questioning the status quo. It doesn't necessarily mean that you'll need to change the status quo, but it must always be open to challenge and future change. Sometimes it is comfortable to think, "You know, the status quo isn't so bad...the community is doing pretty well here...why on Earth would we want to think any differently and change that?"

Here is where it's helpful to be a student of history. Think back to almost any ancient civilization and how civilization would be today if the ancients had remained content with their lot in life. People expected to die relatively early in life because, well, everyone else tended to die young; they might die from an accident or violence or some disease or parasite, it was all part of the natural order, or perhaps god's plan, why would anyone ever question that? These upstart doctors thought that they might be able to increase the lifespan of people with their potions and treatments, but aren't they working against the way of nature, or in defiance of god's plan?

Or perhaps people in ancient times repeatedly injured themselves by continuing to do their job in the same unsafe manner, rather than questioning the way that they did it and devising a better, safer way. If you were only an apprentice, who are you to challenge the master's teachings by suggesting a better way of doing things?

Running parallel with this mindset is the sometimes desirable thought of temporarily putting your cares and woes into someone else's hands. Most adults want to have control of their lives and the daily situations which they face, at least the majority of the time. But with the stress of the daily onslaught (making so many decisions, always having to be in charge, ever being the responsible one, fearful that they may make a poor choice), it is the rare adult who doesn't secretly long for someone else to take over the duties and responsibilities for a while. Perhaps just a brief respite so that they can relax, knowing that someone competent is in charge who will take care of the essential things in their life. So the concept of an all-powerful, omniscient, perfect being who takes care of you and directs things is further reinforced; and the fact that he's a personal god, looking after the details of one's own life is most welcome. After one has worked as hard as they can and have given life their best effort, they are now quite prepared to think, "I have done all I can, the rest is in God's hands..."

But if you are unwilling to question the incredible coincidence of a "personal" god that just happens to see things exactly the same way that you do, or if the possibility doesn't even enter your mind that your own imagination, wishes and desires helped to conjure up this heavenly "answer-to-all-problems", then again, truth is likely not your ultimate goal.

92

You may merely be content to forever agree with your own brain.

And one's religious views are by no means the only place where one tends to agree with their own mind. Biases are a dominant driving force behind one's views and opinions on everything: politics, GMOs, vaccines, child-rearing, alternative medicine, etc. One's biases and mindset help determine whatever they ultimately take as their personal "truths," the "bricks" that form the foundation of one's world-view. In the later chapter entitled "A Collection of Irrational Nonsense," the potency of human biases in forging uncounted complex absurdities is demonstrated, and mercifully abridged.

THE EXTREMIST VS. THE MODERATE

> "My religious faith is very deep; it is at the core of
> my being, it makes up much of what I am. I live
> my life by my faith; it gives me my truths. I am
> happy when I feel that I am living my life by God's
> commandments and fulfilling his will. And I know
> that when I die, I will be welcomed into his warm
> embrace forever."

Upon reading the above statement, do you think that it was
spoken by a religious "moderate" or a religious terrorist?

Regardless of which way you answered, why couldn't you have
answered with the other choice?

These questions and their possible answers point to something
which often misrepresents how supposedly amiable a person's
faith is: that even the most seemingly harmless religious
moderate possesses the same <u>core</u> mindset of a fundamentalist,
an extremist or even a religious terrorist: unquestioning faith.
None of these faithful (at any level of belief) is likely to question
or challenge their <u>own</u> beliefs; they're not even likely to entertain
the possibility that they could be wrong about their beliefs.

Many religious moderates are content to remain moderate in their
beliefs just because of the rationale, "Well, at least I don't act as
fanatical or crazy as a fundamentalist or an extremist."
Meanwhile, the fundamentalist or extremist thinks, "Don't these
'moderates' have any conviction? Don't they ever take the

94

initiative to act on their beliefs? Or do they just expect others to do the hard work for them? How dare they pick and choose which parts of our sacred faith that they will believe and practice and emulate! If they dilute our faith any further, they may as well become secularists!"

And how does the religious "moderate" go about choosing which parts of the canon that they will believe and follow and how devoutly? Isn't their sacred text the same one that the extremist or fundamentalist believes and follows to the letter, without any subtle re-interpretation, no editing, no picking and choosing? Is the moderate saying, "I know better than the author(s) of these texts which parts should be taken literally and which parts are merely metaphorical or allegorical"? If these texts are supposedly inspired by the word of god, aren't they already perfect? Can a mere human edit what's the perfect, inerrant word of a deity?

A common response is, "Well, the text is inspired by god, but it is imperfect humans that write it down, and they may have made a few mistakes..." First, couldn't any all-powerful god at least make sure that their commandments and desires were transcribed accurately? Or if the god wasn't willing or able to put in enough effort on the front end, later on, couldn't they have somehow made it clear to the whole of humanity which version of their holy book got it all accurate? Does it make more sense to have each of the major religions so fractured by various translations, interpretations and Apocrypha?   Is god good with each sect or denomination belittling, persecuting, if not outright killing those with differing beliefs? It's as if god said, "Look, I just created the universe, space and time itself; I'm a little winded, so I'll leave the writing of the book that explains it all to my fallible creations, but heaven help them if they get it wrong..."

So, if god won't make it simple and clear as to the one proper way of being faithful, which fallible human will be the ultimate authority to decide which is the perfect transcription of divine directives? Considering the thousands of denominations of the monotheistic religions of Judaism, Islam and Christianity, the polytheistic religions of Hinduism and tribal cultures and all other forms of religious faith throughout the entire history of humanity, it should be reasonably clear that the answer is that there is no ultimate authority. In fact, there can be no ultimate authority for all people. Each individual ends up deciding the details of what they are going to believe.

HUMANS TEND TO BELIEVE TWO THINGS:
1) WHAT THEY WANT TO BELIEVE,
2) WHAT THEY NEED TO BELIEVE

Both the "fundamentalist/extremist" and the "moderate" have each decided what they want or need to believe and they take pride in asserting that nothing will alter their unshakable faith...The moderate says, "I don't understand these fundamentalists and extremists. They need to calm down and moderate their beliefs and join the present century; they are the ones that give religious faith a bad name." The moderate wonders how a religious terrorist could believe the things they do and commit the heinous acts that they do; when in actuality, their thinking processes are, at their core, substantially the same. At the same time, the fundamentalist/extremist says, "I don't understand these moderates; they go about their lives paying lip service to the most important truth of life, and they don't understand why the rest of the world won't join our faith, or why humanity doesn't change for the better. They need to get serious about their faith and get active about making real change in the world. Until then, they are the ones that give religious faith a bad name".

This badge of a "bad name" is human society's euphemism for "irrational," "not thinking clearly" or just "well-intentioned but misguided." And so, as all of the different religions, denominations, sects and splinter groups of these ideologies argue with each other, victimize each other's followers and occasionally make war or genocide on each other, ironically they are all victims of their own non-critical thought processes. But long before they get to that realization, they draw the line, and they will not cross it; whether extremist or moderate, they won't question their own beliefs, the individual will not make war with himself. The congregation desires solidarity. A proper threat must be found from outside rather than from within. Each congregant is distracted from questioning themselves and focused against some common external enemy; when all the while, the ultimate enemy is between their own ears.

We have met the enemy, and he is us.

—Walt Kelly (d.1973 Cartoonist)

Then comes the day when the moderate hears the "voice of god" in their head, telling them that the day has come and that they must take up swords and slay all who don't believe as they do. Now the moderate has a decision to make; will they believe that this voice is god and do as they are told without question (i.e., become the extremist/terrorist)? Or will they question this experience as a possible hallucination? Or as the devil tempting them to atrocities? Or will they somehow determine with their own innate morality that even if it is god, that somehow, god is asking them to do an immoral thing? Should they disobey this same god that, only a moment ago, they would have sworn was perfect, infallible and moral?

Hopefully, after such an experience, the believer might make the next leap in reason and ask themselves the question, "Well, how can I make sure any faith experience that I've ever had was real or reliable?", and "On what basis have I based my choices of which scripture I will accept and which will I deny?" With ever-increasing levels of honesty, integrity and self-skepticism, each person will eventually realize that they have been following their own desires, morals and biases the whole time and simply labeled it "god."

STATISTICS

Statistics is the branch of mathematics dealing with the collection, organization, analysis, interpretation and presentation of data. When rational argument has failed to make an impression, it is often statistics to which the arguer turns. Statistics have the virtue of being a visual representation, rather than merely an oral or written one. For a species that takes in so much information visually, this gives the statistical representation of data an extra weight of importance and relevance. In addition, statistics seem to imply an investigative rigor that simple rhetorical argument can't. Even so, it's entirely possible for someone to dismiss the implications of even these visual representations if they don't bolster their own view.

However, even on the occasions when the individual is prepared to accept the implications of what statistics indicate, the sad fact is that statistics can be manipulated to apparently demonstrate whatever the publisher wants (or what their underlying biases tacitly convince them must be true). Most people will look at a pie chart, a bar graph or some other representation of statistics and assume that it is a legitimate representation of the outcome of unbiased research and analysis. It isn't typical to question the source or to even to bother to check the source of the statistics. Many readers even ignore the units used on each of the graph's axes; yet taking note of these units is critical in confirming if the reader is actually seeing what they think that they are seeing. Most people approach their viewing of statistics with their biases submerged, and if the statistics confirm their bias, they pay more attention to the statistics and give them more credence. If the statistics seem to argue against their stance or their bias, it becomes evident to them that the data and statistics must have been manipulated and they feel sorry for the masses that have fallen for the deception.

Correlation does not equal causation.
—Anonymous

Another distinction should be made between correlation and causation, as they are often confused for one another. If data is analyzed with statistics and two variables seem to vary in a similar way, it seems to imply some connection between the two; but it is a common mistake to infer that one of the variables causes the change in the other variable. But all that one can say for sure at this early point is that there is a correlation, but not necessarily causation. The association may be caused by a known or unknown third variable, known as a confounding variable or a lurking variable.

The default position is that there is no relationship between two measured phenomena (i.e. chance or random processes alone caused the results); this default position is the "null hypothesis." **Rejecting or disproving the null hypothesis**—and thus concluding that there <u>are</u> grounds for accepting a relationship between two phenomena —is a central task in the modern practice of science.

However, to test for causation takes considerably more scientific rigor, which subsequently takes additional time, effort and money, not to mention a prolonged attention span of the reader. But if someone can appear to make their point with mere correlation, proving causation may not even be necessary. They are banking on the fact that few people are skeptical about the statistics with which they are presented, that they just accept them or discount them based solely on their biases.

Again, approaching any given proclamation of information with a recognition of one's own biases and a skeptical mindset helps to winnow down the chaff and leave only the grain.

100

SHORT LIST OF COGNITIVE BIASES AND LOGICAL FALLACIES (CBLFs)

The following alphabetical list of biases and fallacies has been gleaned from various sources (The Skeptic's Dictionary -Skepdic.com, Wikipedia, etc.) and is by no means exhaustive; nor are the definitions and examples given for each listing the only ones available. Moreover, each entry on the list is not mutually exclusive of others on the list; indeed, these fallacies and biases very often operate in concert with each other, and there may be some overlap in the scope of related biases/fallacies.

It is in fact extremely sobering to realize that this list could easily be extended in length, perhaps three or four times over, to include the sheer scope of poor reasoning created over the millennia by the human mind. For thousands of years, humans have been utilizing these fallacies and biases as the basis of their heuristics: mental shortcuts that facilitate daily life and survival. But the benefit of a heuristic "making life easier" does not endow it with the far more important quality of truth.

Even if this list is abbreviated, knowledge of these biases/fallacies may be an adequate primer for the reader previously unaware of all of them. Moreover, the reader is encouraged to do further reading and research on each entry and hopefully, discover other listings that aren't included. Recognizing different definitions and other examples of each entry is an additional way of increasing the scope of each entry.

After the reader has read these entries and had time to reflect, hopefully they will begin recognizing that their PSB uses many of these shortcuts too. It can be a humbling and even depressing realization that your thinking process is not so different than those with which you disagree. But when you are fore-armed with this self-awareness and knowledge, you don't have to remain a slave to the whims of your brain; you can actively take the necessary steps to overcome these biases and fallacies through the practice of CT.

Ad hoc hypothesis
An ad hoc hypothesis is one created to explain away facts that seem to refute one's belief or theory.

e.g., "Fortune tellers can predict the future!" "Well, why don't they predict the next lottery numbers and become rich?" "Well, they're not in it for the money....."

Ad hominem fallacy

Ad hominem is Latin for "to the man." The ad hominem fallacy occurs when one asserts that somebody's claim is wrong because of something about the person making the claim.

e.g., "This scientist has scientific evidence that proves evolution by Natural Selection!" "Yeah, but you can't trust him because he's from the North!"

Ad populum fallacy

The ad populum fallacy is the appeal to the popularity of a claim as a reason for accepting it.

The number of people who believe a claim is irrelevant to its truth.

e.g., "Billions of people have been Hindus, so Hinduism must be true because there's no way that so many people could be wrong about something so important!"

102

Affect bias

Judgment about the costs and benefits of items can be influenced by a feeling evoked by pictures or words only partially relevant to the actual cost or benefit. The impression one has just before making a decision is a bias that strongly influences that choice and can make it an irrational one.

e.g., People judged a disease as more lethal when it was presented as killing 1200 people out of every 10,000 that had it-- compared to a disease shown as being 24% fatal. So the mental image of 1200 dead people made a more significant impression than a disease that kills twice as many people, merely based on how the morbidity was presented.

Anchoring effect

Our judgment regarding the frequency, probability, or value of items is often determined by comparing the item to an anchor point.

e.g. When buying an item, if two higher prices on the price tag are crossed out, you may feel you're getting a bargain because you use the highest price as an "anchor" with which to compare to the current price (even if that current price were still considered by others to be "too high.")

Anomalistic psychology

Anomalistic psychology (AP) is the study of extraordinary experiences (e.g., the supposedly paranormal or supernatural). AP studies such things as experiences of "telepathy" or "clairvoyance," "UFO"s, "ghosts" or "angels," and "healing touch." AP does not begin with the assumption that a bizarre experience is paranormal or supernatural. AP attempts to explain extraordinary experiences as the inevitable result of known psychological and physical factors, including frauds and hoaxes.

103

Apophenia

Apophenia is the spontaneous perception of connections and meaningfulness of unrelated phenomena.

e.g., Hidden meanings that fortune tellers ascribe to random events, e.g. reading the tea leaves left behind in the cup.

See also Pareidolia, the Gambler's fallacy, Confirmation bias and the Clustering illusion.

Appeals to authority

The appeal to authority is a fallacy of irrelevance when the authority being cited is not an authority. E.g., because Albert Einstein spoke of "god," and Einstein was a genius, that means that a genius believed in god and therefore lends weight to god's existence, even though Einstein's genius (and thus, any perceived authority) was in theoretical physics, not theology.

A different appeal to authority is citing a lone scientist's disagreement with a well-established theory in his specialty as proof that the theory is incorrect. The lone scientist is cited as an "authority," i.e., what this person says MUST be true because he is, after all, a specialist in the disputed area. Ergo, one person may discount he other 99% of his colleagues in the same specialty who have not only accepted the overwhelming consensus on the validity of the theory but can point to how successful and useful the theory has been.

Despite what the media often present, there are no authorities in science and medicine, only experts in various fields. The proclamations of these experts are ALWAYS open to refutation by further scientific investigation. The validity of any pronouncement made in science and medicine is always limited by the implied qualifier: "...to the best of our current knowledge...".

104

(irrelevant) Appeal to tradition

A practice or a belief is justifiable simply because it has a long and established history.

e.g., "That's just the way we've always done it in our family" (as in, they have always been racists, so there is no need to contemplate the matter any further, they will continue to be racists).

e.g., "Our Founding Fathers created our incredible nation, so we should always do as they have done" (even if they kept slaves, withheld the vote from women, forced young children to work in dangerous conditions and believed that bleedings would restore the normal levels of bodily humors).

e.g., Fighter pilots have always been male, so there is no reason even to consider training females for the job.

Argument to ignorance (argumentum ad ignorantiam)

Something is true only because it hasn't been proven false, or that something is false just because it has not been proven true.

e.g., "God must be real because you can't disprove him..." or "Life couldn't have come from non-living chemicals because no one has ever done it in the lab..."

Another form of this fallacy is the "failure of imagination."

e.g., "My spouse must be late because they're cheating on me...what else could it be...?"

Another form is "The argument from personal incredulity," which takes the form of "I can't imagine how that could be; therefore it must be impossible."

e.g., Without the proper education in the biological sciences, it is common to hear, "I don't see how a fish could have evolved into an amphibian." The mere fact that you lack the knowledge or imagination lends no weight at all to your disputation.

Autokinetic effect

The autokinetic effect refers to perceiving a stationary image as moving. Psychologists attribute the perception of this movement to "small, involuntary movements of the eyeball," yet the brain is still continually fooled into seeing motion where there is none, even when the observer knows and accepts the facts.

The autokinetic effect can be enhanced by the power of suggestion and group dynamics: If one person reports that a stationary image is moving, others will be more likely to report the same. The underlying desire to be a part of the "in group" is powerful enough to influence one's perception.

Attribution biases

People tend to attribute their successes to their intelligence, skill, hard work and perseverance, and to other positive personal traits. Failures are blamed on bad luck, sabotage by others, a lost lucky charm, and other uncontrollable forces. These attribution biases are referred to as the dispositional attribution bias and the situational attribution bias. They are applied in reverse when people try to explain the successes and failures of others. Others succeed because they're lucky or have connections and they fail because they're stupid, wicked, or lazy.

Availability heuristic

Most human choices and judgments are made under conditions of uncertainty and immediacy. To determine which belief or action has the highest probability of being the correct one in a given situation, people most often use heuristics, or instinctive yet irrational "rules of thumb," to guide them. One of these heuristics

106

is the availability heuristic, i.e., determining probability "by the ease with which relevant examples come to mind."

e.g., If the news seems to show an increase in child abductions in your area, you are more likely to perceive the threat and take extra precautions, even when the chance of your child being abducted is vanishingly small. When the movie "Jaws" came out, the numbers of beach-goers dropped precipitously, only because the memory of the movie was so recent, its ease of availability in the mind of someone on vacation was enough to change their behavior, even though there was a much greater chance that they'd be struck by lightning.

Baby Moses syndrome (the hope-in-a-basket fallacy)

A psychological defense mechanism of wishful thinking that somebody else will eventually come along to solve your problems for you.

Not to be confused with Moses Syndrome (see) where a perceived authority is seen to offer prosperity to the masses, or the desire that someone has been chosen to lead the masses to prosperity.

Backfire effect

The "Backfire effect" describes how some individuals, when confronted with evidence that conflicts with their beliefs, come to hold their original position even more strongly. The perceived value of continuing to believe that one still hasn't been proven wrong outweighs the benefit of the accuracy of the conflicting evidence. The Backfire effect is strongly associated with Confirmation bias (see).

Barnum effect/Forer effect

The Barnum effect is when a person finds personal meaning and validation in relatively general statements that could apply to many people.

This effect is often seen in horoscopes, fortune telling, cold readings by psychics, graphology and some types of personality tests. It is related to confirmation bias (see) and the file drawer effect (see), where the observer picks and chooses those aspects of the statements that confirm their presuppositions and biases and ignores the aspects that don't. The effect is named for the showman P.T. Barnum whose success was attributed to his philosophy of "have something for everyone." Coincidentally, Barnum is also attributed with the saying, "There's a sucker born every minute."

When the individual begins with the subconscious wish to find something in an idea relevant to themselves, their brain will bend over backward to rationalize a connection, to get a positive affirmation. The alternative of finding nothing relevant to themselves gives no positive feeling of any kind.

Begging the question

"Begging the question" occurs in an argument when one assumes what one claims to be proving. It is related to circular reasoning (see).

An argument is a form of reasoning whereby one gives a reason or reasons in support of some claim. The reasons are called premises, and the claim that one tries to support with these premises is called the conclusion.

e.g. The attempt is made to support the assertion "Paranormal activity is real" by the premise, "I have experienced what can only be described as paranormal activity." The premise presupposes,

108

or assumes, that the claim, "paranormal activity is real" is already true.

If one's premises entail one's conclusion, and one's premises are questionable, one is said to beg the question.

e.g., Past-life memories of children prove that past lives exist because the children could have no other source for their memories besides having lived in the past. [Note how this example also includes the argument to ignorance/failure of imagination (see); different logical fallacies often occur simultaneously].

"Begs the question" is often erroneously used instead of "Raises the question."

Bias blind spot

The bias blind spot is the tendency to perceive cognitive and motivational biases much more in others than in oneself. It is a human trait to give yourself more credit for being unbiased than someone else. Your own biases fall into your mental blind spot.

e.g., 74% of all engineers think they are better than average at engineering, which is by definition impossible since theoretically the highest percentage of engineers that could be better than average only approaches 50%. The additional 24% are by definition biased in their own favor but are unaware of their bias because they are blind to it.

Change blindness

Change blindness is the failure to detect non-trivial changes in the visual field. It is a related to inattentional blindness, both of which have been implicated in the non-reliability of eyewitness testimony. When multiple people focus on different details of an event, their assertions can differ wildly, and they often miss very obvious facts that others saw, and vice versa.

Humans are extremely inefficient in paying attention to multiple things at once. e.g., Texting on a cell phone while driving increases your blindness to the change happening in your visual field (e.g., the child that just ran into your traffic lane).

Circular reasoning (a.k.a begging the question, or circular logic)

Circular reasoning is a fallacy in which the arguer begins with the conclusion that they hope to reach. A circular argument may appear logically valid at the outset because if the premises appear true, the conclusion appears to be true.

Circular reasoning is not so much a formal logical fallacy but a functional defect in the way the argument is constructed:

I.e., the premises are just as much in need of proof/evidence as the conclusion; therefore, the argument should fail to persuade.

or

there is no reason to accept the premises unless one already believes the conclusion.

or

the premises provide no independent ground or evidence for the conclusion.

A classic example: The Bible is the Word of God because God tells us so in the Bible.

Clever Hans phenomenon

A form of involuntary and unconscious cueing. The term refers to a horse, "Kluge Hans," who responded to math questions by tapping his hoof the appropriate number of times. It was

110

eventually discovered that the horse was responding to subtle physical cues (i.e., ideomotor effect) such as involuntary postural adjustments by the questioner, which was his cue to start tapping, and an unconscious, almost imperceptible head movement by the questioner, which was his cue to stop tapping". The trainer was entirely unaware that he was providing such cues. This has been further researched and has been related to the observer-expectancy effect (see).

Clever Linda phenomenon

A form of involuntary and unconscious cueing. The term refers to a speech therapist (Linda Wouters) who responded to questions asked of a patient (previously diagnosed as being in a persistent vegetative state) by guiding the patient's finger to letters on a keyboard.

See Ideomotor Effect and Observer-Expectancy Effect.

Clustering illusion

The clustering illusion is the bias that random events which occur in clusters are not truly random. The illusion is due to selective thinking based on a counter-intuitive but false assumption regarding statistical odds. The illusion is caused by a human tendency to under-predict the amount of variability likely to appear in a small sample of random or semi-random data. e.g., seeing patterns in stock market price fluctuations over time. It is related to apophenia, pareidolia, the illusion of control, the gambler's fallacy and the Texas sharpshooter fallacy. It is also a common way of misrepresenting statistics to bolster a fallacious argument.

Cognitive dissonance

Cognitive dissonance is the mental discomfort (i.e., psychological stress) experienced by a person who simultaneously holds two

111

or more contradictory beliefs, ideas or values. Cognitive dissonance also occurs when confronted with new information that contradicts past beliefs, ideas, and values. It is often augmented by confirmation bias and the file drawer effect in order for the person to continue functioning with their contradiction(s).

Coincidence (law of truly large numbers)

The law of truly large numbers says that with a large enough sample many "odd" coincidences are likely to happen. Because humans rarely find it notable when routine events occur, they will much more likely notice a seemingly "unlikely" event.

The study of this bias helps in dispelling pseudoscience; e.g., the more predictions a psychic makes, the better the odds that one of them will "hit." Then the psychic relies on their clients to forget the vast majority that did not "hit"; this is similar to gamblers tending to remember their wins and forgetting their losses.

Cold reading

Cold reading refers to a set of techniques used by professional manipulators to get a subject to behave in a certain way or to think that the cold reader has some ability that allows him to "mysteriously" know things about the subject. Cold reading goes beyond the usual tools of manipulation: i.e. suggestion and flattery. In cold reading, salespersons, hypnotists, advertising pros, faith healers, con men, and some unscrupulous therapists bank on their client's inclination to find more meaning in a situation than there actually is.

The desire to make sense out of an experience can lead people to many wonderful discoveries, but it can also lead them to many falsehoods. The manipulator knows that his mark will be inclined to try to make sense out of whatever he is told, no matter how

112

far-fetched or improbable. The manipulator knows, too, that people are generally self-centered, that they tend to have unrealistic views of themselves.

Add to this that the manipulator knows that people will usually accept claims about themselves that reflect how they <u>wish</u> they were or think they <u>should</u> be (see Wishful thinking), rather than how they <u>actually</u> are or how they really think they are. He also knows that out of several claims that he makes about his client that they reject as inaccurate, he will likely make one that meets with their approval; and he knows that they are likely to remember the hits he makes and forget the misses.

See Confirmation bias and Barnum effect.

> **Everything happens for a reason...except when it doesn't. But even then, with hindsight, you can come up with an explanation that satisfies your belief system.**
> —Anonymous

<u>Collective hallucination</u>

A collective hallucination is a sensory hallucination induced by the power of suggestion to a group of people, especially if they are in a heightened emotional situation.

e.g. The expectancy and hope of the religious to bear witness to a miracle, combined with the stress, fatigue and sensory exhaustion from extended pilgrimages and/or long hours of staring at religious scenes, increases susceptibility to seeing such things as weeping statues, moving icons or seeing Jesus in a piece of burnt toast (itself an example of pareidolia).

Where belief in miracles exists, evidence will always be forthcoming to confirm its existence. In the case of moving statues and paintings, the belief produces the hallucination, and the hallucination confirms the belief.
--D.H. Rawcliffe (Psychologist and Author)

(In sociology and psychology, collective hallucination is associated with mass hysteria and collective obsessional behavior)

Communal reinforcement

"millions of people can't all be wrong."

Communal reinforcement is a social phenomenon in which a concept or idea is repeatedly asserted in a community, regardless of whether sufficient empirical evidence has been presented to support it. The strength of this bias contributes to the popularity and influence of doctrines, dogmas and mantras.

Often, the mass media contribute to the process by uncritically reporting these claims without skepticism.

It can also explain how the repetition of testimonials within the community of therapists, sociologists, psychologists, theologians, politicians, talk show hosts, etc., can supplant and be regarded as more accurate than actual scientific studies. But the frequency of verbal repetition has no bearing on the truth of a claim.

Conditioning

Conditioning, aka classical conditioning or Pavlovian conditioning, is a form of response to an expectation based on the association between a stimulus and a response.

114

For example, a dog notes that each time a bell is rung, it gets some food. After a long enough period of conditioning (sometimes within minutes), the dog associates the sound with food and so begins to salivate whenever the bell is rung, regardless of whether or not food follows.

Another example: a believer experiences a positive feeling whenever they pray, which increases the chance that they will pray in the future, in order to receive the positive feeling.

Confabulation

Confabulation is an alteration of a memory, involving fabrication, distortion, or misinterpretation of a memory without the conscious intention to deceive themselves or others. People are very confident about the accuracy of their memories, even when it has been proven that the details of a given memory have in fact changed over time.

Examples include "memories" of people claiming to have been abducted by aliens, as well as "false memories" of childhood induced by therapists or interviewers.

Confirmation bias

Confirmation bias is the tendency to search for, favor, and recall information in a way that confirms one's preexisting beliefs while discounting or giving little weight to information that doesn't confirm the belief. People also tend to interpret ambiguous evidence as supporting their existing position.

People display this bias when they gather or remember information selectively, or when they interpret it in a biased way.

It is the peculiar and perpetual error of the human understanding to be more moved and excited by affirmatives than by negatives.

—Sir Francis Bacon (d. 1626 Philosopher, Statesman, Scientist, Jurist, Orator, and Author--- Father of the Scientific Method)

Compare File Drawer Effect.

Conspiracy theories

A conspiracy theory is an unwarranted explanation of an event or situation that invokes a plot, such as might be carried out by a government or leaders of science or industry. Conspiracy theories often produce hypotheses that contradict the prevailing understanding of history or scientific facts.

Conspiracy theories rely on the view that the universe is governed by design, and embody three principles:

1) nothing happens by accident
2) nothing is as it seems, and
3) everything is connected.

When investigated closely, conspiracy theories tend to be a matter of faith rather than proof and have the trait of being unfalsifiable, the latter attribute being a measure of their uselessness in explanatory power.

Of course, there have been genuine conspiracies. However, even if there is a conspiracy, one is still not justified in theorizing a conspiracy just because 1) they can't accept another proven explanation, 2) they can't imagine another explanation or 3) because they have no explanation at all.

116

Continued influence effect

Continued influence is an effect where even after one's beliefs have been found false or unfounded, the beliefs continue to influence one's reasoning.

Compare Confirmation Bias and Backfire Effect.

Denial

A psychological defense mechanism in which a person is faced with a fact that is too uncomfortable to accept and thereby rejects it, despite what may be overwhelming evidence.

Compare Cognitive Dissonance.

Divine fallacy (argument from personal incredulity)

This argument is a logical fallacy that, because something is so incredible/amazing/incomprehensible/unimaginable, it must be the result of a divine/alien/supernatural cause, only because one can't imagine how it could occur otherwise.

This argument is comparable to the "failure of imagination." Humans are limited by their knowledge, intelligence, experience and imagination and when confronted by something seemingly incredible, an easy mental shortcut is to attribute it to something just as incredible; as in, "We no longer need to explain this phenomenon because it was caused by something else inexplicable!".

Dunning-Kruger Effect

The Dunning–Kruger effect is a cognitive bias wherein one mistakenly assesses their cognitive ability or expertise in some area as higher than it is.

> **Real knowledge is to know the extent of one's ignorance.**
> —Confucius (d.479 BCE Philosopher) and Socrates (d.399 BCE Philosopher)

> **The fool doth think he is wise, but the wise man knows himself to be a fool.**
> —William Shakespeare (d.1616 playwright)

> **Ignorance more frequently begets confidence than does knowledge.**
> —Charles Darwin (d.1882 Naturalist, co-formulator of Theory of Evolution by way of Natural Selection)

> **One of the painful things about our time is that those who feel certainty are stupid, and those with any imagination and understanding are filled with doubt and indecision.**
> —Bertrand Russell (d. 1970 Philosopher, Logician, Mathematician, Historian, writer, Social Critic, Political Activist and Nobel Laureate)

False dilemma (false dichotomy)

The false dilemma/false dichotomy (aka "the either-or fallacy") is a fallacy of reasoning which insists that one must choose between only two options and omits consideration of all reasonable alternatives. (There can be false trilemmas, etc.).

An example is someone asking you, "Are you liberal or

conservative?" when there are other alternatives such as libertarian, socialist, etc. If one hesitates to answer, a common ploy is to follow up this question with the admonition, "Quit being wishy-washy...can't you just choose one or the other, why won't you take a stand?"

In psychology, a related phenomenon is "black-and-white thinking," in an area where there may indeed be "many gray areas."

False memory

A false memory is a memory which is a distortion of an actual experience, or a confabulation of imagined experiences. Some false memories involve mixing fragments of memories; some of these memories may have happened at different times but may be confabulated as occurring together. Some false memories are an error in the original source memory. Some involve treating dreams as if they were playbacks of real experiences, and it can be difficult teasing out what was a dream and what was reality.

Other false memories are believed to be the result of the prodding, leading questions, and suggestions of therapists and counselors. The ability to implant false memories in others by these trusted authority figures has been shown to be shockingly simple.

Compare Confabulation.

File-drawer effect

The file-drawer effect refers to the practice of researchers filing away studies with negative or undesirable outcomes. In scientific investigation a negative outcome refers to finding nothing of statistical significance or causal consequence, it does not refer to finding something that affects some aspect of the world negatively. A negative outcome may also apply to finding something that is contrary to one's earlier research or to what one expects or desires.

In confirmation bias, one remembers the hits and forgets the misses. In the file drawer effect, one actively discounts and files away (hides or ignores) that which does not confirm the bias; out of sight, out of mind.

Gambler's fallacy

The gambler's fallacy (also known as the fallacy of the maturity of chances) is the mistaken belief that, if something happens more frequently than usual during some period, it will happen less often in the future, or that, if something happens less frequently than usual during some period, it will happen more regularly in the future. This is imagined presumably as a means of somehow "balancing nature."

Halo effect

The halo effect refers to a bias whereby the perception of a positive trait in a person or product positively influences further judgments about traits of that person or products by the same manufacturer. A simple example is judging that an attractive person is more intelligent and amiable than a less attractive person. And marketers know that if they can get favorable reviews on one of their products, it makes their company and its other products more attractive, regardless of their actual quality.

The corollary to the halo effect is the "horns effect" whereby a perceived negative trait of an individual or brand is spread to all aspects of the individual or company. The "halo and horns effect" is named after religious art that depicts the good with halos and the evil with devil's horns.

This is why first impressions matter so much; they can be extremely difficult to overcome. People love to listen to their

120

intuition or their initial gut instinct when judging someone. It is common practice for defense lawyers to make sure the defendant is clean-shaven and well-dressed to increase the likelihood of the halo effect to be bestowed on the defendant by the members of the jury.

Hindsight bias

Hindsight bias, aka the "knew-it-all-along effect," is the tendency, after a new fact has been discovered or an event has occurred, to see the fact or event as having been predictable, despite having no objective way of predicting it. With it, one can reconstruct one's memory after the discovery or the event (or re-interpret the meaning of something in the past) according to currently known facts and one's current beliefs. It is a way to make the past consistent with the present and therefore seem more predictable than it actually was.

Hindsight bias explains how believers in prophecies and psychic predictions retrofit current events to past claims, which tend to be extremely vague and open to many possible interpretations (retroactive clairvoyance). Typical examples of hindsight bias include explaining world events by the vague predictions of Nostradamus or "bible codes."

Ideomotor effect

The ideomotor effect refers to the influence of suggestion or expectation on involuntary and unconscious motor behavior. The effects of automatic writing, dowsing, the movement of pointers on Ouija boards, of a facilitator's hands in facilitated communication, of hands and arms in applied kinesiology, and of some behaviors attributed to hypnotic suggestion, are due to ideomotor action.

121

Illusion of control

The illusion of control is the tendency for people to overestimate their ability to control events; it occurs when someone feels a sense of control over outcomes even when they know it should be impossible to control the outcome.

Examples include:

Psychokinesis (where one feels they can move objects with their mind)

Intercessory prayer (where one feels they can personally influence a deity to change the deity's original "perfect" plan for the faithful's gain)

Willing your team to win (even when watching them remotely on television)

Gambler's willing their winning combinations to appear (apparently not considering that their competitors are likely attempting to will their own winning combinations to appear).

Illusion of justice

The illusion of justice is the idea that it seems intolerable when bad things happen to good people, or good things happen to bad people. The most popular stories, movies, musicals and operas have good triumphing over evil. The conflict reaches a "just" resolution and the viewer is left satisfied. The golden rule states "treat others as you want to be treated (because that is just)." Generally, humans approve rewarding good and punishing evil.

But in the real world, it is common to see those cheating or breaking laws or committing crimes get away with it or actually being rewarded. Somehow, they escape justice on Earth. But humanity's innate sense of justice couldn't allow it to end there, so humans invented deities that would ensure that ultimately, upon the death of the wicked, justice was served in some other-worldly realm. For some inexplicable reason, the people still living couldn't see this domain, but in their hearts, they knew that it <u>had</u> to be there, otherwise their sense of justice couldn't be ultimately satisfied. Thus, with the illusion of some kind of justice imagined, humans could sleep better at night.

The idea that god is just, is directly contradicted by the idea that god is merciful. Perfect justice and any mercy are necessarily directly in contradiction because mercy is the suspension of justice.
—Matt Dillahunty (Secular Humanist Advocate, Debater, Author and Speaker)

Illusion of skill

The illusion of skill is the belief that the skill alone of the person involved is enough to explain their accuracy in predicting such things as the profile of an unknown criminal, a psychic's knowledge of where a missing person will be found, a stock analyst's long-range predictions for the stock market or the author of a farmer's almanac being able to predict long-range weather forecasts. With a large enough number of predictions, the predictor is likely to get a certain percentage correct just from pure chance outcomes. But by the observer remembering the "hits" and dismissing the "misses" (confirmation bias/file drawer effect), the predictor is given far more credit than is due.

Illusion of understanding

For humans, it is extremely attractive to have the feeling of total understanding of some aspect of the world, or perhaps total understanding of the whole universe Even better if it all made sense. Humans are also far more comfortable with being certain rather than being undecided about various aspects of their world because it makes them feel less helpless. Their alleged understanding and certainty empowers them, and they may even feel like their understanding/certainty gives them some measure of control in their lives.

The ubiquity of confirmation bias and selection bias make this illusion all too frequent. By recalling only the data and information that bolsters your side of the argument and tossing out that which contradicts it, one may form what on the surface appears to be a convincing argument, but it ultimately misleads, not only the listener but also the proposer.

Compare Dunning—Kruger effect and Illusion of Control.

Inattentional blindness (aka perceptual blindness)

This is a psychological lack of attention that is not associated with any vision defects or deficits. An individual pays attention to some specific detail in their visual field while simultaneously failing to perceive an unexpected but obvious visual stimulus that is in plain sight—i.e., a temporary blindness to this stimulus.

The amount of detail in a scene to which the human brain can pay attention is extremely limited. The brain tends to focus on one or two specifics and ignores the rest. This is another reason eyewitness testimony can differ so wildly between multiple witnesses of the same event, and what makes eyewitness testimony such weak evidence.

There was a famous video online that asked the viewer to count how many times a basketball team passed the ball back and forth. When the video ended and asked for the viewer's answer, the "sharp-eyed" would answer "13", which happened to be the

124

correct answer. The questioner continued, "...but did you see the break-dancing bear?" The same video was rewound, and sure enough, someone wearing a bear costume waltzed through the scene in plain sight, not even trying to sneak through. It leaves the viewer stunned that it was so simple to make their brain blind to such a non-trivial aspect of their vision.

Intentionality bias

Even when random, ambiguous events happen, humans tend to assume that they were intended, rather than random. Children are especially susceptible to this. When young children see somebody sneeze or fall over, they think that the person must have meant to sneeze or fall over. With advancing maturity, experience and socialization, humans begin to override their automatic judgment of intent. But the bias is typically only temporarily submerged. And it is often brought back to the surface by imbibing alcohol; an accidental bump, a spilled drink, or an innocent comment all may be misinterpreted into intentionality and may result in retribution.

Intentionality bias is also a core source of many conspiracy theories (see).

Infrasound

Infrasound refers to extreme bass waves or vibrations, those with a frequency below the audible range of the human ear (20 Hz to 22 kHz). While humans can't hear these waves, they can be felt and have been shown in various studies to produce a range of effects including anxiety, extreme sorrow, and chills. One study has suggested that infrasound may cause feelings of awe or fear in humans. It has also been suggested that since infrasound is not consciously perceived, it may make people subconsciously feel that religious, paranormal or other supernatural events are taking place.

Jamais vu

Jamais vu is a phenomenon involving a sense of eeriness and the observer's impression of seeing the situation for the first time, despite rationally knowing that he or she has been in the situation before.

Contrast this with Deja vu where the observer's impression is that they've experienced something before when it's actually their first experience.

Jamais vu most commonly occurs when a person momentarily does not recognize a word or, less frequently, a person or place, that she or he actually knows. After writing down a known word, the writer gets the uneasy feeling, "There's no way it is spelled correctly," or that it is an "actual word."

Magical thinking

Magical thinking denotes the belief that one's thoughts by themselves can bring about effects in the world or that thinking something corresponds with doing it. The belief can cause a person to experience fear of performing certain acts or having certain thoughts because of an assumed connection between doing so and bringing on calamities.

This type of thinking has led to all forms of ritual, prayer, sacrifice, taboo and religious faith. Magical thinking has also been implicated in the occurrence of psychosomatic disease and the placebo effect (see).

Mass hysteria
(a.k.a. collective obsessive behavior, group hysteria or collective hysteria)

Mass hysteria refers to the expression of strong, inappropriate emotional or physical responses such as irrational fears or hopes, or sickness by groups of people to beliefs based on suggestions, misunderstood facts, imagined stimuli, communal reinforcement, or blindly following a false authority.

Recent examples of mass hysteria include the Satanic ritual abuse panic, fear of alien abduction, fear of electromagnetic radiation, milk-drinking statues in India, the monkey-man of New Delhi, the hospitalization of 30 people exposed to a perfume they thought was carbon monoxide, and koro (shook yang) in Singapore.

It is interesting to see how a phenomenon can progress throughout a group even when there is no physical connection between the individuals. By virtue of being social animals, humans tend to interact with, respond to and amplify the emotions of the multitudes with which they share a group. A famous book that deals with this is Extraordinary Popular Delusions and the Madness of Crowds by Charles MacKay.

Moses syndrome

Belief in the promises of others (usually authority figures) to lead one to beauty, youth, wealth, power, peace of mind, or happiness.
Also, it can be the belief that one has been chosen by a god, destiny, or history to lead others to a better place/world.

The Moses syndrome should not be confused with the Baby Moses syndrome (the hope-in-a-basket fallacy), a psychological defense mechanism of wishful thinking that somebody else will

127

eventually come along to solve your problems for you.

Motivated reasoning

Motivated reasoning is confirmation bias taken to the next level. Rather than search rationally for information that either confirms or refutes a particular belief, the individual more actively seeks out information that confirms their belief. Motivated reasoning is clearly emotion-driven, precisely by a desire to avoid cognitive dissonance (mental discomfort from holding contrary opinions). The resulting self-delusion provides a kind of pleasure from psychological relief, and therefore the individual is motivated to continue this faulty reasoning.

> **The most common of all follies is to believe passionately in the palpably not true. It is the chief occupation of mankind.**
> — H.L. Mencken (d. 1956 Journalist, Satirist, Cultural Critic)

> **People apply fight-or-flight reflexes not only to predators but to data itself.**
> —Chris Mooney (Author and Journalist)

Nocebo and nocebo effect

A nocebo effect is an ill effect caused by the suggestion or belief that something is harmful. Sometimes referred to as the "power of suggestion."

More than two-thirds of 34 college students developed headaches when told that a non-existent electrical current passing through their heads could produce a headache.

Compare Placebo Effect and Mass Hysteria.

128

Non sequitur

A non sequitur (literally, "does not follow") is a logical fallacy. One's reasoning is said to be a non sequitur if the conclusion does not follow from the premises or if a given reason for taking an action is completely irrelevant to taking that action. For example, the police chief's reasoning was a non sequitur when he defended consulting a psychic "to help investigators crack the case" based on the premise that "people tried everything else and hadn't solved the case." The fact that the case hadn't been solved using traditional police methods is irrelevant to whether consulting a psychic is a method that should be used. The error in reasoning should become obvious if one substitutes "pick a name randomly out of the phone book to identify the main suspect " for "consult a psychic." The fact that you haven't solved the case using traditional methods provides no support for trying a non-traditional approach. To justify trying a non-traditional process, one needs direct evidence that the non-traditional method has some merit.

No true Scotsman fallacy

This is an informal fallacy related to the ad hoc fallacy in which one tries to protect some aspect of an ideology from refutation by changing the definition in an ad hoc fashion to specifically exclude the refutation.

Person 1: "No Scotsman puts sugar on their porridge."

Person 2: "But my Uncle Angus never left Glasgow and loves sugar on his porridge!"

Person 1: "Well then, no true Scotsman puts sugar on their porridge."

Another example:

1st person: "Members of my group would never kill anyone."

2nd person: "A member of your group just killed someone."

1st person: "Well then, they weren't a <u>true</u> member of my group."

i.e., those who perform that action are not part of their group, and thus criticism of that action is not a criticism of the group.

Observer-expectancy effect

(also called the experimenter-expectancy effect, expectancy bias, observer effect, or experimenter effect)

In medicine and science, a researcher's bias or a subject's bias can lead either to influence the results of an experiment subconsciously.

(This is a significant threat to a scientific or medical study's validity and has lead to the frequent use of double-blind experiments where both subject and researcher are ignorant or "blind" to what factors or desired outcomes are being tested. In this way, any influence from bias can be reduced or blocked).

e.g., Music Backmasking: this is where a subject is given the script of supposedly "hidden messages" only audible when music is played backward. Without a script or without prior notice, the listener will likely fail to hear any intelligible lyrics, but once "hidden lyrics" are suggested, the listener now has increased expectation to hear them and will claim their presence as undeniable.

e.g., Facilitated communication: patients that are thought not to have the ability to communicate in any way are "facilitated" by another individual, usually by "facilitating" or guiding the patient's

130

hands on a keyboard or word-board.

e.g., Dowsing for water or other desirable materials with sticks

Seek and ye shall find. Matthew 7:7

Ockham's razor (aka The Law of Parsimony)

Ockham's Razor should not be regarded as an absolute guide to logic or investigation, but rather as a practical heuristic with which to create a hypothesis. Later on, this mental shortcut may be found to be inadequate and, in fact, may be discarded.

Simpler hypotheses are preferable to more complex ones because they are more testable and falsifiable, thereby resulting in stronger theories.

> **Pluralitas non est ponenda sine neccesitate"**
> **or "plurality should not be posited without**
> **necessity.**
> —William of Ockham (ca. 1285-1349 English
> philosopher and Franciscan monk).

Put simply,

> **"Among competing hypotheses, the one with**
> **the fewest assumptions should be selected."**

Or,

> **"When attempting to explain a given**
> **phenomenon, it doesn't benefit one to**
> **postulate an even more complicated cause."**

Nature operates in the shortest way possible.
—Aristotle (d. 322 BCE Philosopher and
Practitioner of Science)

**When you hear hoofbeats, think of horses, not
zebras.**
—Theodore Woodward (d.2005 medical
researcher and Nobel Prize nominee)

**We are to admit no more causes of natural
things than such as are both true and
sufficient to explain their appearances.**
—Isaac Newton (d. 1726/7 Co-creator of calculus,
Astronomer, physicist, leader of the Scientific
Revolution)

Pareidolia

Pareidolia is a psychological illusion in which the pattern-seeking
human brain responds to a stimulus (usually an image or a
sound) by perceiving a familiar pattern where none exists.

For example: seeing animals, faces or objects in clouds, hearing
hidden messages in music played backward or at different
speeds or hearing voices in constant white noise from fans, air
conditioners, etc., seeing religious icons or celebrities in pieces of
burnt toast or tortilla chips.

Compare Infrasound and Observer-Expectancy Effect.

Perfect solution fallacy (nirvana fallacy)

The perfect solution fallacy is an informal fallacy of assumption: if
an action is not a perfect solution to a problem, it is not worth
taking. It is a type of black-and-white thinking, presenting a false
dichotomy (compare).

Examples:

1) Posit (fallacious): Anti-drunk driving campaigns are worthless because people are still going to drink and drive no matter what.

Rebuttal: Complete eradication of drunk driving is not the expected outcome. The goal is a reduction.

2) Posit (fallacious): Seat belts are a bad idea because people are still going to die in car crashes.

Rebuttal: While seat belts cannot make driving 100% safe, they do significantly reduce one's likelihood of dying in a car crash.

Placebo effect

The placebo effect is the measurable, observable, or personally experienced improvement in health or behavior not attributable to a medication or invasive treatment. This improvement can be due to many things, such as spontaneous improvement, reduction of stress, original misdiagnosis, subject-expectancy, classical conditioning, etc.

A medical placebo is a pharmacologically inert substance (such as saline solution or a sugar tablet) that seems to produce an effect similar to what would be expected of a pharmacologically active substance (such as an antibiotic). They are often used in scientific studies of medication/treatment efficacy as a control, with the aim of reducing patient and investigator bias as much as possible.

Compare Observer-expectancy Effect and Nocebo Effect.

Poisoning the Well

(also known as discrediting, smear tactics)

This is a type of informal logical fallacy where irrelevant adverse information about a target is presented to an audience, with the intention of preemptively discrediting or ridiculing everything that the target person is about to say. This fallacy is a form of ad hominem attack (see).

I.e., Adverse information (be it true or false) about person 2 is presented by person 1.

The audience could then mistakenly assume that any of the claim(s) of person 1 will be false.

e.g., "I have presented my argument with reason, clarity, evidence and honesty. Now, my opponent will attempt to refute my argument by his own fallacious, incoherent, illogical version."

As an audience member, if you allow any of this "poison" to affect how you evaluate the opponent's argument, you are guilty of fallacious reasoning.

A subcategory of this form is the false dilemma (see); one assigns an unfavorable attribute to any future opponents, in an attempt to discourage debate.

e.g., "I have given my reasons why we must go to war with the other nation; therefore, you are either with us or against us."

e.g., "I have given my reasons for contributing to cancer research, so if you don't agree with me, you must enjoy seeing loved ones die."

Compare Ad Hominem and False Dilemma

134

Positive-outcome (or "publication") bias

This is the tendency to publish research with a positive outcome more frequently than research with a negative outcome. Negative outcome refers to finding nothing of statistical significance or causal consequence, as opposed to finding that something affects life negatively.

Positive-outcome bias also refers to the tendency of the media to publish medical study stories with positive outcomes much more frequently than such stories with negative outcomes. Media bias may be due to scientific journal bias, but the latter seems to be due mainly to researchers not submitting negative outcome studies for publication (the file-drawer effect), rather than to bias on the part of the publication or peer review editors.

This bias and other biases contribute to what has been called, "The five diseases that threaten modern science":

Significosis, an inordinate focus on statistically significant results;

Neophilia, an excessive appreciation for novelty;

Theorrhea, a mania for new theory;

Arigorium, a deficiency of rigor in theoretical and empirical work; and

Disjunctivitis, a proclivity to produce large quantities of redundant, trivial, and incoherent works."

Post hoc fallacy

The post hoc ergo propter hoc ("after this therefore because of this") fallacy is based upon the mistaken notion that simply because one thing happens after another, the first event was a cause of the second event. Post hoc reasoning is the basis for many alternative medicine "successes," superstitions and erroneous beliefs.

e.g., A rooster crows immediately before sunrise; therefore the rooster causes the sun to rise.

e.g., The Brazilian footballer Pele blamed a dip in his performance on having given a fan a specific playing shirt; after getting the shirt back, his performance recovered. It was later discovered the shirt returned was not, in fact, the one Pele had given up.

Compare Pragmatic Fallacy and Placebo Effect and Perfect Solution Fallacy.

Pragmatic fallacy

This is an informal logical fallacy implying that, because something works for someone, it can help others.

What the phrase "works for" means tends to be quite vague and ambiguous. "Works for" might mean "I feel better," "It explains things for me," "I'm satisfied with it," "It's meaningful or beneficial to me" or "I really want to believe that it works for me."

This fallacy is often invoked when people are asked for scientific evidence for the efficacy of acupuncture, chiropractic, homeopathy, therapeutic touch, alternative medicine, astrology, numerology, palmistry, etc. Because there are no peer-reviewed scientific studies demonstrating evidence for the efficacy of any of these practices, those questioned merely side-step the issue

136

altogether and rest the "strength" of their case on, "I don't care if there's no scientific evidence for it, it works for me."

See Placebo Effect.

Proportionality bias

The proportionality bias is the tendency to believe that important events with important consequences must have extreme causes. Mundane events must have lesser causes.

E.g. It seems inconceivable that Lee Harvey Oswald could fire three shots in 8 seconds and hit a moving John F. Kennedy with two of the shots. Oswald was a nobody. JFK was President of the United States. The biased observer argues that because it seems unreasonable that a relatively mundane person couldn't by himself remove a powerful person, there must have been a conspiracy (see).

Recency bias

One definition of recency bias is thinking that patterns people observe in the recent past will continue in the future.

Predictions in the short term, based on recent events, work fine much of the time. Predictions in the long term based on recent events have been shown to be no more accurate than flipping a coin in such fields as meteorology, economics, investments, demography and futurology.

The term "recency bias" has also been applied to the tendency of people to recall recent patterns more often than older patterns.

For example, when citing notable people, events or ideas, people are more likely to cite more recent events, ideas or people in the news. Unfortunately, this results in history being given less importance in the current day.

Those who don't learn from history are doomed to repeat it.
—ascribed to multiple people

Regressive fallacy

The regressive (or regression) fallacy is an informal fallacy, a version of the post hoc fallacy. It is the assumption that a phenomenon has returned to normal because of an action taken while the phenomenon was abnormal. This is fallacious because it does not take into account natural fluctuations in the phenomenon itself.

e.g., When her pain got worse, she went to a doctor, after which the pain lessened. Therefore, she must have benefited from the doctor's treatment.

It is possible that the pain lessened due to normal fluctuations. Assuming the pain relief was a result of the treatment is fallacious. This is not to say that the treatment did not lessen the pain (it may very well have), it is the assumption that is fallacious.

e.g., The student did poorly last semester, so he was punished. He did much better this semester. Clearly, punishment is effective in improving student performance.

Excellent academic performance often fluctuates with lesser performance. In this example, the performance may have improved from mere fluctuation.

e.g., The frequency of road accidents fell after a speed camera was installed. Therefore, the speed camera has improved road safety.

Speed cameras are often installed after a particular stretch of road incurs a high number of accidents, but there is the possibility that the frequency of accidents was about to decrease

138

anyway with normal fluctuations.

Representativeness bias

In judging people and items, humans tend to compare them to a representative idea and then rate them as typical or atypical according to how they compare to the representative. This bias can be one of the bases of stereotyping, profiling and "pigeon-holing."

For example, when the only attributes that you are given of a man are "quiet, shy, reserved, and self-effacing," which profession do you think is more likely, an accountant or star athlete? An accountant seems more likely if your stereotype of a star athlete is an outgoing, gregarious person and an accountant as relatively quiet, reserved and methodical. But there are star athletes that are quiet and shy and accountants that are outgoing and talkative. But on a daily basis, people tend to simplify things with stereotypes and will pigeonhole attributes to save on the extra time and energy involved in thinking critically.

Retrospective falsification

This is the process of telling a story that is factual to some extent, but which gets distorted and falsified over time by retelling it with embellishments. These embellishments may include speculations, conflating other events, and the incorporation of additional seemingly related material without regard for accuracy or plausibility.

The brain is driven to find or invent details that fit with the desired outcome, and the process may be done consciously or unconsciously. The newer distorted and false version becomes a "real" memory; it may even be more interesting or entertaining than the original, accurate story; regardless, it is now taken as a reliable record of the tale.

Examples include reconstructions of supposed "miraculous events," psychic predictions, and encounters with UFOs.

Amazingly, time isn't even a necessary constraint with this phenomenon, as those familiar with the children's game "Telephone" may be acquainted: A group of 30 students sits on the floor in a circle. The first student whispers a very short story that they are reading from a page into the ear of the student next to them; this second student then whispers the "same" story to a 3rd student, the 3rd repeats it to a 4th student, and on down the line. Within only 5 minutes, the story that the 30th student repeats aloud bears minimal resemblance to the original.

It is easy to see how rumors, gossip, hearsay, scandals and inaccurate eyewitness testimony occurs.

Compare Confabulation, False Memory, Hindsight Bias.

Selection bias

Selection bias is a bias created by the selection of individuals, groups or data for analysis in a non-random way, thereby increasing the likelihood that the sample obtained is not representative of the population.

Selection bias most often refers to the distortion of statistical analysis, resulting from the biased method of choosing samples. If the bias is not taken into account, then the conclusions of the study are less likely to be accurate.

A related informal bias is "cherry-picking," where someone selects only those items that bolster their argument while ignoring those items that argue against it.

Compare Confirmation Bias, File-Drawer Effect, Availability Heuristic.

140

Selective thinking

Selective thinking is the process whereby one selects out favorable evidence for remembrance and focus while ignoring the unfavorable evidence for a belief. This kind of thinking is the basis for most beliefs in the psychic powers of so-called mind readers and mediums. It is also the basis for many, if not most, occult and pseudo-scientific beliefs.

It should be noted that selective thinking works independently of wishful thinking and should not be confused with biased thinking, whereby one seriously considers data contrary to one's belief, but one is much more critical of such data than one is of supportive data.

Compare Confirmation Bias.

Self-deception

Self-deception is a process of denying or rationalizing away the relevance, significance, or importance of opposing evidence and logical argument. Self-deception involves convincing oneself of a truth (or lack of truth) so that one does not reveal any self-knowledge of the deception.

People tend to hold overly favorable views of their abilities in many social and intellectual domains. This overestimation occurs, in part, because people who are unskilled in these areas suffer a dual burden: Not only do these people reach erroneous conclusions and make unfortunate choices, but their incompetence robs them of the meta-cognitive ability to realize it.

Compare Confirmation Bias, File-Drawer Effect, Selective Thinking, Dunning-Kruger Effect.

<u>Shoehorning</u>

Just as a shoehorn can force a foot into an ill-fitting shoe, shoehorning uses evidence or events to support an idea, even if the data don't fit the idea's conclusion. The process requires either a very loose use of the facts and vague definitions or incorporating selection bias and selective thinking or cherry-picking of the facts.

Shoehorning is often used to force-fit some current affair into one's personal, political, or religious agenda. Psychics frequently shoehorn events to fit vague statements they made in the past.

For example, the prophecies of Nostradamus are hopelessly vague, although many current events can be shoe-horned to fit some of his prophecies.   The same can be said of biblical prophecies, especially in the Book of Revelation.

Compare Barnum/Forer Effect.

<u>Single cause bias/ fallacy/ illusion</u>
(aka the fallacy of the single cause, causal oversimplification, causal reductionism, and the reduction fallacy)

The <u>single cause </u>**bias** causes one to think that there is a single cause of a complex phenomenon.

The <u>single cause </u>**fallacy** is the belief that there is a single cause for some complex phenomenon based on no evidence, and thus is a fallacy of assumption.

The <u>single cause </u>**illusion** is the belief that there is a single cause for some complex phenomenon based on testimonials, biased scientific evidence, or communal reinforcement for the single cause. The illusion is based on confirmation bias and the fallacies of omitting relevant evidence, hasty conclusion, and false cause.

142

The single cause **bias** is exemplified by the tendency to think that such complex phenomena as alcoholism, autism, cancer, mental illness, extreme weather conditions, or economic recessions are each due to a single clear cause.

The single cause bias can be traced back to the earliest attempts to understand the world. Whether there was too much rain or not enough rain, too much wind or not enough wind, a safe voyage or a disaster, it had to be due to spirits or gods. The scientific method has successfully chipped away much of this irrational conjecture. But even so, Scientologists still believe they have scientific evidence that all mental and physical illnesses are due to engrams. There are many psychotherapists today who think they have scientific evidence that all psychological problems are due to their patients having been abused as children.

It is more straightforward, easier and far more attractive only to have to deal with one cause and rally others to its solution. It takes much more effort and thinking to admit that few problems are so simple to cure; as has been stated elsewhere in this book, humans like an answer, sometimes any answer...and preferably a simple one.

Special Pleading

Special pleading is a logical fallacy in which the speaker pleads for an exception to a rule in a special case, but without proper justification. Most often, it is used when the speaker has been caught in a logical inconsistency.

Classic case: Something had to create the universe, and that is god.

So what created god?

Well, god is special, he didn't need to be created, he's always existed.

(There is no justification for accepting that god is special in this way, it is simply asserted)

Another case: Science has never been able to detect god.

Well, science can only detect natural things, and god is supernatural.

The monotheistic religions (Judaism, Christianity and Islam) all claim that morality comes from their holy texts. Their followers pick and choose which parts they follow (e.g. shunning homosexuality) and which they don't (e.g. stoning unruly children to death or selling daughters into slavery). This arbitrary selection process is an inherent necessity since the texts don't specifically say which commandments are to be taken literally and which are to be analyzed allegorically or metaphorically. Special exceptions for some commandments are asserted, usually based on the particular biases/interpretations of each denomination, sect or cult.

Bear in mind, there are cases where special pleading is logically consistent, but each case must be proven to be justified.

Strawman Argument

A straw man argument is a common form of argument and is an informal fallacy based on giving the impression of refuting an opponent's argument while refuting an argument that was not presented by that opponent. One is said to be "attacking a straw man" that they've constructed rather than attacking the real man.

The typical straw man argument creates the illusion of having thoroughly refuted or defeated an opponent's proposition through the covert replacement of it with a different proposition ("stand up a straw man") and the subsequent refutation of that false argument ("knock down a straw man") instead of the opponent's actual proposition.

Examples:

A: We should relax the laws on beer.

B: No, any society with unrestricted access to intoxicants loses its work ethic and will create a community of drunks.

The original proposal was to relax laws on beer. Person B has misconstrued/misrepresented this proposal by responding to it as if it had been something like "we should have unrestricted access to all intoxicants." It is a logical fallacy because Person A never advocated allowing unrestricted access to all intoxicants.

In a bank robbery conviction, a prosecuting attorney said in his closing argument:

"I submit to you that if you can't take this evidence and find these defendants guilty, then we might as well open all the banks and say, 'Come on and get the money, boys,' because by setting that precedent, we'll never be able to convict criminals."

This was a straw man argument designed to alarm the jury; the chance that the acquittal of defendants on a lack of evidence would literally make it impossible to convict any bank robber is ludicrous.

Subjective validation
(a.k.a. personal validation effect)

Subjective validation is a cognitive bias by which a person will consider a statement or another piece of information to be correct if it has any personal meaning or significance to them. Subjective validation can lead one to perceive two unrelated events (i.e., a coincidence) to be related because their personal belief demands that they are related. Closely related to the Forer effect, subjective validation is an important element in cold reading (see), astrology, fortune telling, personality tests and various kinds of paranormal phenomena.

Sunk-cost fallacy

In making decisions in financial investments and other business decisions, sunk-cost refers to the cost that has already been incurred and cannot be recovered.

If an investment isn't going well, it's normal to think, "I can't stop now; otherwise I'll lose all that I've already invested." While true, the loss is irrelevant to whether you should continue to invest in the area concerned. Everything you have invested is lost regardless of your next decision. If the prospects continue to look bleak, your past losses should point you to abandoning the investment.

This fallacy can apply to any area of human cognition, where one has invested much time, e.g., an ideology such as politics, religion, behavior, etc. Even when one has been shown where they have wasted time (even for years) in unprofitable pursuits or been proven wrong in their thinking, they may continue anyway solely for the reason that they "can't turn back now, I've invested too much of my time and thinking in this, I don't want to admit to having been wrong all of this time."

Compare Backfire Effect.

Testimonial (anecdotal) evidence

Testimonials and vivid anecdotes are all too familiar and, unfortunately, convincing forms of evidence presented for beliefs in the supernatural, paranormal, and pseudo-scientific. Misuse of anecdotal evidence is an informal fallacy and is sometimes referred to as the "person who" fallacy ("I know a person who..."; "I know of a case where..." etc.) which places undue weight on personal experiences of close peers. Of course, these

146

anecdotes may suggest further scientific investigation and eventually may even result in solid science; however, it is when the anecdote alone is deemed "enough" to represent the truth that the fallacy occurs.

Anecdotes and personal testimonials are unreliable for various reasons. Stories are prone to contamination by beliefs, later experiences, feedback, selective attention to details, etc.   Stories can get distorted in the telling and the retelling. Details get exaggerated or muddled. Time sequences get confused. Memories, as a product of an imperfect brain, are imperfect and selective; memories are often filled in after the fact.

Experiences are later modified by one's biases, memories, and beliefs. Most people aren't expecting to be deceived by others, let alone by their own brains. Anecdotes are inherently problematic and not falsifiable and are therefore usually impossible to test for accuracy.

Due to cognitive biases, people are more likely to remember notable or unusual examples rather than typical examples. So that even if accurate, anecdotal evidence is not necessarily representative of the typical experience. Statistical evidence is necessary to determine whether or not anecdotal evidence is "typical" or not.

Anecdotal evidence is also frequently misinterpreted via the availability heuristic (see), resulting in an overestimation of its prevalence. Anecdotes can also lead to faulty conclusions via the post hoc ergo propter hoc fallacy (see), the tendency to assume that if one event happens after another, then the first must be the cause of the second.

See Confabulation, False Memory, Hindsight Bias, Retrospective Falsification.

Texas-sharpshooter fallacy

This is an informal fallacy which is committed when similarities in data are stressed, but differences are ignored. Interpretations of the predictions of Nostradamus often use this reasoning.

The term refers to the story of the Texas sharpshooter who shoots holes in the side of a barn and then draws a bulls-eye target around the bullet holes.

Example: The "fine-tuning" of the known physical laws and parameters of universe (i.e. a minuscule change in any one of which would make the existence of the universe impossible) being used to argue for "intelligent design" when all scientific evidence shows that the "appearance" of "fine-tuning" was actually inevitable though the random results of the local physics of the Big Bang of the only known universe.

If, as mathematics and astrophysics suggests, there could be an infinite number of universes coming into existence (or attempting to come into existence) with their own combinations of physical laws and parameters, and a considerable number of them never even get started because their specific combination of laws/parameters won't physically allow it, then the universes that actually come into being (humanity's being the only one currently detectable) are going to seem special or significant because their parameters appear fine-tuned, when in reality, their random combination of parameters were simply the only combinations that actually resulted in physical existence. In other words, "fine-tuning" is easy to find when you have no other universes with which to compare yours.

This kind of weak reasoning typically leads to the anthropic principle, that the inevitable result of such a "fine-tuned" universe is to end with humanity. The strong anthropic principle states that the universe is somehow forced to result in sapient life. The weak anthropic principle states that the universe's "fine-tuning" is the result of selection bias (especially survivor bias); i.e., only in a universe capable of eventually supporting humans would there exist humans capable of observing and reflecting upon supposed "fine-tuned" parameters. These arguments draw upon some notion of a multiverse, which provides a population of universes from which to select and thereby leads to the selection bias.

Compare confirmation bias, file drawer effect, the clustering illusion and apophenia.

> **Imagine a puddle waking up one morning and thinking, 'This is an interesting world I find myself in, an interesting hole I find myself in, it fits me rather neatly, doesn't it? In fact, it fits me staggeringly well, must have been made to have me in it!' This is such a powerful idea that as the sun rises in the sky and the air heats up and as, gradually, the puddle gets smaller and smaller, frantically hanging on to the notion that everything's going to be all right, because this world was meant to have him in it, was built to have him in it; so the moment he disappears catches him rather by surprise. I think this may be something we need to be on the watch out for.**
> —Douglas Adams (d. 2001 Author, Scriptwriter, Essayist, Humorist, Satirist, and Dramatist)

Unfalsifiability

If a theory or hypothesis cannot be contradicted by an observation, by the outcome of any physical experiment or by good reasoning, it is said to be unfalsifiable.

Making unfalsifiable claims exits the realm of rational discourse since they are not founded on evidence and reason. Unfalsifiable claims are often faith-based, as is the reciprocal.

Exception: All unfalsifiable claims are not necessarily fallacious; they are just unfalsifiable. As long as proper skepticism is retained and proper evidence is given, the claim could be using a legitimate form of reasoning. But by still being unfalsifiable, the worth of the unfalsifiable claim is minimal if not non-existent.

Karl Popper (a philosopher of science) proposed a scientific epistemology which stressed the problem of demarcation—distinguishing the scientific from the unscientific—and makes falsifiability the demarcation criterion, such that what is unfalsifiable is classified as unscientific, and that the practice of declaring an unfalsifiable theory to be scientifically true is pseudoscience.

wishful thinking

Wishful thinking is an informal fallacy when it is assumed that because someone wishes something to be true or false, it is actually true or false.

Wishful thinking is the formation of beliefs and making decisions according to what might be pleasing to imagine instead of by appealing to evidence, rationality or reality. It is a product of resolving conflicts between belief and desire.

Wishful thinking should not be confused with positive thinking, which is trying to make things happen by willing them to happen.

150

PART II

THE FRUSTRATION OF MOST DEBATES

Through the internet, anyone can watch videos of debates. How can so many intelligent people not solve more contentious issues when discussing important topics and making seemingly convincing arguments? Yet here people are, after centuries, still debating the same old controversies with seemingly little progress being made. Why is this? Inevitably, if reason and logic and CT are used, an uncontested answer may finally be enabled for a given question. Still, at the end of most debates, some of the audience will think that one side won it, some will think the opposite side won it. But how can both sides be right? Does this presuppose that only one side can be right?

Even if it appeared to all "reasonable" people that one side did "win" the debate, or that they had more provable or at least more agreeable points than the other side, the "losing" side is not likely to acquiesce or capitulate. In such a public domain, to admit defeat would be to lose too much face. The "loser" will simply go home and think to themselves, "They simply don't understand...they have closed their minds to the truth...nothing that I could have said would have swayed them....they have clouded their minds incontrovertibly...."

Listen to a debate. You will often hear one side bring up a very good point, perhaps one that is irrefutable, it's truth is patent. So what does the opposing side have to say about it...? "Well, yeah...but what about [my next point]...?" Note that the opposing side has just acquiesced to the challenge made, yet they keep trying to win points with the audience by shifting attention away from the original (potentially damaging) point and moving on to another point. Quite often, the winning point that was made is quickly forgotten, even by the presenter of the winning point, and why? Because they have been distracted by having to address the new point that the opposition brings up. It is a way of brushing aside a threat to one's position, to minimize the damage. To the audience, even if the challenge hits home (i.e., the "punch was landed," as in a boxing match), all they seem to see is the "loser" staying in the ring with their foe. As long as the "loser" can keep fighting (by bringing up one point after another), they gain <u>some</u> credibility in the eyes of the audience. As in,"Hey, I might have been crushed by the heavyweight champion of the world, but I did stay in the ring with him for the entire fight! Therefore on one level, we are equals, and you should give me <u>some</u> respect, as I have earned the right for my arguments to continue to be heard."

This is one reason some feel it is a losing strategy for secularists to debate theists. No matter how many ways the secularist shows the theist's arguments to be poor, the theist can always bring up <u>another</u> point and "stay in the ring" with their opponent. Those who side with the theist ignore or brush aside the damage done to their points, thinking, "These secularists just don't understand the wonderful message we're trying to bring." They will instead focus on their champion still on their feet at the end. Ergo, "We can argue just as long as you can, and we'll keep repeating the message until you accept it." No concession ever given, progress rarely made. And of course, this occurs in debates of politics, ideology, morality, etc.

The individual is usually very motivated to maintain their position and their beliefs no matter how many reasonable and logical assaults have overturned them. The individual always has, in the back of their mind, the mindset of "No matter what happens, I've got to get my position accepted. I can't give it up, I've invested too much time, energy, thinking and emotion into it. To give up at this point would be devastating to my psyche. Come what may, I will use every means at my command (possibly, even dishonesty) to keep my position afloat and to save face."

Think of a given ideology: one that has been espoused for centuries, responsible for atrocities, war, misery, the very stagnation of human progress. What do its current adherents say in its defense? "Well maybe it led to those bad things, but look at all of the good that it has done too...you can't just judge it by its bad parts!" And because many have focused on the good parts (they've remembered the positive "hits" and forgotten the negative "misses"), somehow this ideology is given equal footing with all others. Thus, a seemingly damaging ideology gets new life, it lives to fight another day, the debate is perpetuated, history repeats itself, frustratingly futile.

So, if these debates are in so many cases futile, does that mean that all such discussions should be eliminated? By no means. Arguments are essential to the weeding out of weak ideas. But to make these discussions more constructive, to make them worth one's time, attention and contemplation, one must first be versed in the discipline of CT. By forearming oneself with a working knowledge of CBLFs, one can recognize their use in these debates and discount the failed arguments outright. Consider if the moderators of these debates were to score each point made and behind them on a display, show the fallacy or bias that was just employed by a debater so that the viewers could recognize and confirm it for themselves. By the end of the debate, the resulting list of fallacies and biases used by each debater would make it easy for the viewer to see and decide for themselves who made the most uncontested points thereby maintaining intellectual integrity. Minds in the audience could actually be changed and progress made. If this scoring were employed universally, very quickly, debaters would abandon the fallacies and biases in their arguments and practice more elements of CT. The discussion may not necessarily lead to an ultimate truth, but at the very least, the motion wouldn't be hopelessly bogged down in non-productive casuistry as it has for centuries.

This is an excellent example showing why science and engineering are based on CT. The moment someone brings up a questionable idea, it can be subjected to rigorous testing, with additional experiments, design changes, testing and more testing. Those ideas that survive the onslaught of testing and experimentation live to fight another day, only to have to face the onslaught again and again in the future. There is never a point where some ultimate idea or design is put on a pedestal with the sign that reads "Perfection: No More Testing Required; Do not Disturb." Why should any idea or design be considered the final word or be kept sacred? Why wouldn't you invite more and more challenges to it? What is the worst that could happen? A poor design is exposed or a bad idea defeated? What is the best that could happen? A superior design is found or a superior idea discovered, that which is called "progress"! So what if your treasured idea was proven wrong? At least you don't have to continue to labor under its limitations or misdirections. You're free of being shackled to the idea, you may continue with a view of your world that is a little clearer, a little more accurate. And perhaps best of all, you have made the conscious decision that finding a better truth, one closer to reality was more important than merely saving face or keeping alive your poor idea/design for its own sake.

I think, therefore I am.
—Jean-Paul Sartre (d.1980) Philosopher,
Playwright, Novelist, Political Activist, Biographer,
and Literary Critic.

I THINK, THEREFORE I AM...RIGHT.
—every other human that has ever lived.

You are a human...a higher primate, a mammal, an animal that finds itself on the surface of this planet. You are essentially alone and physically cut off from every other sentient being. It's you against the world, you have an instinct to survive, and beyond that, perhaps, a desire to thrive. You are defenseless and have no external resources to use or exploit. What do you already possess that may help you in this situation? In reality, about 3 pounds (1.36 kg) of grayish-pink gelatinous tissue perched atop you spinal cord, your brain.

As mentioned in the preface, your brain isn't just your built-in personal computer; it is your mind, your every thought, your every emotion, your opinions, your preferences, your personality, your psyche, your every intention. It is...you. The remainder of your body is only there to contain and convey your brain to another location, to allow it to interact with your environment, to nourish and sustain your brain. And ultimately, in most cases, your body will enable you to interact with other humans to increase the chances of spreading your genes to another generation to create a remarkably similar brain.

This similarity between brains isn't just from parent to child, but between the entirety of humanity, living and dead. Of course, to a certain level, each person is unique, with different personalities and views on various issues. But the way that brains are wired, and the way that people tend to use these organs, are strikingly similar.

This wiring is how nature has made humanity; this is the route of survival and reproductive success that evolution found through a few million years of environmental change and adversity. But evolution never ends, it is an ongoing process, and it doesn't end with "perfect" forms. In fact, it doesn't even <u>need</u> to end with perfect forms. All evolution leads to is a form that is "good enough" to reproduce itself, or a form "slightly better" than the other competing forms to increase its competitive edge toward reproducing in its given environmental niche. When the environment changes, the progeny whose chance genetic mutations result in a design that is "slightly-better-modified" for that environmental change have a slightly greater chance at reproductive success than the "slightly-worse-modified" or "unmodified" progeny. So it follows that modern human brains are likely just "good enough" or perhaps "slightly-better-modified" to survive for reproductive success. Nowhere is it written or even implied that human brains must be perfect. Let that sentence sink in...

The fact is, reproductive success hardly even requires a brain, let alone a slightly better or even superior brain. The vast majority of mammals or even vertebrates have fantastic reproductive success utilizing much more "limited" gray matter than humans possess. As for the invertebrates that outnumber humans both in numbers and sheer biomass on this planet, most of them exist and reproduce splendidly with simple nerve networks that operate on only the most rudimentary scales (compared to yours). On Earth, bacteria far outnumber/outweigh humans and have no brains at all (although scientists are discovering that when they marshal their numbers, they can achieve very impressive things). So it could be argued quite convincingly that as far as successful species go, bacteria, which have been around for billions of years (compared to humanity's mere millions of years) are a far more successful species than Homo sapiens sapiens by several orders of magnitude. When it comes to life, all nature favors is reproductive success; intelligence turns out to be an interesting but ultimately superfluous quantity. But of course if you have intelligence, you're more likely to be enamored with it.

158

It is tempting (and very human) to be impressed with and even be in love with your own brain. People rely on them for so much, day after day, minute by minute, every second of their lives. Most people probably don't walk around thinking to themselves, "Why was I born with this organ in my head? What good does it do me? Its workings are pretty limited, and it is very prone to imagining things and making bad decisions...." What is much more likely is that, at a certain age, people think that they have learned enough about their world that they will always make good decisions about how things should be. At some point, people tend to default to a position that states, "The person that just made that statement is wrong, and I <u>know</u> this because I think about it in a different way." That is, "the person must be wrong for no other reason than, <u>I am right!</u>".

Jean-Paul Sartre said, "I think, therefore, I am." But the default position of most humans is: "I think, therefore, I am right!" Remember, you're alone, naked on this Earth, so whose brain are you going to trust if not your own? If you don't have faith in your own mind, in whose mind are you going to put your faith? Will you live your life with someone else making every single decision for you? Making every choice for you? Feeding you every opinion you'll ever have as if your own mind didn't even matter? Likely not. No matter how confused each person may be in their given circumstances, no matter how overwhelmed with new information they may be, no matter how limited their knowledge in a given area may be, they are likely to put the most trust in their own brains.

But is this trust justified?

For millennia, humanity trusted what their brains perceived as "obvious," that the sun orbited the Earth. Rain or shine, the sun "rose" in the east, "set" in the west. It had never failed to do so. The solar revolution around the planet got to be so reliable, humanity could base the calendar on it, even sow and reap their crops by it. It was a useful and reliable pattern. And it was so "obvious" that the sun revolved around the Earth, after all, it was the sun that was moving across the sky; "common sense" said that the immovable Earth always remained "terra firma" under one's feet. This scheme was also an attractive prospect in an anthropocentric sense: humanity seemed so important on this Earth that the sun, the planets, the very stars themselves revolved around them. People must be the most important things in the universe since they appeared to be at the center of it, the very reason in fact for its creation and existence.

And of course, all of these people's brains were wrong.

Yes, despite the "obvious" nature of the sun's proposed movement, despite the "common sense" that it made that people are firmly planted on an "immobile" Earth while the heavens revolve around and admire them, despite the usefulness of this concept and its predictability...the perception was still wrong. With further skepticism, questioning and investigation, it was eventually discovered that it is the Earth and all of the planets instead that revolve around the sun. This apparent "movement" of the sun is, in reality, the Earth rotating around its own axis once every 24 hours while the sun remains fixed in relation to it. But to humans, in their plane of existence, held to the Earth by gravity and spinning on its surface at the same rate that it rotates around its axis, all that surrounds them in the cosmos seems to revolve around them; much like the spectators watching a spinning carousel seem to zip past the rider while the carousel appears immobile in relation to the rider.

It is the truly rare individual that actually enjoys admitting when they're wrong; or perhaps worse, admitting that they don't even have an answer to some question. Hopefully, by the end of this book, the reader will not only be willing to admit when they are

160

wrong or when they are ignorant about something but will enjoy admitting when they are wrong or ignorant and are thus, ready to learn.

And a common mistake is to assume that the reason your opponent is wrong or lacks knowledge is a lack of intellect; or even that <u>you</u> are wrong because of a lack of intelligence. Even the most brilliant minds that have ever existed and given birth to extraordinary discoveries have made these mistakes in cognition. The human brain is merely a thought-processing machine that will begin running askew when not adequately controlled, much like a high-performance automobile running askew when its driver gets distracted by something other than his driving.

After reading this book, the honest reader should agree: the self-questioning of an individual's thought processes isn't just a good idea, it is an absolute imperative. The mistakes, the errors and yes, even the evils that the average mind is capable of must at least be reduced, if never entirely eliminated. Humans must reign in the awesome power of their brains; only in this way may humans realize their full potential and expand their future wisdom, while reducing harm and malevolence.

When asked, "Are you a critical thinker?" or "Are you capable of thinking critically?", most people would answer unhesitatingly "yes" to either question. "Critical thinking" sounds different than just the word "thinking," that adjective "critical" seems more specific, more rigorous, more complex. However, if one is asked the subsequent question, "How would you define CT?", it is most illuminating to hear the answers. Some may respond by defining CT as "thinking long and hard about something" or thinking about an issue in a different and better way than everyone else...even if they arrive at the same conclusion as everyone else. They assume that they arrived at this same conclusion simply by using a superior thinking method.

Alongside these questionable definitions, another assumption is often made: "Since I'm a critical thinker, your thinking must by definition be inferior, and therefore most likely wrong." Right from the start, this is a bad assumption and an all-too-human one. When it comes to scrutiny of the human thinking process, it is much more attractive to direct the attention away from one's self and onto the thought process of someone else, <u>anyone</u> else.

And the misdirection is often ironic; many mature individuals will readily admit that they make mistakes, even that they can be fallible in the way of their thinking. Yet, when pressed on their stance on an issue, they dig in their heels, they defend an indefensible position, they deflect criticism, and they would rather die rather than admit to being wrong: "Yeah sure, I've been wrong about many things in my life many times before, but there's no way that I could be wrong about THIS thing right now!"

There are many different definitions of CT, most of them overlapping in their essence. For this book,

> CT is "The process by which any human may
> avoid being misled by their <u>own</u> brain."

By redirecting the emphasis from someone else's thinking back to where it belongs, on the individual's <u>own</u> brain, the discipline of CT overcomes simple biases against other people. When one is alone and brutally honest with themselves, when there is no audience, no peers to impress or convince, no social stigma of backing down, no embarrassment of admitting being wrong, then genuine progress can be made.

Even if an individual lies to them self for a while, or misleads them self, or just ignores their own internal contradictions, a seed of doubt can still be planted, lying submerged within their mind,

162

nagging at them during quiet moments. One cannot run away from their conscience hibernating within their own brain, it is always there, and it cannot be ignored forever. In the end, this self-doubt, this self-skepticism, this self-questioning has far more weight than any argument that one's opponent might offer. When and if the individual can correct themselves, the change in their psyche will be more profound than any change forced upon them from an outside source. In addition, they will have earned the self-esteem and self-respect that is an inevitable consequence of an examined life.

This book is by no means suggesting that the human brain isn't capable of translating the detection of patterns into amazing achievements: art, music, literature, architecture, mathematics, science, engineering, flight, reason, logic, computers, space travel. These are considerable attainments, and their importance should not be diminished. However, what often isn't tied to these achievements is that the same brains came up with inequality, slavery, war, torture, genocide and other forms of injustice and malevolence.

But how could this be? How could an organ capable of constructing particle accelerators and supercomputers have failed humanity so magnificently over and over again, across the ages? This book proposes an explanation: the limitations of that same brain. The "hard-wiring" of the brain tends to mislead a given person in their daily life, resulting in daily, even hourly mistakes in cognition. These errors may occur in either trivial or crucial scenarios, but regardless, they are either accepted as accurate or at least "good enough" as a kind of mental "short-cut" to simplify survival and get through each day. Often the cognitive errors made are relatively benign, not resulting in any real or lasting harm (depending on how one defines harm). Indeed, these mistakes often occur side by side with the genuine and considerable achievements mentioned above.

163

But quite often, these errors in cognition lead humans down the wrong path, and often a very dark path. It may not seem an attractive proposition: examining one's own thought processes and the potential damage to which they may lead. This potential is examined in the next chapter Epistemic Responsibility.

A conclusion is where you got tired of thinking.
—Steven Wright (Comedian)

EPISTEMIC RESPONSIBILITY

The majority of this book deals with epistemology: The study of how people come to their beliefs, and the theory of knowledge, especially with regard to its methods, validity, and scope. Epistemology is also the investigation of what distinguishes justified belief from opinion. Herein is presented the proposition that CT is the most practical way of beginning one's investigation of the world to form valid beliefs, opinion and knowledge. Practical and crucial.

Examples given of non-CT have concerned everything from minor harm to humans to serious consequences and even death. So one might bring up the point that most human beliefs and choices don't entail a life-or-death result. For example, one might ask, "What's the harm in my belief if it doesn't hurt anyone?" "Why can't people respect each person's personal beliefs?" "Why can't people just let people believe what they want?"

THE ANSWERS:

    I. Because one's beliefs do not exist in a vacuum. The faulty reasoning that led to one of your incorrect beliefs may lead to other incorrect beliefs.

    II. Because your beliefs inform your actions.

    III. Because your informed actions may not have any direct, immediate effect, but over time, the consequences are potentially devastating.

If someone is convinced to believe in one falsehood on the basis of little or no evidence, or only because it's what they are comfortable believing, then what is to stop them from using this same mindset in other areas of decision-making? For example, because they believe in creationism, they may vote for a candidate who doesn't support teaching accepted science (e.g. evolution) in public schools and the result is that the community doesn't foster the next generation of scientists and engineers. Perhaps because they identify as anti-vaxxers, they don't immunize their children, resulting in an outbreak of measles where innocent children die. If because of their faith-based views, they fail to take their sick child to a medical doctor, and their child dies, who accepts responsibility for the death? The adults making the decisions often refer it upward, "It's our belief to allow this", "It is the will of our deity", "we had no choice, our doctrine demands it."

In each of these cases, the human with the personal belief has demanded the right to believe as they want, but it is rare that they will accept the responsibility for the consequences. The consequences may not be to them directly, but to their family members, or to their child's classmates, or to their community as a whole. In some cases, entire countries are affected by the beliefs of an individual, sometimes even to humanity globally as a species. These are just a few examples of why it isn't wise to "just let people have their own beliefs"; if harm comes to anyone, from the believer themselves to actual innocents, the beliefs must be challenged.

For example, if you read a headline that antiperspirants had been connected with an increase in lymph node cancers, you might make an initial, provisional judgment that it sounded reasonable. Your first reaction is to accord it a certain level of provisional acceptance or belief. Keep in mind that you haven't read anything further about it, you haven't read the original science article for its methods, procedure, results, analysis or conclusions. You haven't actively looked up anything on the internet to see if this announcement is a hoax, or if this paper is in an extreme minority to others concerning the same topic. You haven't seen if any other lab has been able to replicate the results. You haven't bothered to research if other investigators have cited the study as a basis for their continuing experiments. All you have done is decided that it sounds reasonable to you.

People do this all of the time when reading things, whether it is in a book, magazine, on a webpage or just an internet meme. Rarely is skepticism, logic, reasoning or CT employed. You simply decide either that you agree, or think it's reasonable, or at least that it isn't unreasonable. But what are you engaging to make these judgments? Quite likely your own built-in biases.

If you persist in asking "what's the harm....?", there is an entire website devoted to the answer:

www.whatstheharm.net

This website includes innumerable specific documented cases where someone's faulty thinking processes caused real harm, even death, to them, to those in their immediate circle, or to innocent strangers who had no control over the situation. All this after some person asked the seemingly reasonable question, "What's the harm...?"

Included are such examples as:

> After an astrological prediction of a planetary alignment that would cause a devastating cyclone in India, over 60,000 workers fled a port town in fear. This caused the ship-breaking yard there to shut down at a loss of up to $60 million.

A homeopath telling a patient to give up her asthma medication. The patient later died of an asthma attack.

A child had a congenital condition that could have been easily treated with conventional medicine. Unfortunately his family belonged to a church that believes in faith healing rather than medicine and he died from the condition. His cousin also died in related circumstances.

When one looks back in history, the damage done from mankind discriminating against, persecuting, punishing, torturing, executing and even burning alive those who didn't believe as they did is nothing short of appalling. And when the modern believer is reminded of these pogroms, they often brush them off as, "That was so long ago, it's ancient history, why do you have to keep bringing that up?", or "We don't believe that way anymore, so you can't hold us accountable for past atrocities", or "That was how all people thought at the time, so no one could've have thought any differently."

Taking one at a time:

"That was so long ago, it's ancient history, why do you have to keep bringing that up?"

With this mindset, there is apparently a statute of limitations on the persecution, torturing, execution or burning alive of innocents. So if the believer makes it to the afterlife, they will be able to meet with these victims and say with a straight face, "Great news! The wretched agony that you went through doesn't matter any more! It's been so long, we've forgotten all about it and

168

we've learned from our mistakes. Hope that makes up for things. Oh by the way, now that we believe so much better than in your day, we're not going to be held responsible for our beliefs then or now..." <u>That</u> is why it keeps getting brought up.

"We don't believe that way anymore, so you can't hold us accountable for past atrocities."

Okay, you don't believe that way any more, you've stopped believing as those past people had. Over the years, you've somehow <u>reasoned</u> past their beliefs and learned to do better. There is the answer to "what's the harm in believing a certain way? Why question what's worked for you?" It took reason to improve your mindset. And if you could go back in time and hold those people accountable for the way that they believed, you'll hopefully see why you are now being asked to be accountable for the consequences of your current beliefs.

"That was how all people thought at the time, so no one could've have thought any differently."

Actually, if history recorded any of the thoughts of the <u>victims</u> of these monstrous acts, you'd have probably read many eloquent mindsets that thought <u>very</u> differently than their executioners at these time periods in history. Those that thought differently than the powers in force then either learned to keep their mouths shut to avoid persecution or they worked covertly over the centuries to get the populace to question their beliefs and the harm that came from those beliefs.

To learn who rules over you, simply find out who you are not allowed to criticize.
—Voltaire (d.1778 Writer, Historian, and Philosopher)

Humanity must never forget the atrocities of which it was (and still is) capable with the worldview of "What's the harm of letting us believe as we wish?"

"What's the harm?" indeed. These examples and the pre-existing mindset of "What's wrong with everyone having their own beliefs?" bring up a relatively new idea: epistemic responsibility. Humans are the only species that possess the potential to determine fact and truth for all other species on planet Earth. Knowledge cannot exist without a species who are the possessors and determiners of that knowledge, Without humans as carriers of that knowledge, the whole idea of knowledge is moot. If humans rely on questionable data, experiences and faulty reasoning to make important decisions, not only can it cause financial damage, the consequences can be fatal, for individuals, species-wide (as well as for other species besides *Homo sapiens sapiens*) as well as planet-wide.

Epistemic responsibility asks two central questions:

1) To what degree should humans be held morally responsible for the consequences of their choices?

2) Who determines the criteria for the justification of holding a belief?

Epistemic Responsibility has been defined as,

> *"The obligation to engage in rational investigation in the search for truth, the ability to give valid reasons and evidence for one's position, and the readiness to revise one's beliefs in the light of new evidence to avoid negative impact."*

Epistemic Responsibility means acknowledging direct control and accountability for the quality of your personal, subjective experience of reality, as well as the impact that your beliefs, desires and actions have upon others in ever-increasing circles of association. This obligation must be honored even when you aren't comfortable acknowledging it.

If you refuse to acknowledge your power and your responsibility for your beliefs, you will always be a passive subject to the experiences of others or of any given circumstances. And you will never be able to take control of your own life; i.e., you will be a victim of mental enslavement.

All humans occupy a shared reality, which each individual is continually interpreting through their own filter (biases). And at the same time, everyone else is filtering the same reality with their own different biases. Everyone is swimming in this vast ocean of consciousness, in which they are all impacted by the waves of beliefs and actions of everyone else. When you accept total Epistemic Responsibility for the quality of your own beliefs and opinions and how they may impact others, the waves created by your biases are reduced/eliminated, and all inhabitants of the planet can exist in a becalmed ocean. It may not lead you to an ultimate destiny safe on an island, but it will increase the chance that you and others aren't drowned by a tidal wave of biases.

For those that are able to find there way out of the ideologies that result from non-CT (cults, conspiracies, religious faith, simplistic political affiliations, pseudoscience, the paranormal), their realizations are astonishingly similar. Looking back on the truths that they used to cling to and the certainty that they held of these phenomena, they talk of a "fog that is lifted" or a "veil that is raised." Rather than having a difficult time understanding how someone else could believe such things, they have a difficult time

171

understanding how they themselves could have believed such things and the harm that they caused by their resulting actions.

They remember the comfort, happiness and solace that their former beliefs gave them, but they also acknowledge that they hadn't approached the tenets of their world-views with adequate skepticism, they'd simply followed where their pleasant biases had ultimately led them.

They also had not taken any responsibility for the consequences of their beliefs. If they believed that the leader of their cult, church or temple would protect them and the earth, they tended to not worry about their personal impact on other people, other species or the planet. For example, if they believed that their behavior and investment in this mortal life mattered little because they would be rewarded with another eternal, perfect life after death (simply by believing), their mindset was likely to impact not only them but others on the planet.

> Teaching kids to ask magical beings to solve their problems in the form of prayers creates irresponsible adults who fail to find their own solutions.

But with their newfound clarity of mind, those newly freed from their dogmas reasoned that there was no evidence of a celestial bail-out that would save them and their planet. And if there was no afterlife, that meant that their current life was the only one that they'd ever get. Understandably, their initial reaction may be one of dismay, as if a parent had promised an amazing gift to their child for behaving well all through childhood, only to renege on the promise once their adulthood was achieved.

But once the reality of the situation set in, some profound truths were discovered. If one's planet is the only home that any species has and nothing supernatural will ultimately save it, you'd

172

better take more responsibility and maintain it as well as possible. And if you find no reason to believe that you'll receive any kind of afterlife, the few decades that you are afforded in this life become oh so precious. The mind becomes focused on maximizing the productivity, presence and pleasure of every moment of every day--the philosophy of YOLO, you only live once. And there is genuine pleasure and pride in taking total responsibility of your life and its impact in the world.

But even after finding a way out of their previous worldview, the individual isn't guaranteed a clear new direction. Years and decades may have been spent thinking in comfortable, familiar satisfying patterns, and simply dispensing with them doesn't necessarily imply a way forward. For religious faith, thousands have obtained help through the Recovering from Religion Foundation, where former believers help those that are questioning their mindset and world-view.

A special case involves those that lead congregations and have found a way out of the pattern of faith, but are now in the precarious position of having no other means of support. After years of repeating the cycle of faith to members of their congregations, they may in essence lack the skill set to contribute to society in a secular fashion. In some cases, they are forced to continue leading their faith-based communities in faith while keeping their transition to doubt and skepticism to themselves. The Clergy Project currently helps hundreds of these leaders to deal with the real-world problems that years of indoctrination have created.

The table of contents of www.whatstheharm.net covers many of the same topics listed under the next chapter of this book.

ORGANIZED COLLECTION OF IRRATIONAL NONSENSE

This list is pulled from a Venn Diagram available online entitled "An Organized Collection of Irrational Nonsense." The dimensions of the diagram do not easily lend themselves to printing in a book, but the overlap and intersections between its various categories are compelling enough to reproduce them in list form here.

The collection is assembled from a substantially Western point of view, though there are entries from all world cultures. Sadly, it is hardly an exhaustive list of the subject matter; there are millions more of these entries available from all cultures throughout history; and, of course, the collection is being added to all of the time. Still, while this collection only scratches the surface of the subject of irrational phenomena, even this abbreviated list serves the purpose of showing how rampant and widespread these beliefs are and have been throughout history and how easily the human brain is fooled into seeing patterns that aren't necessarily there.

To devote the time necessary to investigate each listed phenomenon fully to determine its validity would be impractical. It is a far more pragmatic, constructive and intellectually honest to approach each phenomenon with skepticism and to withhold one's belief and respect until presented with verifiable evidence from scientific and critical investigation. There is no time limit on how long the individual may withhold belief and respect.

One man's theology is another man's belly laugh.
—Robert A. Heinlein (d. 1988 Dean of Science Fiction Writers)

Anyone reading this list is going to find multiple things that they both recognize and find humorous..."...how could anyone believe in such foolishness...?" And yet, every single one of these items (and the millions unlisted) has its staunch adherents. To them, the phenomenon(a) they believe in are as real and true as any truth accepted by the whole of humanity. Are these adherents mad? Are they unintelligent? Are they uneducated? Or are they simply too ready to accept some interesting explanation to a perceived pattern, rather than taking the skeptical position, "I don't currently know if this is real or not"?

BAD MEDICINE

Snake Oil. Colonic Irrigation. Aphrodisiacs. Bee Pollen Superfood. Emu Oil. Rhino Horn. Oil Pulling. Past Life Regression. Breathwork. Urine Therapy. Rumpology. Aromatherapy. Cupping. Ear Candling. Primal Scream Therapy. Ayurvedic Medicine. Therapeutic Touch. Blue-Green Algae. Hijama. Bloodletting

BAD MEDICINE/PARANORMAL

Albino Body Parts are Magic. Vibrational Medicine. Chakra. Rebalancing. Reiki. Qi. Moxibustion. Psychic Surgery. I Ching. Charms. Touch Pieces .Crystal Healing. Feng Shui

BAD MEDICINE/PARANORMAL/RELIGION

Faith Healing

BAD MEDICINE/RELIGION

Circumcision. Healing Relics. Talismans. Fertility Statues. Extreme Unction. Amulets. Angel Therapy. Virgin Birth. Castrati

RELIGION

Gods. Messiahs. Resurrection. Animal Sacrifice. Day of
Judgment. Prophets. Baptism. Heaven. Doomsayers.
Mortification of the Flesh. Cults. Destiny. Eschaton.
Reincarnation. Shamanism. Nirvana. Heresy. Ragnarok.
Pilgrimages. Kahuna. Taboos. Angels. Sacrilege. Victim Souls.
Demons. Glossolalia. Blessings. Confession. Curses. Buddhas.
Satan. Penance. Miracles. Afterlife. Fate. Seraphim. Hell.
Blasphemy. Protective Temple Garments. Immaculate
Conception. Fundamentalism. Druidry. Vigils. Age of Aquarius.
Second Coming. Private Revelation. Cherubim. Spirits. Prayer.
Antichrist. Divine Grace. Sacraments. Holy Places. Divine Plan.
Damnation. Holy Water. Providence. Holy Books. Fakir Magic.
Hagiography. Ancestral Sin. Predestination. Eucharistic Fasts.
Public Revelation. Holy Wars. Souls

RELIGION/CONSPIRACY

Opus Dei. Freemasonry. Doomsday. Jewish Media Control. One
World Government. Mark of the Beast. Globalism. Knights
Templar. Illuminati. Satanic Rock Music. Pope Joan. Dungeons
and Dragons. Pokemon. Promise Keepers. The Vatican. Black
Volga. Darwin's Deathbed Confession. Protocols of the Elders of
Zion. NASA and the Missing Day. Harry Potter Books. Lavender
Mafia. Halloween

RELIGION/CONSPIRACY/PSUEDOSCIENCE

Fomenko's Chronology. Holocaust Denialism

RELIGION/CONSPIRACY/BAD MEDICINE

Jihad against Western Vaccination. Abstinence-only Sex
Education

176

RELIGION/PSEUDOSCIENCE

Alchemy. Intelligent Design. Enneargram Supremacism.
Gematria. Noah's Ark. Numerology. Creationism

PSEUDOSCIENCE

Nutrigenomics. Expanding Earth Hypothesis. The Hundredth
Monkey Effect. Hidden Messages in Water. Rorschach Inkblot
Method. Starfire Water. Superhumans. Pseudolaw. Reverse
Speech. Korean Fan Death. Geocentrism. Self-Transforming
Machine Elves. Hollow Earth. The Mozart Effect. Myers-Briggs
Type Indicator. Koreshanity. Pseudolinguistics. Worlds in
Collision. Graphology. Japanese Beliefs about Blood Type.
Geomancy. Pseudoarcheology. Facilitated Communication. Ica
Stones. Mermaids. The Boggy Creek Monster. Modern
Dinosaurs. Gaia Hypothesis. The Face on Mars. Quantonics. The
Loch Ness Monster. Thunderbirds. Long Range Locator Devices.
Yeti. Bigfoot. Time Travellers. Abiogenic Petroleum. Schumann
Resonance. Negative Calorie Food. Lepus Tempermentalus.
Perpetual Motion. Dimensional Travel. Mass/Global
Consciousness. Dowsing. Speed Reading. Spontaneous Human
Combustion. Krilian Photography. Electronic Voice Phenomenon.
Polygraph Tests. Lunar Influence. The Dyatlov Pass Incident

PSEUDOSCIENCE/BAD MEDICINE

Hypnosis. Esogetic Colorpuncture. CieAura Transparent
Holographic Chips. Ionized Bracelets. Alkaline/Acidic Diets.
Detoxification. Iridology. Laser Therapy. Reflexology. Neuro-
Linguistic Programming. Qigong. Perkl-Light Energy Spa.
Naturopathy. Alternative Chelation Therapy. Freudian
Psychoanalysis. Wet-Cell Healing. Live Blood Analysis.
Subluxations. Whole Body Vibration Training. Cymatic Sound
Therapy. Bee Venom Therapy. Magnet Therapy. Kangen Water.
Isopathy. Dianetics. Oxidative Therapy. Homeopathy.

Bioharmonics. Colloidal Silver. The Haramein-Rauscher Metric. Vega Testing. Baking Soda Cancer Cures. Binaural Beats. Cytotoxic Testing. Vitamin Megadosing. Electronic Hypersensitivity. Chromotherapy. Phrenology. Craniosacral Therapy. Chiropractic. Acupuncture

PSEUDOSCIENCE/BAD MEDICINE/RELIGION

Transcendental Meditation. Auras. Conversion Therapy. Timewave Zero. The Celestine Prophesy. Alphabiotics. Yoga. Chakras. Rebirthing Therapy. Narconon. Meridians. Lawsonomy. Generational Healing

PSEUDOSCIENCE/BAD MEDICINE/PARANORMAL

Multiple Personality Disorder. Palmistry. Mei's Hole. Kirlian Photography. Nibiruan Council. Quantum Magic. Biorhythms. Vitalism

PSEUDOSCIENCE/BAD MEDICINE/PARANORMAL/CONSPIRACY

Trepanation. Possession. Recovered-Memory Therapy. Deliverance. Exorcism. The Evil Eye

PSEUDOSCIENCE/PARANORMAL

The "Sixth Sense". Mistpouffers. Bermuda Triangle. Time Shifts. Slips. Ley Lines. OOPArts. The Hum. Die Glocke. El Chupacabra. Werewolves. Rods. Mokele-Mbembe. Therianthropy. Dreamreading. Mothman. ESP

PARANORMAL

Luck. Vampires. Nymphs. Gnomes. Bat Boy. Trances. Wights. Shades. Jinxes. Omens. Mares. Fairies. Runes. Giants. Pixies. Wishes. Genies. Muses. Scrying. Fetches. Zombies. Telepathy. Levitation. Superstitions. Shadow People. The Coso Artifact.

Spring-Heeled Jack. Gef the Talking Mongoose. Clairvoyance. Entombed Animals. Doppelgangers. Yurei. Tutankhamen's Curse. The Kamchatka Gears. Bad Things Come in Threes. Magnetic Hills. Backster Effect. Magical Thinking. Bringers of the Dawn. Superluminal Communicatino. Djinn. Psychokinesis. Death Clicks. Xenoglossy. Making Wishes. Will o' the Wisp. Remote Viewing. Automatic Writing. Torsion Field Energy. The Baigong Pipes. Star Jelly. The Cassiopaean Experiment. Quantum Holograms .The Dropa Stones. Black-eyed Children. Elves. Celebrities Always Die in Threes. Zana E Malit. Slate Writing

PARANORMAL/RELIGION

Ifa. Ghosts. Apparitions. Wicca. Past Lives. Incorruptible Corpses. Voodoo. Hungry Ghosts. Near-Death Experiences. Succubi/Incubi. Hauntings. Karma. Stigmata. Poltergeists. Oracles. Seances. Enchantments. Familiar Spirits. Fatima. Bilocation. Necromancy. The Occult. Ouija Boards. Mantras. Acheiropoieta. Transubstantiation .Prophecies. Santa Claus. Divination. Weeping, Bleeding or Blinking Statues. Incantations. Channeling. Ecstacies. Stichomancy. Cambions. Skinwalkers. The Veil of Veronica. Rains of Blood. Wendigo. The Astral Plane. Astrology. Mecalito/Mescalita. OBEs

PARANORMAL/RELIGION/PSEUDOSCIENCE

Atlantis. The Bible Code. The Spear of Destiny. Raelism. The Quran Code. Ancient Astronauts. Orbs. Crystal Skulls. Kabbalah. The Flood/Deluge Mythology. Chariots of the Gods. Pyramidology. Tarot Cards. Ectoplasm. Lemuria

PARANORMAL/RELIGION/PSEUDOSCIENCE/BAD MEDICINE

Trepanation. Possession. Exorcism. The Evil Eye

PARANORMAL/RELIGION/PSEUDOSCIENCE/CONSPIRACY

The Holy Grail. Shroud of Turin. Georgia Guidestones. MK Ultra and Jonestown. The Works of David Icke. The Grand Grimoire. Backmasking

PARANORMAL/PSEUDOSCIENCE/CONSPIRACY

UFOs. Roswell. Nibiru Cataclysm. Ummo. Alien Abductions. Bovine Excision. Crop Circles. Area 51

PARANORMAL/RELIGION/CONSPIRACY

Satanic Ritual Abuse

CONSPIRACY/PSEUDOSCIENCE

Monsanto. Apollo Moon Landing Hoax. Free Energy Devices. Genetically Modified Organisms. Cold Fusion Cover-up. NASA's Anti-Gravity Machines. Water-Fueled Automobile Engines. Power Line Diseases. Monosodium Glutamate is Toxic. Secret Alien Bases in Antarctica. Daylight Savings Time. CARET. Camp Hero's Montauk Project. Nikola Tesla's Suppressed Work. The Vile Vortices. The Tunguska Event. Black Helicopters. Military Weather Modification. Gravity Control Propulsion. The Philadelphia Experiment. The Flat Earth Society. Climate Change Denial. Time Cube Theory. Numbers Stations. Alien Autopsies. Renewable Oil. Aspartame. Planet X. HAARP. Vril

CONSPIRACY/PSEUDOSCIENCE/BAD MEDICINE

AIDS Denialism. Asbestos in Tampons. Vaccines and Autism. Rife Machines. Fluoridation. Chemtrails

CONSPIRACY/BAD MEDICINE

SARS Conspiracy. Cancer Cure Coverups. Manufactured Diseases. OPV and AIDS Conspiracy. HPV Vaccine

180

BAD MEDICINE/RELIGION/PARANORMAL

Faith Healing

RELIGION/CONSPIRACY/PARANORMAL/PSEUDOSCIENCE/ BAD MEDICINE

Scientology. Indigo Children

Again, by no means a complete or exhaustive list. Depressingly, this only scratches the surface, it is the mere tip of the iceberg when it comes to the imaginative nonsense cooked up by a brain hard-wired to find patterns and then work overtime subconsciously to "make sense" of the patterns.

Take, just as an example, "Crop Circles": when they began appearing, seemingly out of nowhere, they were speculated to be the result of alien visitation. It was explained that an alien technology/ phenomenon (such as a flying saucer) was smashing down crops in interesting, usually circular, patterns. Over time, the "designs" of the crop circles became more elaborate and complex. There were even paranormal "experts" that would vouch for their authenticity, stating that it was impossible for humans to be able to create their intricacy and complexity, without leaving tell-tale traces. These "experts" had even "investigated" the suggestion of a hoax and been able to disprove even the possibility of it. Thus, an "authority" had spoken, and many of the credulous were eager to accept its veracity. Here, finally, physical evidence of alien visitation that the skeptics couldn't ignore, and seemingly couldn't deny. The faithful were finally vindicated, their long years of belief that aliens had visited finally "proven." Before, they were always having to deal with the scorn and ridicule from the unbelievers. Crop Circles and their various explanations brought some interest and excitement into people's relatively mundane, repetitive, drab lives. Inevitably, within a few years, several people stepped forward and admitted to the original hoax. They also demonstrated on video how simple it was to create them with a simple piece of board and some string/twine, and without leaving a trace (unless you knew where to look, of course).

It was similar to a magician revealing how he performed a fantastic illusion; the audience that one moment before, would have sworn that they just witnessed something impossible, something truly "miraculous," is embarrassed to realize the ease with which they could be fooled. The magician had merely exploited those areas of the human brain that strive to come up with an explanation for its experience, and upon that brain's failure, just attributed it to the supernatural or the paranormal. After all, better to come up with an interesting, exciting and satisfying supernatural answer rather than merely admit ignorance or approach any phenomenon with skepticism.

And still, even after having been shown how easy it is to be fooled, there are still those who adhere to the alien explanation: "OK, these human hoaxers may be responsible for some crop circles, but we still believe that aliens made some other crop circles. Those that deny any alien visitation are just part of a conspiracy to keep those of us in the know quiet, or perhaps to keep the public from panicking at the government's powerlessness to deal with this superior culture and technology." It's as if the believers had invested too much time, energy and belief in the proposition and they couldn't quite let go of it. The novel is so much more entertaining and satisfying than the routine. The believers still actively looking for some loophole, some exception, some undiscovered evidence that will allow them their continued belief, a vindication of their time, imagination and their original faith. Their brains grasping at straws, their presumption hanging by a thread, their minds repelling the incessant onslaught of skepticism and reason, all to save face and keep their explanation in the ring somehow.

182

Another reason that humans seem to enjoy explaining away the unknown with the supernatural or the paranormal is that they love to upstage those experts who are often held up in veneration in society precisely because of their science education and investigative abilities, as well as their past successes. They love to think that they can embarrass the legitimate scientists, the medical doctors, the researchers who currently may not be able to give a scientific, logical or reasonable explanation for a given phenomenon. If the believer at least has some "answer," they can point to these experts and justifiably claim that they are "ignorant." This "answer" or premature conclusion is an example of why admitting and accepting one's ignorance is so essential and even desirable; otherwise, you are more likely to jump on the first explanation that seems interesting, exciting or merely satisfying.

Perhaps these devotees of the paranormal/supernatural had a difficult time with learning science or math (or were merely denied it by the powers that be), and would like to say, "See? I didn't have to waste all that time to learn math and science! I can live my life just fine without them; and what's more, I have an explanation for a phenomenon on which researchers and scientists have admitted ignorance! Having an answer makes me feel good about myself, I enjoy the feeling of superiority over these so-called 'intellectuals,' these 'experts,' these 'great thinkers,' so I feel a sense of vindication. If they can't come up with a scientific explanation, then it is entirely valid for me to continue to believe in this way. After all, I have an answer, whereas they do not! And in the future, if the scientists and researchers announce that they have finally found a proven explanation for the phenomenon, I can take solace in the fact that their explanation is very probably the result of a conspiracy because they want to take my favored explanation away from me!"

Those who believe in the paranormal, religion, pseudoscience, conspiracies and bad medicine will often ask, "Okay, we may make some fantastic claims, but so does science; if everyone is making incredible claims, shouldn't they all get equal time and equal respect?" While on the face of it, this seems a reasonable question, there is a single word that shows why only science should be respected: evidence. Science rises or falls on this solitary concept. The only thing that the five pillars of irrational nonsense can offer as an explanation for their phenomena is personal experience, and that varies from person to person even within the same ideology. In science, if individuals have different experiences, their conclusions are called into question and ultimately, any hypotheses generated by the experiences are discounted.

These devotees don't seem to be able to grasp the simple proposition that those who employ logic, reason, science and CT are more than comfortable admitting where they are still ignorant. It is far wiser to make this admission and to continue to search for evidence of an actual answer than to just say, "For the time being, I have discovered an answer that makes me happy!"

184

AN AUTHORITY ON ABUSE

An important note to make on the subjects of the previous chapter: Of Conspiracy, Pseudoscience, Bad Medicine, the Paranormal and Religion, only one of them is implicated in the thousands of years of intentional maltreatment, abuse, enslavement, torture, murder and war on humanity, and that is the latter. Of these five main pillars of irrationality, what is so unique about religious faith that makes its potential for these banes of humanity so inevitable? If, as this book contends, all five pillars are the outcome of the same PSB, committing similar CBLFs, what sets the discipline of religion apart from the rest?

No matter how long any of the other four pillars have existed, no matter how many adherents they have had, they never managed to come up with an ultimate authority. There is no one, for example, in any of the pseudosciences listed that can be pointed to and introduced as "Mrs. So-and-so, who wrote the final definitive text on our subject, so there will be no other competing theories." There have, of course, been many branches of these other four pillars, and each of them has had many "prophets" (not to mention "profits"), but still, no ultimate authority.

Even if any of the other four pillars had come up with an authority, it still would be unlikely that any of their followers would inflict any of the abuses listed above on a rival doctrine. That is, the believers in crop circles aren't likely to wage jihad on believers in gnomes. It is far more likely that they would accept each other's followers since both groups possessed a similar mindset and both used questionable thought processes to arrive at their conclusions.

Where religion went beyond mere irrationality was by finally declaring authorities: gods. In the hierarchy of human leadership, there is always someone higher up than the last leader. But with religious faith, at some point, the highest human supervisor must point to an even higher authority, an ultimate one, and it must be above mere humanity, and it would be best if it weren't limited by nature. And it would be most convenient if it was also an authority whose desires and decrees could not be questioned. And so the gods were imagined into being. So if a king felt that war on the next kingdom would be desirable, it was astonishing to see how often his god agreed. In fact, most often, it was declared by the human authority that the god had the idea of war even before he did. And who set the king on his throne and gave him his authority over his vassals? His god.

But all-out war wasn't always necessary for the highest human authority to meet their agenda. Sometimes a simple murder of a rival would do for the nonce. Torture of an apostate might suffice. Enslavement of a subjugated people could fit the bill for a while. Abuse or maltreatment of non-believers might also be a compelling illustration of why you should fall in line with the rest of the faithful. And if the human authority is ever called to task for these questionable acts, he can dismiss the admonishment with a wave of his hand as well as an emphatic, "Our god hath said so."

186

AN ANSWER TO FEAR

One of the most primal of human emotions is fear. No matter how experienced, how educated, how intellectual or how rational a human may be, they are still subject to the feeling of fear. By its virtue of being a primal emotion, it also has the potential of being a primal driver of the thinking process, even superseding the higher levels of cognition. It is, therefore, an enormously influential emotion. In other words, even the doctor, the scientist, the rationalist can still change their mind from a position of reason to one of irrationality if they bow to a sense of fear. Fear is an emotion and instinct ingrained in the animal conscious and unconscious as a result of the evolutionary wiring of the brain. And it has served a useful purpose: it can be a warning when something happens outside of the control of the animal. For example, lightning thunders above the early human and she knows from earlier experience that others have been killed by this light flash, so she heeds her resulting instinctual fear and retreats to a safe shelter as soon as possible. Thus, she increases her chances of living to see another day as well as increasing her chances of procreating and therefore further spreading her genes (as well as this fear instinct) onto her progeny. Or, if she is past child-bearing age, she can impart her hard-won wisdom to her grandchildren or the children of other families.

By being instinctual, ingrained, and hard-wired into the human brain, fear is extremely difficult to ignore or to keep from influencing many of an individual's choices and decisions throughout their lives. Think of a leader in your culture who strives to be elected or stay in power or influence merely by appealing to your fear. "If you don't support me and my ideology, you are inviting some malevolence into your life." They prey on your fear for your safety by suggesting that only they can keep your enemies from taking your possessions or from hurting you

187

or from damnation to an everlasting fiery torture in hell. Or only by following their suggestions can you avoid retribution from your deity/deities (all other suggestions to the contrary from others being, of course, misguided, deluded or evil). It is far easier to influence humans by appealing to primitive areas of their brain than by appealing to the higher reasoning areas of the same brain.

> **Religion is regarded by the common people as true, by the wise as false, and by the rulers as useful.**
> —Lucius Annaeus Seneca (d. 65 C.E.
> Philosopher, statesman, dramatist and humorist)

And though humans may not commonly think of it this way, one of their greatest fears is that of being powerless in a given situation, or even more simply, being ignorant of the facts of a scenario. Using the lightning example, humans, as a rule, are fearful that they don't know when and where the lightning will strike; therefore, they feel powerless because they can't control or predict this aspect of nature. But even upon accepting this fact of powerlessness, deep down in their psyche, the human may convince themselves that they may still gain <u>some</u> control over the situation by at least knowing why the lightning occurs in the first place. For example, someone saw one of their clan killed by lightning; the observer remembers a past pattern and makes a possible connection: they once saw a member of their group kill another member as a punishment for a transgression (e.g. stealing food). So it seems reasonable to think the person killed by lightning from the sky was being punished by someone up in the sky, possibly for some transgression not yet recognized by the remainder of the clan. Thus an early sin is designated and an early god (or agent) was imagined. The observer then feels duty-bound to inform the others of their tribe that they know the reason why the member was killed by lightning: "The sky god

188

punished him for not planting his crops as early as I'd recommended. If only he would have followed the rites as I had laid them out, he might be alive today!" Thus an early religion and its first prophet were possibly born.

Again, humans feel empowered when they feel that they have an answer. The feeling of wallowing in ignorance robs them of the sense of control of a situation. And any answer (even a weak answer) is better than no answer. Someone seeks out a practitioner of "alternative medicine" for their malady, and sure enough, the practitioner gives them an explanation for their problem and has a treatment that conventional medicine has belittled, ignored or overlooked. And this patient is, after all, receiving the information from an "authority." The "authority" is perceived to have more learning and experience in this area than the layman, so it is presumed that the "authority's" expertise is to be given deference. Yet, the success rate of this alternative treatment appears no more successful than taking no intervention at all, and in many cases, the malady worsens or is accompanied by new symptoms. But the successes are remembered more than the failures, so the alternative practitioner gains credibility.

For these and a multitude of other reasons, science became necessary. People were tired of watching loved ones suffer and die due to the continued ignorance of bodily processes, or they never wanted to go through another famine due to the continued ignorance of horticulture to successfully feed their community. They were fed up with the fear, powerlessness and lack of control that they had over their own lives. They finally became skeptical enough of taking any answer merely on faith, no matter from what authority, especially when it had a track record very close to that of random chance. And so they decided to go outside the monopoly of control of the perceived authority. They questioned the established dogma and began to put various hypotheses to the test. Those hypotheses that withstood the onslaught of skepticism and testing and reproducibility and which resulted in usable, practical and desired outcomes were accepted and used and were perpetuated, only to be tested yet another day. Those hypotheses that failed the tests at any stage could be instantly discarded. Over time, the original "authorities" were either overruled, ridiculed or simply ignored, replaced by the experts of scientific experience who could prove their findings and their ability to control aspects of their world time and time again. And thus, science inevitably took its rightful place as the best discipline to remove as much ignorance and the accompanying fear in the human experience.

Even if a human can avoid a premature death, they know that death comes to everyone eventually. Virtually all humans have a fear of death and its inevitability, and to avoid that fear, a few have invented a place where they can avoid a final end: a "better" place than this Earth, perhaps somewhere with their god; or if you prefer, some sanctuary, a heaven. With this invention, you wouldn't have to feel fear anymore because (after your earthly death) you would live on forever, possibly side by side with your beloved deity. Undeniably appealing. Even modern-day parents (who would otherwise consider most faith-based claims of supernatural powers and occurrences to be ridiculous), may still be inclined to raise their children with a belief in heaven. On the face of it, it doesn't seem to do any harm, and maybe there is an outside chance that, by their children professing belief in it, they might indeed have everlasting life. Or at least they might avoid non-existence, limbo, purgatory, hell or even just separation from their deity's "grace." In this way, they may see themselves as "good" parents doing everything that they possibly can for their offspring. Moreover, others in their peer group consider them good parents and approve, therefore reinforcing the behavior. Add to that, the children have ready-made playmates, and everyone is in a familiar social circle that shares

190

common beliefs. No questioning, skepticism or critical thinking encouraged or even considered.

On the other side of the aisle, humans found that the fear of a final death and an ultimate misery or even eternal torture for the sinful or immoral (or merely the unbeliever) made a most powerful (and useful) incentive to behave in a way that embodied a benevolent society, that is, morally. Eventually, morals themselves seemed to become inextricably linked to religious faith. And when the believers grew large enough, they become emboldened enough to declare those who didn't believe as they did as sinners and the immoral. Of all groups, the one that is most often shown by polls to be the least trusted are the atheists.

THE OTHER SCARLET LETTER "A"

The fool hath said in his heart, "There is no God." They are corrupt, they have done abominable works, there is none that doeth good.
—Psalm 14

All children are atheists, they have no idea of God.
—Baron D. Holbach (d. 1789 Author, Philosopher and Encyclopedist)

All humans are born as non-believers, i.e., atheists. Humans are not born with an innate concept or belief in a god. A newborn babe may quickly imprint on and bond with their parents and other caregivers, but the concept of an ultimate being is something that must be introduced from somewhere outside that child's mind. No baby or infant's first words were, "Praise God!", unless of course, the people that raised them were continually repeating that mantra in front of them.

It can be said that humans <u>are</u> born with an innate sense of curiosity and wonder about the world around them, and a very reasonable question to ask once they've attained a certain age and level of experience of the world is, "How did all of this get here?" In the early history of humanity, if any adult or elder were intellectually honest, they would have simply answered, "I don't know how all of this got here." After all, in the early history of humankind, there were no scientific disciplines such as geology, biology, chemistry, physics, cosmology, etc. to give one at least a

192

rudimentary understanding of the world. But answering the question with "I don't know" at that time would have been giving up too much respect from the younger generations. After all, once bodily strength diminishes, what does an elder have over a youth except more experience, knowledge and wisdom. An admission of ignorance couldn't be countenanced. The elder had to come up with some answer to save face. Seeking for a pattern, their brains may have made a connection: all of their possessions were hand-made, so everything in the world must have been made by someone too. But since the world is so much bigger than just their possessions, the maker must be much bigger too, so out pops the "answer": "A god did it."

Now, who is the infant going to trust? They are totally ignorant of all things and have little experience; and here, they have their parents, their caregivers, their elders, likely their entire community relaying consistent information to them. Very few infants will have enough self-confidence and inborn skepticism to question this information from their elders and peers even for an instant. And with the constant, daily repetition and reaffirmation of this information, it would be challenging for a child to avoid becoming wholly indoctrinated. The idea of a god becomes a familiar, recognizable, even comfortable pattern. And it may seem to answer how things are the way that they are. One isn't left struggling anymore with the ignorance and uncertainty that comes with the original question of "How did all of this get here?"

But even if an individual can somehow avoid this indoctrination, and they make it to the "age of reason" without the belief in a deity, being an atheist is not necessarily an easy life. The label of "atheist" is an incredibly narrow one; it is merely a single, isolated position describing whether or not that individual believes in a god(s). An additional problem is that it is also a term that has had many negative connotations attached to it by its opposition down the centuries.

193

There is the mistaken belief that atheists "don't believe in anything at all." Most atheists probably believe in the majority of the same things that believers do, such as the existence of the universe and everything in it; they simply don't believe that there is a god necessary to explain it. That's it. There's no need to assume all the other negative baggage that is traditionally lumped in with atheism. There is nothing in the term "atheism" that implies or even suggests nihilism, amoralism or anarchy for example.

Some have suggested that many of the despots in the last 100 years or so (Mussolini, Hitler, Franco, Salazar, Tito, Hirohito, Stalin, Mao, Pol Pot, etc.) who killed millions with seeming impunity, did so because of atheism. Still others say atheists won't believe in god because they don't want any higher authority telling them what they can or can't do, or even perhaps that the atheist wants to be a "god" them self. But deeper research reveals that these despots either committed their atrocities with the blessings (or capitulation) of the faith-based or the otherwise credulous. Still, for those despots who were avowed atheists, they simply felt too much deference was being paid to unearthly gods, and that too much money and power was being held by theistic institutions and their authorities. They finally decided that they wanted those benefits redirected to them and their own earthly purposes. But robbing, punishing and disbanding traditional faith-based institutions doesn't make one an "atheist," it makes one an oppressor, a tyrant, a despot.

Atrocities cannot be committed "in the name of atheism" when atheism is nothing more than a single position on a single question. The lack of a belief in a god isn't attached to any particular ideology or worldview; it has no mandate for any action, moral or immoral.

It would, however, be a wonderful experiment if a society, perhaps an entire country were created in the name of CT and secular humanism and all of their ideals. No truths assumed, no group assuming domination over another, no unquestionable ideology, no uncontested authorities. A society with a moral system that is always searching for that which is best for all, actively avoiding harm to any faction; an entire populace actively questioning everything, looking for their own answers, always being aware of their own biases. As peoples came to the New World to avoid the religious tyrannies in their homelands, people would likely flock to this brave new world where all minds were open and free, yet voluntarily disciplined.

Since the term "atheist" describes a single position on a single question, it has no ability to describe the other attributes of the individual. You could even be an atheist and wish that you could still believe that there was a god. Atheism is a word for an incredibly narrow range of belief, basically a single, isolated stance on a single issue, one of the millions of issues that a person may decide upon in their lifetime. But over the centuries, it has been a convenient label on which to heap the many woes of believers. Humans want an answer, any answer and the simpler, the better. How could anyone kill millions of people? It would be convenient to imagine that an atheist (who couldn't believe in any final judgment by a god), would reason to themselves, "Why not kill millions? Nothing will happen to me..."

But the position of atheist contains no other implied judgments on any other issues; no warrant for action, no description of politics, personality or character. Atheists can be philanthropists or misogynists, mass-murders or humanists. They can be affable or antisocial. An atheist could believe in unicorns, leprechauns, fairies or any other supernatural being. An atheist could be a denier of global warming or someone who thinks vaccines cause other medical conditions like autism. Some people actually take pride in their atheism, possibly thinking that because their lack of belief in a god somehow makes them smarter than the average believer. But if a person is an atheist only because they are holding onto the default position with which they were born (with no additional thinking involved), it's not a particularly laudable stance.

It would make for a much more useful and constructive discussion if, instead of the label of atheist, that one labeled one's self as a critical thinker. After all, you'd be describing yourself by the process by which you think, rather than labeling yourself by a single conclusion that you have come to. One's position of atheism would be much more laudable if it were the byproduct of CT, the form of thinking which has the additional desirable outcome of discounting all the other irrational nonsense mentioned in brief in the earlier chapter.

Some have argued that the presence of some form of god/supreme power in virtually every society and culture ever known somehow lends weight to the validity of theism in general. It is said that each religion interprets the "fact" of a supreme power through the lens and filter of their own culture and that, in the end, all of the cultures are pointing to the same ultimate truth.

Others have postulated an actual "god gene" that humans may possess that makes each individual's search for a supreme being and the resulting satisfaction in finding one almost inevitable.

Both of these contentions become specious upon reflecting on the default position of the human brain: ready to be fooled, forearmed with heuristics based on those omnipresent CBLFs. Seek (the pattern) and ye shall find (the pattern), especially if you've already got a pretty good idea of what you'd like the pattern to look like. If one approaches any given occurrence with a slurry of mental shortcuts and inherent biases, attributing agency to one's experiences is practically unavoidable. When all

196

known societies throughout history have done this, what you would predict is exactly what is seen: an incredible variety of irreconcilable religions, faiths, sects and cults; all imagined by biased humans in their bubbles to give some "answer" to continually-asked questions.

Those who are antagonistic to atheism often imply that if you have no belief in god, you must have no morals. Or perhaps, without a belief in a god, you couldn't have any sound basis for your morals; therefore, you must be a moral relativist and must make up your morality to suit you as you go through life.

This contention will be explored in the next chapter.

MORALITY

**From the point of view of a tapeworm, man
was created by God to serve the appetite of
the tapeworm.**
—Edward Abbey (d. 1989 Environmentalist,
Author, Essayist)

Nature itself may not appear particularly moral in a human sense
considering that the vast majority of living things are <u>eaten alive</u>
by their rivals or predators. That is an unimaginable amount of
horrific suffering all on its own. But because they are usually
spared these scenes, humans just don't tend to dwell on this
common, ubiquitous pattern.   However, upon contemplation,
even if a human considered this fact cruel or even tragic, the
unsettling fact is, nature doesn't care what humans feel. This
repetitive pattern is simply nature's way of increasing the
chances that the better-adapted individuals will spread their
genes to the next generations more often than the unadapted
ones. This ensures that the overall fitness of a given species for
its particular environment is maximized over time.

The lion isn't the "bad guy" because it kills and eats the
"innocent" gazelle. And the gazelle isn't "innocent" because it
might get eaten. They are both merely parts of the mechanism of
nature, performing their roles that evolution allows them.
Evolution has no consciousness and therefore, no intent. It is an
ongoing process, not a "grand design." The ultimate end of
evolution wasn't necessarily to have lions eat gazelles; they are
merely the current step in this phase of the process. Neither
animal has any choice in the role it plays, any more than when
the *Tyrannosaurus rex* ate the *Triceraptops* during their phase of

this process.

Nature has no obligation to be "moral" or "nice" or "pleasant" in any human sense, and because it also is not an "agent," nature doesn't have any intent either. An erupting volcano may bury the animals, people and cities around it in ash or lava, a tsunami may destroy human and animal life on a vast scale. But this is not nature being "cruel" or "evil" or "immoral" or even "indifferent"; all of those terms refer to an agent with consciousness or at least sentience, of which nature has none. These events are nature operating as it has for billions of years, long before there were any humans present to judge or label it.

In many cases, some animals abuse or even kill others in their own group to establish an order of dominance; again, this increases the stronger animal's chances of access to food and reproductive partners, ultimately to increase the overall fitness of the descendants and the species as a whole. To humans, it seems mean, unfair, even cruel, especially if the individual recalls a similar pattern of abuse perpetrated on them by members of their own species. Opponents to evolution by Natural Selection have often used these examples to suggest that those who accept the validity of Natural Selection think that in human society "only the strong should survive or dominate." Some have suggested that the genocidal despots of the last century used Natural Selection as the basis for "Social Darwinism" which suggested that it was only "natural" for the stronger leaders (or stronger races) to overcome and dominate others and to kill with impunity.

But the Theory of Natural Selection (NS) is simply a description of how nature has operated for the last few billions of years; it is not, however, meant to be a description of why it operates that way (which may end up being a nonsensical question). NS is an explanation of how plants and animals evolve, but it does not contain any sanction for why they behave as they do. The fact of evolution, and it's most currently accepted explanation, NS, have never implied that their inherent indifference and seeming cruelty are to be a guide for the way that humans should treat each other. Humanity has overcome and superseded some aspects of the lethality and cruelty that would ordinarily happen to it from NS (with solidarity and morality), in a similar way to how humanity has overcome and superseded the lethality and "cruelty" that would ordinarily occur to it in outer space (by protecting themselves with spaceships and spacesuits).

A moment's thought brings the realization that most mammals, indeed most animals, possess the rudiments of morality without any theism at all. While Natural Selection continues in nature, with its "cruelty" and its seeming indifference to suffering, there are still animals that supersede this supposed callousness and hardness. Many animals share their resources with others in their group; they also tend to care for members of their own flock who are in pain, in sickness or distress and to protect them from predators. Evolution of their brains has imbued them with the instinct that cooperation and species solidarity yield the best situation for as many in the group as possible. The members of the group whose brains cause them to behave in ways uncooperative to the common good are the ones driven out of the group. Thus, a rudimentary morality was instilled in many species as the simplest way of ensuring that the most "good" outcomes and the fewest "bad" outcomes would predominate in many animal groups.

Even beyond simply "doing what's best for the herd," there are uncounted recorded instances of cross-species altruism, where a member of one species will help another species. There are also numerous examples of members of one species befriending those of another species, sometimes even when one is a prey species and one is a predator.

200

With this potential for solidarity, cooperation, morality and even altruism in many animal species, it is not unusual that the human species would have inherited these qualities as well. Human society as a whole benefits when its members cooperate with each other, look after one another and treat each individually and collectively as worthwhile members of their group, regardless of their individual abilities. Having evolved from the common ancestors of other animals, humans had this form of morality in their instinct as well. Then, they took the next step; a leap in human culture possible with a more "advanced" brain: mankind was able to conceive of treating each with an even "higher" morality than that which nature had already imbued them.

Somehow, over the course of history, religion claimed morality as a gift bestowed only on those who believed in a certain way, a truth "written on the hearts" of each person by a supreme being. Many believers were always ready to relate their personal experience of feeling this divine cardiac manuscript. Repetition of this pattern over centuries resulted in this "truth" being taken on faith, part of a dogma. Later on, it was accepted almost as a given that one needed religion or faith to be moral.

But no evidence was ever supplied for this supposed truth. It was handy to have a book (a physical written "authority") that one could point to that supposedly contained "the word of god." Anyone who admitted ignorance of god's will on morality could read it for themselves in the scriptures (or much more often, have it interpreted to them by a priesthood).

But somehow, over the centuries, what was considered moral in these holy books seemed to evolve, the god appeared to be changing his mind. In the beginning, it was proclaimed to be moral to consider women inferior, to own people as slaves, to mutilate the genitals of defenseless infants and to execute children by stoning if they became unruly as adolescents.

Homosexuals deserved death. At that time, entire tribes of people could be put to the sword, massacred down to the last babe and pregnant mother for the "sin" of believing in the wrong god or living in the wrong land. And each swordsman would surely have felt no compunction as he plunged the sword into the expectant mother's belly while saying, "You can relax, ma'am, the lord assures me that this is moral and holy."

In later iterations of these holy books, when the implied deity had had every opportunity to correct and improve his code of ethos, slavery, the subjugation of women and infant genital mutilation were still condoned. But other questionable aspects of morality were added on top of this onus, such as substitutionary atonement for sin, vicarious redemption, compulsory love of all others (including one's enemies), dissuasion from aspiration, investment and education as well as the threat of never-ending, unlimited torture for a limited transgression: the "thought-crime" of doubt. In any version of these books, morality was determined by whatever the god had supposedly inspired humans to write down. There was apparently little human discussion on whether it made sense or not, but if it didn't make sense, the answer was that humans simply couldn't understand or weren't meant to understand the wisdom and morality of this god. The divine fiat was declared, and obeisance demanded. What mere mankind thought was moral wasn't even a consideration, morality was determined by the superior omniscience (or caprice) of the deity.

But the longer humanity looked at these scriptures, the more they began to pick and choose which divine commandments sounded reasonable; which should be followed literally and which figuratively; which could be ignored, or explained away as allegory, metaphor or something that was "moral for that time, but not moral in our time." There seemed to be a moral relativism where different people could interpret the same books in very different ways, leading to many religious schisms,

202

denominations, sects and cults. And no matter which version of the divine edicts were proclaimed holy writ, or at what different time in history they were declared, each denomination professed their current edition the rock-solid, unalterable, unquestionable "foundation of morality." Considering the thousands of denominations and sects past and present, that's a lot of incompatible/irreconcilable "rock-solid" moral authorities.

But just as progressing scientific discovery shrunk the areas of knowledge that necessitated a god or the supernatural as an explanation, the increasing use of reason and CT shrunk the necessity of a supreme being to explain how and why humans should behave morally: it is simply and instinctually the best way for humans to get along.

It also seems to be instinctual that when the individual treats someone else (or another species) with respect, care, kindness or love, they experience an internal sense of gratification.

Virtue is its own reward. —John Henry Newman (d. 1890 Anglican and Catholic theologian and poet)

Morality doesn't have to be dictated by an authority or a dogma; in fact, it's typically inherent.

Ethical behavior is doing the right thing when no one else is watching- even when doing the wrong thing is legal.
—Aldo Leopold (d. 1948 Author, Philosopher, Scientist, Ecologist, Forester, Conservationist, and Environmentalist)

So what would cause someone to "do the right thing" even if the action wasn't acknowledged or appreciated or rewarded by some other being? Is it conscience? Is it the internal feeling of being virtuous? Is it merely the chemical reward of a discharge of endorphins in the person's brain? The answer could be one or more of these (and other possibilities besides), yet all of these possibilities are still part of the <u>natural</u> order; what is evident is that this morality doesn't require anything supernatural.

The irony is that, over the eons, the same increase in brain mass that has imbued humanity with superior cognitive abilities and a potential for a superior natural morality has also ingrained the human species with the potential for negative personality traits, warped imagination, and incredible immorality. The likelihood is that all humans have this potential, the quiescent possibility of abuse and cruelty that goes far beyond what is typically found in nature. It has lead humans to maltreat and torture members of their own species as well as other species. In some cases, humans actually feel pleasure in committing these acts. Humans alone in the animal world have the imagination to even conceive of the idea of genocide, let alone to implement it. These more "imaginative" or "sophisticated" examples of immorality and sadism are rarely seen outside the human species. When it is, it is usually the species with "more advanced brains" (such as orcas and chimpanzees); yet still, the sadism is not anywhere near the extent or the degree as seen within the human animal. Even these "lesser" animals wouldn't stoop that low.

LIVING LIFE BY SHORTCUTS

Humans share the phenomenon of instincts with other animals. Humanity couldn't have survived to the present day without them. Why is the tall grass moving? You might assume that it's the wind and be wrong and suffer the consequences when the hidden lion (who was stalking you in the grass) attacks. You can always assume it's a lion and run in the opposite direction and be wrong but still be safe, even if it was just the wind. In other words, you will still survive even when your instinct was wrong and compelled you to do something unnecessary. The reward (survival and increased chance of passing on genes) goes to assuming a threat, yet still being wrong most of the time.

Since more animals survived in the same kind of potentially life-threatening situation assuming a threat (and being wrong) and always running than those animals that assumed no threat (and were wrong) and stayed put (and got eaten), through thousands of generations of successful reproduction of the survivors who always assumed a threat, but were still wrong, it became an instinct to err on the side of caution. Assume the worst and always run, because the cost of the consequences of being wrong is very low (just wasted time and energy, but still surviving to reproduce).

But assuming the best and being wrong could result in the high cost of injury or death (and therefore, less chance of survival to pass on your genes). It became a "knee-jerk," rule-of-thumb to run away from moving grass. This rule-of-thumb is an example of a heuristic, a mental shortcut that facilitates daily life, and sometimes, survival. These heuristics don't have to be accurate or correct, they just have to make survival more likely on average or to make living easier or more straightforward. By being so automatic and instinctual, heuristics don't take much energy or take up much space in the higher reasoning centers of the brain.

CT, on the other hand, takes far more energy and focus in the higher reasoning centers of the brain. It's slower and much harder to employ: if you want to avoid being eaten, it's better not to delay by self-questioning. It slows down the routine of the everyday. It doesn't necessarily provide the instant gratification, the immediate, and sometimes practical payoff that a heuristic can. Thus, for many, heuristics become the automatic, default solution to daily life. Don't do any more thinking than is absolutely necessary to get through the day.

Furthermore, CT isn't even necessary for 98% of your daily life. Heuristics do work well enough for many of one's daily routines. If you've used the same route to work or school for years, your mental shortcuts and "rules of thumb" can lead you accurately to your destination with very little conscious thought. In fact, for daily purposes, heuristics are very often the far more practical approach. Using CT for these particular everyday purposes would needlessly bog down your actions. You would always be wondering if you were being fooled by certain visual cues. CT would have you skeptically questioning whether gravity, even though it had always been in effect in the past, would necessarily be in effect the next time.

But there are those times when things aren't routine, and when CT is necessary, even if it does take a bit longer. For example, when it comes time for an election. In the past, you've always voted only for the candidates in your party, and the results (regardless of which party won) have so far, always led to a continued high quality of living for you. You could have read the in-depth positions on the issues of both the candidates of your party as well as those of candidates from other parties, but why? That would take a lot of time and mental effort, and why bother? You've heard them give speeches before where they touch on their positions. Voting your party is a comfortable mental shortcut and based on previous experience, it seems likely that it will continue to lead to a comfortable living for you. Voting in this way has always resulted in the reward and comfort before, and therefore, the use of your heuristic gets further reinforced.

However, unbeknownst to you, the voting records and actions of several of the elected representatives that you voted for have differed in some regards to their position on which they ran their campaigns! Your shortcut (forgoing reading in depth on their positions) would've made you miss this breach of promise by your representatives. Yes, you receive the same reward, but not for the reasons that you assumed. The world didn't work in quite the way that you thought it would; in essence, you continued to be rewarded, even when you were deluded.

Another example: for years, you've always taken the same way home because it's a straight shot, you can let your mind wander and don't have to worry about missing a turn. But in the name of the expediency, your mental shortcut of using this literal shortcut has made you miss a slightly longer and more convoluted route with much more beautiful scenery. The longer, more scenic route is fraught with more turns, more unexpected traffic signs, which takes much more attention, and thus, more mental effort. You're not able to let your mind wander (i.e., to let your brain fall back to its default position of non-CT). Taking the new route would simply be more of a mental challenge.

Consider that if for your whole life you've listened only to your preferred genre of popular music, and only your preferred genre of music; it's sounds and rhythms are familiar, soothing, expected, it becomes an accustomed pattern (for entertainment purposes, it's a mental shortcut). But you've missed out on the depth and richness of other music genres and their respective cultures. These other music forms and patterns may initially feel alien to you, not nearly so familiar; they may not be initially as pleasing or even as satisfying as your familiar genre; they may take a much longer attention span, they may take much more mental processing and evoke different, unexpected feelings and emotions than your preferred genre. Initially, the feelings these new genres evoke may not even be expected or welcome; they challenge your brain in a way that it's not used to being challenged.

But over time, a new genre can become satisfying, bringing a new, different pleasantness. The new patterns also become welcome. But with your range of appreciation expanded, you realize how limited you were in your tastes and experiences and how much you had been missing. You may lament the time lost, but you console yourself with the increased bounty of the future.

Likewise, you may have always assumed a creator because it felt like a handy mental shortcut to explain how the world works, and that something greater than you cared about you and would take care of you, including after your death. It gave you a moral authority that could set the bar for behavior and ethics and that simply by following that authority, you could feel like you were a good person leading a moral life. What's more, you were considered a member of a large group of other people who saw things very much the same way as you did.

It can be an extremely comfortable way to live life, feeling loved, accepted and agreed with, and it's a wonderfully familiar pattern. But by this shortcut, you've missed out on the wonders of nature and science that explain the world and the universe far better and that have the added benefit and integrity of being provable, reproducible, and far more useful. You've missed out on how logic, reason, CT, normal instinctual human solidarity and the ubiquity of human conscience can explain and provide the morality and ethics essential to progressing as a species and ensuring the survival of the planet. You take the shortcut and yes, you survive and perhaps prosper somewhat another day.

208

And of course, it doesn't take nearly the mental effort, but you miss out on the much larger, much grander world of truth.

BIAS BUBBLES

The ideal starting point for your position on any issue, be it within science, politics, faith, morality or anything else should be "I don't know" or "I'm not sure." This confession of ignorance at the very beginning of your inquiry would be intellectually honest when being confronted throughout your life with so many possibilities and unknowns. There are thousands, even millions of ideas and phenomena that each human is inundated with throughout their life, and it would be extremely impractical to have to research every one before deciding on a given stance on any single one. It's much more practical and conducive to fall back to the position that says, "I'm not certain, but I'm going to maintain a healthy skepticism toward each of these things, and I will wait until I have sufficient evidence for any given position before I adopt a position of acceptance or rejection." Unfortunately, it is the rare human who is brought up in such a skeptical environment, freely allowed by their family and community to go through their own skeptical thinking process. It is far more common that the average human is raised within certain "bias bubbles."

All humans have biases, whether they like to admit it or not. For this book, a bias is not the same thing as a prejudice. A bias is just the pattern that the individual is most used to sensing, and the environment in which the individual is raised has a huge influence on the patterns with which they will be most familiar and comfortable. The more often the person is presented with a given position on an issue, the greater the possibility that their PSBs can ease the transition from that position staying a mere possibility to becoming hard-wired in their brain as an actual bias. A bias doesn't necessarily have to be intrinsically negative, detrimental or harmful; it may simply be another pattern, a false assumption generated by repetition and familiarity. However, this bias may make the transition to an active prejudice when the owner of the brain doesn't actively question the bias. And the prejudice becomes discrimination when the owner acts on the prejudice.

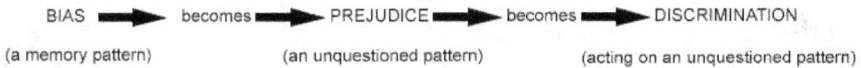

BIAS ➡ becomes ➡ PREJUDICE ➡ becomes ➡ DISCRIMINATION

(a memory pattern)   (an unquestioned pattern)   (acting on an unquestioned pattern)

How often when you question someone on their bias/prejudice/ discrimination do you hear the defense "Well, that's just how I was raised?" or "This is the way that it has always been within my culture". This is what passes for reason? This person is, in essence, saying, "I am helpless in this discussion, my upbringing and experiences have so molded my brain and the patterns that it is used to that it is a <u>waste of time</u> for me to actively question my position, my opinions or indeed, my entire thinking process. After constant bombardment with and reinforcement of this bias, I have decided that the bias is valid, and <u>I have no choice</u> but to succumb to the pattern that my brain now rather comfortably recognizes."

This is an example of a "bubble," the ongoing, immediate, repeated stimuli in a person's proximal environment to which that individual will begin to assign the label of "the usual," the "normal," even the "moral."

If you are brought up on a tropical island with the ocean and jungle supplying you with food, you are much more likely to come into constant contact with people that think that there are gods in the sea, the forest, the sky. If you were brought up in Ancient Egypt around the Nile River which supplied you with fish and birds and irrigation for you crops reliably every year, you are very likely to be told that the Nile has divine attributes. If you were brought up near the Fertile Crescent in ancient times where food was more plentiful around large rivers than around other places, you were very likely told that there is a "specialness" to your homeland. And this was the reason that so many of the most important events in history were all clustered (conveniently) in your homeland.

No matter what your religious faith, you are more likely than not to have come by it merely by the chance of your birthplace. If you were born in India, you're more likely to be Hindu; in Saudi Arabia, more likely Muslim; in Mexico, Christian. Of course, there are exceptions, as there are religious minorities in any country. But again, you are more likely to be of the same faith as your family; or the same as some other community with which you've regularly come into contact.

And the longer that you live in a place, the greater is your chance that you will come to the same faith-based conclusions as those with whom you've interacted during all of that time in your community. This is an example of a faith "bubble." And the longer that you are kept in that bubble (or any other bubble discussed below), the more ingrained that its tenets and "truths" are likely to become in your brain. At a certain point, these patterns may become so ingrained in your thought process that nothing can overcome them: not logic, not reason, not evidence, not science. It simply becomes a long-established pattern that your brain likes to revisit over and over and over again, the pleasure of the familiarity of the pattern constantly reinforcing the bias in your brain. "I believe what I believe, and nothing is going to change my mind!" "I'm happy with my beliefs, why should I even consider questioning them or changing them?"

However, if you can question and perhaps someday even overcome the influence of a given bubble, it can still be a painful process. As the years go on, you will have myriad experiences piled onto and connected to your bias through association,

212

emotions, memories, and communal reinforcement. Eventual eradication of the bias can be as difficult as digging out an old tree stump whose roots have grown around and intertwined with underground pipes and electrical lines, shackling the stump to the Earth. Yes, the stump can eventually be torn from the ground, but the hole that remains has very ragged edges and the hole contains many damaged pipes and wires. Apparently, it was a traumatic eradication event that resulted in this leftover, painful, gaping wound in one's world. And a common question asked afterward is, "I've always had this space in my psyche filled with something comfortable, familiar and dependable; with what am I now supposed to fill this sensitive void?" The answer is, hopefully, something a little closer to the truth.

Unfortunately, there are many possible bubbles in any individual's life. The bubbles of one's politics, one's language, one's home, one's income, even what web pages and apps that a person visits on a daily basis. Forgoing the comfort and pleasure of the familiar pattern is, well, uncomfortable and unpleasant.

If you are raised in a household with one dominant political ideology, you are more likely to subscribe to it. Later, no matter what your politics may be, you are much more likely to read information from political sources on the internet that agree with your current bias. By this constant exposure to like-minded opinions, your own similar opinions are thus strongly reinforced. You actively pursue viewpoints that vindicate yours.

You are much less likely to actively seek information from the opposing political party, especially when they present a valid argument against your stance that you can't refute. You get a negative vibe from this pattern, this challenge, and it definitely doesn't trigger the pleasure centers of your brain like reading information that already agrees with your bubble.

You aren't spurred to pursue investigation into things that give you a negative feeling; at least not nearly as often as those things that you're reasonably sure will provide you with a shot to the pleasure centers of your brain.

There have been mammal studies where the animal subjects can stimulate their brain's own pleasure centers, and they will choose this stimulation over food and water, even to the point where they die of thirst and starvation. Given the same opportunity, humans will tend to do the same, but the human mammal usually has the advantage of a family member or co-worker to remind them when it's mealtime.

If you are raised with one language, you are far more likely to be irritated by or merely be suspicious of those speaking other languages to each other in your presence. You may disparage them for not having the courtesy to speak your language in front of you so that you can understand them more easily, or at least know about whom or what they are talking. Welcome to your language bubble.

If you were raised in the city, you are more likely to think that those raised in rural areas are less educated, less sophisticated, less experienced in worldly matters. This is your home bubble.

If you are fortunate enough to have been raised in an affluent household, you are more likely to look down on those who are poor, reasoning perhaps that they didn't work hard enough, so they deserve their plight. Your income bubble.

When one is raised in an urban/suburban bubble, they are likely to think of the things in that bubble as the "ordinary" and things outside the bubble as more "extraordinary." If someone raised in the city walks along the street and sees a sparrow, they may not even pay much attention to something so "common." But the first time that that same person sees a picture of the Bird of Paradise, they are likely to think of it as "extraordinary" or even "exotic." But is this justified? As far as nature and reality are concerned, the Bird of Paradise and the sparrow are equally ordinary. Each of them is simply the species that results from the environmental pressures of their respective ecological niches. It's all too human to come across some novel discovery like this and then to consider it somehow "special." But it will be instructive to take that expression "all too human" and substitute the phrase "typical for a PSB succumbing to one of its bias bubbles."

Humans become very comfortable with all of their bias bubbles. School is an excellent place to be regularly exposed to those who were raised in different bubbles than you were. If one can go to college, they're even more likely to come into contact with people from another city or even another country, as well as their respective bubbles. These are excellent opportunities to challenge the thinking patterns that your bubbles have imprinted on your mind. The whole idea of school is to become more educated, to add to your knowledge base and yes, to challenge your thinking and perhaps even have your mind changed.

What is the point of going to school or college just so that you can maintain the exact same opinions and "truths'" that you had before you began? Have you learned anything new about other people, other ideas, other phenomena? Was there ever even a chance that you might change your mind?

And yet, these bias bubbles are purposefully being perpetuated when students are sent only to a religious or faith-based school, whether at the primary/secondary school level or the college level. Does it make sense to start in a bubble and move onto an institution expressly designed to solidify that bubble? There are even some ideologies that insist on having a communal enclave unto themselves precisely so that they won't be exposed to the differing ideas of the outside world! As if to be confronted by questions and challenging thoughts is an actual threat!

Fortunately, a phenomenon has occurred that has had the effect of bursting many of these bubbles: the internet. Now, the vast majority of inhabitants of the world have access to a resource that contains virtually all of human knowledge and it comes with that handy addition that so many ideologies lack: evidence. The individual may access the net on their own, often without outside surveillance or supervision (except in those areas where access is denied, by some authority [parents, religious leaders or the government] that wishes to keep individuals in their bubble).

When access to the net is finally achieved, the individual can ask themselves questions that have been bothering them about their viewpoints and beliefs and get feedback. They may sample the cultures, experiences, upbringings and education (and the corresponding bubbles) of others all over the planet, instantly, without even having to go to a school or university. In essence, they can self-educate and contemplate, all without physical confrontation with their conversant, without having to back down when proven wrong or without having to save face in the immediate vicinity of their challenger.

There is no going back. Humanity has drunk from the fountain of the Information Age; they have become spoiled by its availability, now they expect it, and they relish it. They prefer knowledge over ignorance. To maintain healthy engagement and stimulation, the human brain yearns for variety over uniformity. It only remains for each person to be on the lookout for their own biases as they take their own long draught.

With the advent of the internet has come a virtual Second Age of Reason. Bubbles are shattered, conflicting ideas are exchanged, and challenges are made to comfortable thought patterns; one is finally shown all possibilities in a very complicated world. And in quiet moments of private contemplation, with no impinging

216

influence from one's family, party or community, one is allowed to question one's own beliefs and opinions. There is only so long that you can respond to your family or community in a way that they will accept; you may even be able to submerge your doubts about your own positions and beliefs temporarily, or sometimes even for years or decades. But during all of this time, your uncertainties will keep nagging at you. The doubts will not leave you alone because at the very core of your being, you don't want to believe something simply because you already believe it, you want to have good, demonstrable reasons for your position, backed up with as much evidence and reason as possible. It is your own conscience demanding intellectual integrity from you, and your conscience will not remain silent forever.

GOOD BYE, KRIS KRINGLE

Many people in faith are kept there partly because they fear life without their greatly venerated icon. What will they do without the great love that they feel for their symbol? But have they ever thought about what took the place when they ceased to believe in other beloved icons like Santa Claus? Or the Easter Bunny? Or the Tooth Fairy? Or any other icon in its given culture? Initially, they possibly felt a certain measure of loss followed by a brief melancholy, perhaps about the loss of some aspect of their child-like innocence. And then later, upon reflection, they likely realized that something else must have taken the special place of these icons in their lives; possibly their increased knowledge and experience and recognition of the reality of life.

In most cases, their appreciation of these associated events didn't so much diminish as change to a new, more mature appreciation. They took on the additional responsibility of wanting a more mature truth in their life. Perhaps after achieving adulthood, they smiled while looking at the next generation of children, thinking to themselves, "Look at them, so innocent, so willing to accept these fantasies, it makes them happy just to believe. I hope that they enjoy this aspect of their childhood, for all too soon, they too will grow up to become reasoning adults, and they will also discard these cherished beliefs in favor of reality."

Then there are the children who have somehow discovered the truth relatively early in life: there is no Easter Bunny, there is no Tooth Fairy, no Father Christmas; it was actually the adults creating and providing these things. But upon this discovery, these more informed children are admonished by the adults, "You must not tell the other children about the truth, you will spoil the joy of their illusion if you educate them too early about reality. Let them bask in their illusion for a while longer until they discover it for themselves." It seems that the more informed and realistic the individual is, the closer they are to being a social pariah.

For many ideologies, the long-held cherished beliefs don't stop even in adulthood. As they mature and educate themselves about the reality of the world and the beliefs of other humans, it slowly dawns on many that their seemingly dependable stances on any variety of issues and beliefs begin to lose their luster. The integrity of a given position doesn't seem so unquestionable anymore; there may now be some uncertainties, some gray areas and many other possibilities. It often becomes difficult to find reliable footing for one's stance any more. Yet, the individual may maintain their precarious footing because it is comfortably familiar, the arguments in favor of their positions are well-rehearsed, their mantra is a pattern that they have memorized. Questioning of the position presents the possibility of a pattern too different from the norm to be comfortable. Those whose beliefs differ are now the social pariahs who are expected to keep their opinions to themselves lest they taint the next generation. Or they are brushed away as hopelessly ignorant, "you just don't understand..." It may simply be more pleasant to remain shackled to one's patterns of a lifetime.

Consider a scenario where, after generations of slavery, a slave is offered freedom; the door is opened and the world outside beckons. There have been instances when certain slaves hesitated to leave. While freedom always seemed desirable, when it was finally offered, the slave is filled with anxiety about the prospect. Even if their captivity was oppressive and initially unwanted, it still provided a measure of security and routine. They were provided with a "home" of sorts, provisions such as food and clothing, as well as a community where their position was well understood and constant. And they didn't have to be responsible for creating their purpose in life because they were provided with a purpose by the master. They weren't allowed to aspire to be anything else; their days were fairly predictable. Some slaves saw freedom as a kind of "threat" to that security. Unlike the free man, the slave may not have been allowed the opportunity to gain the life experiences, abilities and opportunities to achieve the maturity, self-confidence and self-esteem necessary to strike out on their own. The thought of taking full responsibility for one's choices and actions and purpose (after a lifetime of having it done for them) may have seemed all too daunting. They aren't used to this new pattern; it's simply too different. Some slaves may have declined the offer or asked for a "modified freedom" where much of their daily routine remained the same, but they gained some rights of the free. This milder change in the pattern of their life was acceptable. The patterns in one's life can seem relentless, tenacious, concrete.

Irrespective of which pattern that one finds acceptable, most people still tend to seek community with the like-minded whom they now also consider friends. That to even question a common ideology (let alone to abandon it) is to invite a dreaded social ostracism. This phenomenon will be covered more fully in the next chapter.

"IN" GROUPS AND "OUT" GROUPS

Humans are social animals. There are exceptions of course, which prefer to be loners, but generally, humans prefer to be around other humans. They also have a strong tendency to seek out those that are like them in some way: similar in outward appearance, similar in language, culture, social strata, similar in mindset, in beliefs. There is the feeling of solidarity from having your similarities reinforced, your beliefs somehow validated by being with others who share your traits. And of course, you feel security and strength in numbers. You don't have to be in a minority; you can be in the majority. You feel empowered by it, and if there are more in your group than outside of it, your group must be correct in some aspect, after all, how could so many people be wrong about the same thing?

As soon as you're accepted into some club, some congregation, some family, it's as if a switch was turned on and you immediately changed from an "outsider" to an "insider." As a person, you are identical to the person that you were a second ago before this change, before the acceptance. But somehow, now you're perceived as being different. You're more acceptable, you have an instant support network that will help you much more readily, willingly and unquestioningly than they might have helped you as an outsider, the very person that you were a moment ago. Humans love to create "in" groups and "out" groups; they love to pigeon-hole, to classify something as "acceptable" or "unacceptable," something to welcome, or conversely something to separate if not ostracize.

Once you're a part of the "in" group (that particular political party, that particular faith, that certain mindset) you typically solidify several things: your stances on various issues, your ready-made responses to probing questions, your mantras that you repeat over and over again. All these things continue to be familiar, comfortable patterns.

You might imagine how cozy and even appealing it is to repeat the same beliefs, prayers and mantras that have been repeated by you and repeated to you throughout your life. These repeated "truths" become memorized, even comforting as an expected, familiar pattern, you feel satisfied once they have been repeated. It's even easier to continue in your current mindset when you're surrounded by an entire family and community repeating the same things over and over. Humans are social beings. There are few things more comforting to a human being than being part of the "in" group..."you're one of us now." You have the most welcome feeling of belonging, of acceptance, of being loved by a large group, every one of whom believes substantially the same things that you do. All of this is understandably attractive. What's more, you don't have to be identified as someone in the "out" group, an "outsider," an apostate, an unbeliever, the mistaken, an undesirable.

In the best of circumstances, those who have decided that they don't believe the same as the "in" group are permitted or tolerated, perhaps merely endured. But quite often, the dissenter is met with disappointment, disapproval, if not outright disowning by members of the "in" group. Depending on the depth of exclusivity of the "in" group, the nonconformist may even be shunned, excommunicated, vilified, punished, abused, tortured, and in the case of some religious faith, executed. Murdered. For nothing more than thinking differently. Thought crime.

The "in" group is saying, "You have no choice in this, you aren't allowed to question our truths, to let your mind stray and begin to think of alternatives, other possibilities. You are forbidden to use your imagination. The only proper use of your mind is to agree with our way of thinking; come to think of it, you don't even have to do any thinking at all, we've already done the work for you.

222

We have found a pattern that works well for us; it is simply up to you to recognize and agree with the same pattern." Alliance with the "in" group has now moved from attractive to imperative. In some cases, it has become a simple matter of survival.

Imagine if a pet dog taught itself many skills and wanted to impress and please its human caretaker with its abilities to jump far distances, to do backflips, to run an intricate obstacle course and to dance on its hind legs, but each attempt is met with a beating and the human yelling, "Sit! Just sit! That's all that I want you to do, sit!" And if the dog decided that it couldn't hold back the desire to demonstrate its potential, the human tortured and killed it, "I warned it to behave only the way that i wanted it to. I had no choice; it wouldn't obey."

If you are the only person who holds a particular position on an issue, and everyone else holds a contrary position, will you be more likely to switch over to their position just because you are outnumbered? After all, a consensus seems to carry so much weight in human lives. Whether it's the science that people accept, the laws that the government enacts and the morals by which society lives, most humans go with the majority, whether they choose to or because they feel coerced.

As with a theory, a consensus has a different significance between the colloquial and the scientific. In common parlance, a consensus simply means that a large enough group of people agree on some point that the point is practically taken as a given. But as has been touched on earlier, there is no particular trick to getting large numbers of humans to agree on anything. Appeal to their biases, repeat to them what they already want to believe and your task is nearly done.

You can sway a thousand men by appealing to their prejudices quicker than you can convince one man by logic. —Robert A. Heinlein (d. 1988 Dean of Science Fiction Writers)

The difference with science and its great advantage is that the entire process begins by acknowledging that all humans (including the researchers) have biases and that the experiments, data and analysis must be protected from these biases at all costs. Once enough rival scientists have performed the same research and obtained the same results, a scientific consensus may be reached. And while this scientific consensus may not be an absolute totally accurate description of reality and truth, it will be the closest that humans can attain with the limitations of their current technology and their level of intelligence. And it will be far ahead of any common consensus based on what humans merely want to believe.

Choosing to be part of a minority merely to be a contrarian, an iconoclast, or a rebel, is not a particularly respectable position either. But if your minority position results from the use of reason, logic, science and CT, and you recognize that the majority has arrived at their majority position by some other means (coercion, faith, jumping on the bandwagon, not wanting to rock the boat, avoiding retribution, etc.), then the only way for you to maintain personal and intellectual integrity is to continue to hold to your minority position. The popularity of a position has zero significance in its truth.

Great minds think alike, but fools seldom differ.
—Anonymous

COMMON SENSE(S)

Believe nothing, no matter where you read it or who has said it, not even if I have said it, unless it agrees with your own reason and your own common sense.

—Buddha (d. Circa 480 B.C.E)

Given the time period in which he lived, this was the most sage advice that the Buddha could impart: don't take anything as granted just because some "authority" said it or wrote it. This Buddha (who some consider an "authority") even recognized that he had his own biases, and that his followers should avoid the mistake of blind adherence and obedience. Without the benefit of future scientific inquiry and technical advancement, all that his followers had to fall back on at that time was reason and common sense.

And therein lies the limitation of his advice.

Humans are most comfortable dealing with the world on their own scale. You're much more likely to consider your immediate environment when determining the actuality of things and making decisions on issues. It is not an intrinsic habit of humanity to consider the microscopic or the astronomic when dealing with everyday life. Without the necessary education, it isn't common sense to accept that 99.999% of everything that humans see is hollow. Yet, it is has been proven with science that the vast majority of each atom that makes up everything that is visible is hollow.   Scale up the typical atom, where the outer electron shell is represented by the circumference of a professional sports stadium, and the nucleus will be a golf ball on the center of the field. All the rest of the space of that atom is empty. Humanity knows this is true because scientific instruments and mathematics prove it, and humans have exploited this truth in medicine, science and engineering.

But it can be a hard reality to accept when you use your knuckles to knock on a "solid" block of steel. This "common sense" that the steel block is "solid" allows you to get through your daily life quite nicely even though you're laboring under a falsehood, a delusion created by your senses. What "common sense" and your common senses tell you is your "solid" knuckles knocking on a "solid" steel block is, in reality, electrostatic interactions of the electrons in your knuckles being repulsed by the electrons in the steel block; essentially, one mostly hollow object repelling another mostly hollow object, without actually touching.

Is it common sense to accept that 99.9999% of the known universe is empty space and that a spaceship traveling near the speed of light would take years to reach the closest star to ours (let alone millions of years to reach the nearest galaxy)? Is it common sense that stars and planets are merely "suspended" in the "fabric" of space/time? Are humans comfortable that in space, there is no "up," no "down"? Does it make sense that the very fabric of space/time continually expands the size of the known universe at incomprehensible speeds?

Humanity's body of knowledge and its increasing ability to control its destiny would have been virtually paralyzed if inquiry always ceased whenever something didn't seem to "make sense." While impressive to humans, human imagination is far too limited by itself to "make sense" of everything in the universe. Skepticism, science and other aspects of CT are required to leap beyond that restriction.

The more that you learn about astronomy and cosmology, the more it begins to dawn on you that not only are you an infinitesimal speck on the Earth, but that the Earth is an infinitesimal speck in the solar system; which is, in turn, an infinitesimal speck in the Milky Way galaxy; which is, in turn, an infinitesimal speck in the local group of galaxies; which is, in turn, an infinitesimal speck in all of the known universe. And this isn't even considering the possibility of a multiverse (multiple universes). It may be difficult to accept how minuscule your individual existence may seem.

This isn't to say that your existence has to be meaningless, worthless or without purpose. No matter how small your existence may be, you still have full potential to give your life these qualities. Perhaps it's the <u>difference</u> that you make in the world that gives you life meaning, worth and purpose. In the end, when your obituary is read, would you rather it <u>only</u> listed the fine meals that you enjoyed, the hobbies that occupied your time, the travel that you experienced? Or would it seem to imbue your life with more purpose, worth and meaning if your obituary also listed the peoples' lives that you helped transform, the difference that you made in the part of the world that you touched, the ideals that you embodied and practiced?

Arguably, it is undesirable merely to be provided your worth, purpose and meaning by some outside agent; it is much more fulfilling and satisfying to decide for yourself what your purpose and meaning should be and earn your worth for yourself.

Still, on a practical day-to-day basis, one doesn't even have to dwell on one's scale compared to the universe. It serves humanity well enough that on a human scale, humans consider themselves as solid and the objects that they interact with as solid. In essence, **people can successfully function in daily life while remaining deluded or ignorant to certain absolutes of reality.**

What an extraordinary statement!

And from this all-too-human ability to set aside reality in favor of the immediacy of practicality often springs the contention, "well, it's 'real enough' for me, so I don't care about what it is in reality," so that one may have their own "personal truth." Or, to paraphrase: "Well, I can still function well in this society while remaining deluded or ignorant."

This aspect of humanity's "common sense" is based on their common senses, which are surprisingly limited. Human vision and it's limitations were touched on earlier. Vision is, after all, humanity's primary sense, the one that has the most gray matter devoted to it, the sense to which humans pay the most attention and the last that most people would choose to lose.

But humans don't realize how "blind" they are. Each eye has a built-in blind spot which the brain has to fill in with the corresponding portion of the other eye's visual field, taking extra brain processing power. In humans, only the central vision is sharp, the remaining 99% of the retina is devoted to low-resolution peripheral vision. Vast amounts of gray matter are involved in all levels of visual processing, which wouldn't be necessary if any competent engineer had designed the human eye. Humans can't distinguish between different polarities of light.

Add to that, humans are blind to 99% of the electromagnetic spectrum! The wavelengths that *Homo sapiens sapiens* can detect occupy such a narrow range of the electromagnetic spectrum that if you stretched the length of the EM spectrum from Maine To California, the portion that humans could see would be the length of a couple of football fields. And yet, with this pathetic level of vision, a person will still say that they've seen all of the United States. But the average human continues to marvel at their sight because it's the pattern that they're used to, or that is to say, it is to what they are biased.

Most birds of prey such as hawks, eagles, falcons and owls have much more extensive percentages of their retinas devoted to acute vision, and for some reason, relatively small areas of brain dedicated to their processing. Snakes are sensitive to the infrared, insects to the ultraviolet, some birds and bats to different polarities of light, but humanity was denied these faculties.

The remaining senses that humans are most commonly conscious of are hearing, touch, taste and smell. Human hearing is far more limited than that of dogs and cats. These animals also possess far superior senses of smell. A butterfly shames

228

humans with the sensitivity of its sense of taste. The human sense of touch is far less sensitive than that of the star-nosed mole. 100,000 nerve fibers are packed into the mole's fingertip-sized nose; this is five times more nerves than an entire human hand.

Why were these animals gifted with superior senses to humans, didn't a deity deem humanity worthy of their incorporation? Still, if these sensual limitations are all that you've ever known, how are you expected to know any differently about your sensual inadequacies? You rarely get the chance to compare your senses with another animal, and when you do, you tend to marvel more at the animal's abilities than at your own limitations. You think to yourself, "Well, my senses are good enough for me, I don't need any more accuracy to interpret the world."

And yet with all of the limitations of your senses, and with your professed ignorance or delusions concerning reality, you still feel like you know how the world works to an impressive level of accuracy. Or perhaps you're thinking, "I know how the world works well enough....for me. This is my truth, though it may be different from your truth. It gets me through the day, and it's gotten me this far successfully".

On a daily basis, using what senses and brains with which you were born, you have to construct a mental model of the world and universe so that you may make some kind of sense of it (common or not) and interact with it, and attempt to control certain aspects of it. But because each human is saddled with imperfect senses and an imperfect brain, the way that humans perceive the world is always going to be imperfect as well. The best that any human can hope to do is to approximate how the world works by creating an internal model in their mind. The basis for this model relies on the quality of the incoming data to that brain, what the limited senses detect, the observations, the interactions, the perceptions and their inevitable distortions created by the brain. What this amounts to is: Humans don't see the world as it actually is, they instead see the world distorted as their limited, biased brain allows them.

229

And yet, this realization is no reason to become despondent. Even if the brain is susceptible to errors in cognition and limited in its abilities, one does not need to throw up their hands and say, "Great, there's no reason even to try anymore..." Just because human legs are limited in the speed with which they allow one to run, humans don't typically lament their inefficiency; they just learn to use them within their abilities, avoiding situations where, for example, they cannot outrun a wolf, a falling tree or an automobile. Likewise, once you've learned the limitations of your brain, you learn to use it within its abilities, avoiding the dangers of its inborn biases and distorted perceptions.

For millennia, humans had to struggle with their ignorance of the world that they interpreted through their limited common senses. Fortunately, thanks to science and engineering, humanity has been able to augment its perception of its world and universe with the help of scientific instruments such as telescopes, space probes, microscopes, radiation detectors, etc. Of course, these devices have their own limitations, and while the model to which they contribute is superior to an exclusively human model, it is still limited and imperfect. Any given model is simply the best humanity can produce at any given time. And the resulting technology and abilities with which it endows humanity will improve over time as will humanity's understanding of the universe; but alas, it is humanity's fate always to be dealing with an imperfect picture.

> **The universe is not only (stranger) than we imagine, it's (stranger) than we can imagine.**
> —J.B.S. Haldane (d.1964 Physiologist, Geneticist, Evolutionary Biologist, Mathematician, Statistician and Biostatistician)

When a sculptor is creating a stone sculpture, she typically starts with a mental image of the final piece. To create her final sculpture, she is essentially chipping away from the material all of those parts that don't accurately represent her subject, that is, tossing aside the distractions and the inaccuracies. She begins

230

with an extremely roughly-shaped (or inaccurate) block of stone that looks very little like her mental model, but over time, the sculpture begins to resemble the image more and more. But no matter how long she sculpts, no matter how much detail she puts into it, it will always be an imperfect approximation of the original idea. However, when she finishes the sculpture, she can say that it is a much more accurate model of what she originally envisioned, and it may be sufficient for her present purpose.

And so it is with how humans interpret the universe with their own models, i.e., their scientific theories. For the best practice of science, step one is to discard as many of humanity's CBLFs as possible, ignoring these distractions and inaccuracies, so time isn't wasted in inefficient pursuits. By discarding these as well as throwing out scientific studies whose results can't be replicated by others and ignoring studies whose results don't lead to predictive usefulness, the scientific investigator chips away from their model of the universe all of the things that don't accurately explain their universe. As time goes on, the model (or scientific theory) gets more and more accurate, more predictive, more useful, but it will never be a perfect model/theory, it will only be as good as possible considering the current level and detail of knowledge. It can always be further refined, augmented, made more accurate, more predictive, more useful with future work, investigation and questioning.

And while the pursuit of these models and theories is necessary and laudable, the sobering truth is that in the final analysis,

> **There is no guarantee that the universe is understandable by a human level of intelligence.**

That statement doesn't mean that scientific investigation is a waste of time, only that its theories must always be viewed with humility and with an admission of their limitations.

SCIENCE

People tend to believe either 1) What they want to believe, or 2) What they need to believe.

Science isn't good or bad, it's only true.
—William Henry "Hank" Green (entrepreneur, musician, educator, producer, vlogger, and author)

Intelligence is the ability to take in information from the world and to find patterns in that information that allow you to organize your perceptions and understand the external world.
—Brian Greene (Physicist, Author)

When faced with the destruction, death and misery of widespread catastrophes such as volcanic eruptions, earthquakes and tsunamis, it is understandable how a human might have employed wishful thinking. "If this is the result of a god that is displeased with us, maybe if we behave better, the god won't put us through this again." This had the effect of the populace attempting to be more moral or at least more orderly, offering some illusion of control over the situation by the humans involved. Subsequently, if the populace <u>was</u> spared any calamities for a time, the interpreter of the catastrophic events becoming a wise man, an augur or priest.

232

One thing that cannot be said of science is that it begins its pursuit of fact with wishful thinking. Before the sciences of geology, vulcanism and plate tectonics were developed, the early practitioners of what would come to be called the scientific method may have been ignorant of the mechanisms involved. But they most likely did not think to themselves, "I hope that we find out that these events are caused by immense pockets of magma deep underground that cause catastrophic upheavals in the Earth's crust over which we will have absolutely no control!" They simply followed the observations and data to their ultimate conclusions and accepted them as the most accurate theory based on current information. Their hopes or wishes never even entered into the discussion.

The discipline of science doesn't care what an individual believes or wants to believe. Science actually begins by ignoring these human biases, in order to accelerate the deciphering reality.

> **Reality is that which remains even after you stop believing in it.**
> —Anonymous

How should one define science? To the layman, science may just be those courses in school that they didn't like, didn't understand well or in which they performed poorly. To some, it is what scientists "arrogantly" tell the populace is fact. Still others consider scientific theories as simply "hunches" or "best guesses" that may explain how parts of the world work, but they're no better than anyone else's "hunches." There are even those who take science as a worldview that was developed merely to refute their beloved, long-held beliefs. Such a scheming world-view could even have the trappings of a conspiracy, its findings and pronouncements not to be trusted (or maybe trusted only when the results are of benefit to the believer, but not to be trusted when it defies their beliefs). Many regard as science only that which they see in the popular media reported as science. Still others consider aspects of science detrimental because it has been used in a negative way against humanity, such as in the form of bombs and human experimentation.

All of these definitions are arguably inadequate and distracting from a much more fundamental and ultimately illuminating definition presented here:

SCIENCE--a human method of investigating reality that overcomes the limitations of a pattern-seeking brain.

Over the course of human history, humankind began to accumulate examples of fallacious explanations based on the pattern-seeking nature of the brain:

e.g., After noting the recurring pattern and seeing the sun "rise" in the East and "set" in the west for millennia, the human brain concluded that the sun revolves around the Earth. But using the approach of science, humanity later found that the human brain had fooled its owner; instead, the Earth rotates, and the sun only appears to revolve around it.

e.g., After the human brain saw a pattern of leftover meat, followed by maggots, followed by flies, it initially concluded that spontaneous generation was the cause---the meat literally transformed directly into maggots. But by using the approach of science, the investigator later found that it was flies laying their eggs on the meat (a pattern to which the brain hadn't seen or paid attention) that actually resulted in the maggots/flies.

234

Humans had been fooled by their brains again.

When there was a plague, people thought it must be the work of witches/demons/an angry god or foul air or the work of a traditional enemy that had poisoned the wells. But using the approach of science, when these biases were ignored, and certain aspects of hygiene, community waste removal and clean water measures were implemented, the rate of plague fell dramatically. The undisciplined pattern-seeking human brain had once again been duped, rescued only by the discipline of science.

Over time, the scientific approach resulted not only in a higher quality of life, but it also increased human understanding of how the world worked. Mankind was able to chip away at the mysteries of the universe, perhaps never resulting in an entirely accurate model, but always increasing the accuracy. Science was not developed to counter religious faith; it instead arose from a sincere desire of humans to overcome the biases and faulty perceptions with which their PSBs were continually inundating them. After humanity saw the usefulness and accuracy provided by the scientific approach, the less-reliable, less useful, distracting and misdirecting phenomena of an earth-centered universe, spontaneous generation and religious faith could be discarded as unnecessary burdens to the pursuit of ultimate truth.

It may come as a surprise to many who disdain science that it isn't merely an endeavor relegated to academicians in white coats in laboratories. Even the greatest doubters in the scientific method are active practitioners! What they may be doubting or suspicious of is the formal practice of science with its established institutions of higher learning, hierarchy of professors, lab technicians, engineers, field scientists, peer-reviewed publications and reports of discoveries in the media as well as roll-outs of resulting improvements in technology and quality of life.

What they are far less likely to doubt is their own <u>informal</u> practice of science, a practice that, they would be stunned to realize, they execute on an almost daily basis. After all, one does not need to don a white lab coat, light a Bunsen burner and pour chemicals between test tubes to discover that ants are having a banquet in the human's food pantry. At this point of the discovery, would it be considered reasonable for the human brain to automatically assume that the food had magically transformed directly into ants? Or that ants simply materialized there out of thin air? Or that a god had placed them there? The imagination of the human brain is all-too-ready to see such a pattern and, on-the-spot, develop an interesting or even exciting hypothesis as to explain it.

Ockham's RAZOR: Don't make an explanation for a phenomenon any more complicated than necessary, the simplest explanation tends to be the correct one.

Fortunately, in many cases, the human brain is content with noting the original observation of ants on the food, then investigating a bit further. Perhaps someone will retrace the trail of ants path to the outdoors and discover the actual source, the ant mound that had formed in the last couple of days up against the outside wall of the dwelling. Reasonable explanation made, no fantastic or supernatural involvement required, corrective action may be taken; the way the world works was explained in a little more detail, improving the quality of life---science triumphs again.

But how can that be science? There were no white lab coats involved, no test tubes; there was no journal publication made of the discovery, no press release, no interesting contribution to the body of science, just an ordinary, everyday discovery that was simply noted and ultimately, explained. Welcome to science at its core. In its essence, that's all science is: observation of a phenomenon, forming a hypothesis (an informed, provisional guess that may be further tested and readily disproved if false), testing the hypothesis by further research, obtaining the resulting data, analyzing it and making the most reasonable conclusion while actively discounting unnecessary, though possibly exciting and imaginative explanations. And now that additional knowledge has been gained, intervention can be taken to change and hopefully improve the original situation. The answer may be mundane; it may not be as exciting or awe-inspiring or entertaining as postulating some mysterious energy field, or some supernatural agent or the paranormal, it is merely something closer to the truth. Better living through science.

Humans have the potential to use this informal scientific approach all of the time, every day, mostly without even acknowledging it. Fortunately, with practice, it often doesn't even take conscious thought for the brain to switch gears to a scientific approach, because the brain subconsciously makes note that this method has produced the most reliable results throughout its owner's life. But this suggests that, to utilize some subset of critical thinking, such as the scientific method, the brain must switch to it from some other default setting.

The wiring of the brain has humanity locked into pattern-seeking, which in the example above of the ants could have resulted in the hypothesis that food spontaneously turns into ants. However, after this initial hypothesis, it is possible to switch from the brain's default setting of "I'm ready to be fooled" to the new setting of "I realize that I am quite possibly being fooled at this moment, so I will switch to some method of investigation that overcomes my default ability to be fooled (i.e., utilizing the scientific method)." By consciously avoiding the distractions of false patterns and biases, you have a better chance of perceiving the more accurate pattern of "ants gathered around food...connected to a trail of ants...connected to an ant mound outside...connected to a lack of an ant mound two days ago", and ultimately, coming to a more accurate model of your world, something closer to the truth.

Yes, science has been associated with the creation of bombs and questionable human medical experiments and atrocities which have been a stain on the history of humanity. But one must ask, "Is it science itself or the scientific method that mandates or even suggests that these things be used against man? Or is it the human brain itself that, through non-critical thinking, has decided these experiments and atrocities were allowable, and merely uses the tools of science against man?

Again, science is merely a process to obtain data by bypassing the inefficient methods of the average human's daily use of heuristics: the handy, yet often inaccurate rules-of-thumb that speed up the navigation of everyday life. Science and the scientific method (and the technology that results from them) contain no implied morals (good or bad) or mandates for action. It is up to the human utilizing the science and technology to employ morals in their use and for the human to provide a mandate for the human's actions. But as has repeatedly been shown in this book, that same human is subject to their own imperfect brain. And throughout history, humans have been content to unquestioningly follow their brains, overburdened with biases as they are. If CT is actively engaged to recognize and discount the biases, any warrant or mandate for immoral action is significantly reduced, if not outright eliminated.

Science will ultimately allow the tailoring of the human genome.

238

But there is nothing implied by this potential that then suggests, "Now, we should create a perfect human race that will supplant the imperfect!". Only a biased and fallible human with unquestioned thinking processes could contemplate or indeed pursue such an end. When humanity finally controlled the technology of fire, it accomplished great things such as cooking food, illuminating their surroundings at night to extend the time available for necessary tasks and protecting itself from nocturnal predators; humankind advanced. But on occasion, humanity conceived of the horrific idea of taking over the land, woman and possessions of other peoples and decided to use the existent technology of fire in a wholly new, insidious way: to burn people out of their homes to expedite their atrocities. So, is the technology of fire "evil"? Not inherently. When appropriately utilized it makes things better for humanity, not worse. But when used improperly or immorally, humanity suffers. Thus it is with the use of all science and technology.

Then there are those who bring up the "theories" that scientists keep creating as explanations for how the world works. What's more, these scientists seem to keep changing their minds and changing their theories saying, "We weren't 100% correct on this theory, and so we need to update what we were thinking about it". If they keep changing their minds and their theories, does it mean that scientists never have anything actually correct? You may even have your own "theory" that explains how the world works and it is very different from the "theories" of these scientists. And you may think that since all of these "theories" are simply "hunches" or maybe even just "educated guesses," that they should all be treated with the same amount of skepticism and respect, right? All of these theories deserve to be taught in the classroom and we'll let the children decide what they'll believe, right?

Wrong.

The scientific theories that are taught in science classes have earned their right to be taught to all children. They have stood the test of time, withstanding all skeptical inquiry and have proved accurate, predictive and beneficial for decades if not centuries. As soon as a rival "theory" shows the kind of accuracy, reproducibility, predictability and benefit to humanity as the Germ Theory of Disease, the various Theories of Gravity and the Theory of Evolution, they will have earned the right to be taught side-by-side with these scientific theories...but not until then.

It will be productive to define this term "theory," and then you may be able to draw your own conclusion. The colloquial term "theory" does imply a person's "hunch" or "educated guess." For example, your friend has been late to meetings every day for a week because he has to battle traffic to get to the meetings. He is also late to today's meeting, so your "theory" (i.e., your "hunch" or "educated guess") is that he is late once again because of traffic. Given recent history, your "theory" is entirely reasonable, and may even be accurate, so it's a valid "theory," right? Except that this time, your friend's car broke down and he wasn't even able to drive to the meeting. So regardless of how reasonable your theory was, it was inaccurate and not wholly predictive. The term "theory" that you used to label your "hunch" (your "educated guess") refers to a "colloquial theory," or that which in science more closely resembles a hypothesis, as opposed to what is meant by a "scientific theory."

Humans are often misled into thinking that in science, there is a kind of linear hierarchy where first, scientists collect observations/facts; they then form a hypothesis (an educated guess informed by these observations/facts); they then test the hypothesis through research and if certain things are "proven",

240

the hypothesis becomes a "theory"; and then, later on, some additional testing and proving must go on so that the theory somehow "graduates" and becomes a scientific "law". You may have heard of some so-called theories like the "Theory of Evolution by Natural Selection," and thought, well, it's "just a theory," a "hunch," an "interesting idea." It must not have been "proven" because it hasn't become the "Law of Evolution by Natural Selection" yet. So you don't have to pay any attention to it because it's still "just a theory," right?

Wrong again.

This kind of misinformation has retarded the education of billions of humans on the planet. The reality is, in science, facts are a dime a dozen and not necessarily particular useful individually or even that interesting. Scientific laws are NOT the highest echelon of scientific pursuit; while they are often used in science, they aren't particularly descriptive, useful or even predictive when used in isolation.

Ironically, it is the scientific theory which holds the highest echelon, the greatest value in all of science. It is the most useful, the most predictive, the most interesting of scientific constructions. Why? Because it incorporates everything discovered by science, all of the observations, all of the facts, all of the supported hypotheses, all of the laws that have come before it. It is an intricate model that puts all of the pieces of the jigsaw puzzle currently known together into one coherent picture. Plus, it can be tested over and over and over again when new observations and phenomena are discovered, to see if it still holds up, to see if it still reliably explains all new discoveries. Scientific theories also have the strength of being predictive. Once the theory is constructed, any investigator can use the theory to predict future discoveries, phenomena and observations, further testing the strength of the theory. This makes a scientific theory the most powerful, the most desirable, the most useful of all scientific constructions. Instead of denigrating a scientific model as "just a theory," a much more appropriate phrase would be, "Hey, this model is complete and strong enough to deserve that prestigious title '**theory**'!"

But like any jigsaw puzzle, a scientific theory may have some pieces missing. After all, there are still unexplained phenomena in the universe (i.e., the missing puzzle pieces). And sometimes, a researcher discovers a piece that was temporarily forced into a space, but was later found not to be the correct one, and so that piece must be removed, either to allow the correct piece (fact/observation or law) into the space vacated, or for the space to be left open and incomplete until the correct piece is found, if ever.

Now, if one has built a puzzle that is 97% complete, but not 100% complete, is this puzzle (this model, this theory) <u>useless</u>? To continue the metaphor, if the puzzle is the picture of a cat, and the cat is 97% filled in, but there are 3% of the pieces still missing, does this puzzle tell the viewer nothing of what subject is represented? The reasonable person would likely say, "We know it's a fairly good representation (or model) of the original cat picture, just a few details to be worked out."

And this is how it is with a scientific theory. It can not be and is never intended to be, the final, absolute, perfectly accurate model of how the world works. It is just the best current model of which the human mind can conceive and understand with current proven knowledge and the limitations of human intelligence; a scientific theory utilizes all available data, observation, confirmed hypotheses, scientific laws, etc. It is the most reasonable approximation/explanation of a given phenomenon; it has predictive power of how future observations ought to look if the theory were correct; it agrees with <u>all areas of science</u> not just the specifics of its own discipline, but also physics, chemistry, biology, geology, astronomy, paleontology, genetics, etc., etc. It has amazing explanatory power and thereby is genuinely useful.

But it is still limited by being a model, only a human brain's representation of reality. It is a jigsaw puzzle put together by the limits of the same brain. And when new observations and data conflict with or are seeming anomalies to the long-established scientific theory, that theory must either be augmented, modified, reorganized or outright discarded in favor of a new theory. But any new theory must be an even better explanation of the phenomena, with even greater reproducibility, greater predictive power, greater usefulness to humanity than the previous theory in order to supplant it. What reasonable person wouldn't welcome such an improvement and wish for its establishment? When scientists announce a change to a prevailing theory, instead of denigrating them and the science for having been wrong, not perfectly accurate or incomplete, humanity should applaud them for their persistence and perseverance in teasing out these details, admitting past inadequacies and filling in the missing puzzle pieces and continuing to increase the accuracy of the model of the world.

Consider if one was to say that the Theory of Gravity is "just a theory." This statement sounds like you should be doubtful that there is some force keeping you on the ground, despite the daily evidence to the contrary. The statement implies that if someone finally shows that gravity itself is a hoax, the obvious consequence is that all unsecured objects should immediately begin floating off the ground unchecked into outer space.

The reality is, gravity is a fact. It is a physical phenomenon that manifests itself throughout the known universe. But explaining how it happens (i.e., the theory of gravity, a.k.a. the model of gravity) is where there is and ought to be constructive debate.

243

Over the centuries, several people have come up with theories (models) for how gravity occurs. In the 4th century B.C., Aristotle had an early theory of gravity explaining that the heavy bodies were not attracted to the Earth by an external force of gravity, but tended toward the center of the universe because of an inner gravitas or heaviness, determined by their size or density. In the 9th Century, the theory of Indian astronomer Brahmagupta said it was merely the "nature" of the Earth to draw things to it, as it was the "nature" of fire that it burns things and the "nature" of wind to move things.

Still later, Isaac Newton added to the work of Robert Hooke and Johannes Kepler and created a law of gravity whose mathematics worked even better and more predictably than the previous theories. That is, it did until some of the missing puzzle pieces of Newton's model were exposed with new observations and hypotheses, and then Albert Einstein had to add some more puzzle pieces to augment the theory. And now many modern astrophysicists are adding onto and sometimes changing or refuting some details of Einstein's long-held and useful theory. They each changed pieces and added other pieces to the puzzle, and by virtue of these investigator's hard work, this model has been amazingly useful and predictive, but always just an approximation that the human intellect can comprehend. Someone will add more puzzle pieces to the model, and the picture will get clearer and more complete. But the very fact that there is gravity is never seriously questioned. The current Theory of Gravity is not "just a theory," it's actually strong enough to achieve the pinnacle, the zenith of human achievement: a **theory**!

Then there are those who readily acknowledge the validity and usefulness of most scientific theories, but still will pick and choose which parts of science they will accept or deny. And what is the reason they give for not accepting certain aspects of science? That it doesn't fit in with their beliefs or desires. Regardless of the fact that the piece of science they deny fits in perfectly with all other areas of science, irrespective of the fact that the piece has withstood the most rigorous testing by rivals, has been duplicated by competitors, has been shown to be predictive of future discoveries and perhaps most importantly, has been shown to be genuinely useful to humanity (regardless of their individual beliefs) and to the planet as a whole, the science denier will still readily excise any part of the otherwise cohesive body of scientific information, simply because they can't comfortably reconcile it with their own biases.

THE ENEMIES OF SCIENCE:

1) THOSE THAT DENY A PART OF UNIVERSALLY ACCEPTED SCIENCE BECAUSE IT CONFLICTS WITH THEIR OWN PERSONAL BELIEFS,

2) THOSE WHO RESPOND TO AN AMAZING SCIENTIFIC DISCOVERY WITH, "YES, GOD MADE IT THAT WAY..."

3) THOSE WHO START WITH POSITION 1) AND AFTER CONCEDING THE VALIDITY OF THE SCIENCE, CONVENIENTLY SHIFT TO POSITION 2)

We do not rely solely upon science and reason, because these are necessary rather than sufficient factors, but we distrust anything that contradicts science or outrages reason.

—Christopher Hitchens (d. 2011 author, columnist, essayist, orator, religious and literary critic, social critic, and journalist.)

Humans often feel comfortable falling back on an authority. After unsuccessfully arguing a point, the arguer will point to someone either well-known or well-regarded in a given field and say, "Well this important person says the same thing that I do, therefore, you have to respect my opinion..." It's yet another weak way of arguing, yet another logical fallacy, and it has no place in any mature discussion, but particularly not in the discipline of science. There have never been and there never will be authorities in science and medicine. There is no one in science, at any level, with any amount of experience, clout, or peer admiration that can make a pronouncement and have it accepted unquestioningly by all. The mere idea of such an unquestioned authority is utterly anathema to science.

Of course, there are experts in various scientific fields, but the proclamations of these experts are always open to skepticism and subject to repetition, confirmation and often refutation by further scientific investigation. Even an elementary school student could overturn the longest-standing theory of the most revered scientist if that student produces the necessary evidence. And while the scientist may be disappointed (years of work may be undone), if the scientist maintains integrity in their pursuit of truth and knowledge, they will ultimately welcome having their theory overturned. The media, however, is fond of citing a given expert in a news story as an "authority" as it implies to the viewer that they should take special notice of what is thereafter presented. But the validity of the pronouncements made by these experts is always limited by and followed by the omitted-but-implied qualifier: "..to the best of our current knowledge..."

The fact that people receive most of their ongoing scientific "education" from popular media is both a blessing and a curse. It can be a positive thing that the public is made aware of scientific discoveries and progress both from the simple enrichment that this knowledge adds to their lives, but also so that the public can appreciate the advantages that these developments and improvement can lead to in life.

The negative aspect comes from the fact that the popular media is not in the education business; they are in the entertainment business, and their ultimate goal is to make a profit. The media were never designated as the "fact-checkers" of science; if reporting on an exciting scientific discovery will momentarily engage or entertain their audience, the popular media will report it. Nowhere in their reporting is it implied, let alone guaranteed, that they have personally verified what they are saying, or that they have searched out whether other independent researchers have reproduced the same findings, or even necessarily whether the results agree across other scientific disciplines.

The popular media's intent is to catch the viewer's/reader's eye, first with the headline, and then with the following article; hopefully they can get the reader's eye to stray to the advertising that they connect to their reporting. After all, it is from their advertisers that the media makes their money, not from the scientist's on whose work they are reporting. And you may imagine that the advertisers have their own biases, both on what science that they want published and if the science agrees with the products and services that they want you to buy. And always, if either the media or the advertisers can appeal to and exploit your own biases, all the better. They know that you will get a more positive feeling from having your own biases mirrored and seemingly confirmed.

The most responsible scientific researchers don't make their announcements through the popular media, they make them in the scientific papers that they propose to peer-reviewed journals where their colleagues and rivals can attempt to pick apart and disprove the analysis of a given paper far better than any layman reading a random news article could. These responsible researchers know only too well of the biases of the layman as well as their own biases.

Using health science experiments as an example of scientific research, below is the hierarchy of increasing strength of conclusions drawn from various styles of scientific health studies:

Beginning with the weakest:

a) Case Reports   Detailed histories of a small number of individual cases

b) Cross-sectional Survey   Assesses the prevalence of an outcome in a broad population at one point in time

c) Case-Control Study   Compares histories of a group of people with a condition to a group of people without the condition

d) Cohort Study   Follows a group of people to track risk factors and outcomes over time

248

e) <u>Quasi-experiment</u>   Non-randomly assigns groups of patients to receive either a treatment or a placebo

f) <u>Randomized-controlled Trial</u>   Randomly selects a group of patients to receive a treatment and another to receive a placebo

g) <u>Systematic Review and Meta-analysis</u>   Collects all previous studies on the topic and statistically combines their results

As can be inferred from this order of studies, the reliability of the information obtained increases as the sources of human bias are further and further eliminated. The patterns that any investigator is going to sense must be put to the test by comparing their observations with others who may sense a slightly different (or wholly different) pattern. And any hypothesis that an investigator proposes to explain the effect of a medical intervention must be valid only for those test subjects receiving the treatment and not those who received the placebo. After all, if the placebo causes the same effect as the treatment, then there must be nothing novel about the treatment. It must instead be some human bias from the subject or investigator allowing the Placebo Effect.

Under the category "Randomized Control Studies," "double-blind" studies are another common research technique where both the test subjects and the investigator are "blind" to whether a placebo or the drug in question was given to each subject. That way the biases of both subject and investigator are lessened. Scientific investigation has been designed with these safeguards because it has long been conceded that the human brain is too easy to influence with expectations, too easily fooled, too ready to sense an imagined pattern. Since humans can't automatically shut off this aspect of their brain, the next best thing is to eliminate its potential effect with some aspect of CT. The more that one is aware of the CBLFs that are inherent in the human brain, the better the particular design of a scientific experiment. Once the human bias has been eliminated as a contaminant, and after years and sometimes decades of diligent work, the summation of all that has been learned can finally be incorporated into a medical or scientific theory; and then, ultimately, all of humankind may benefit from it.

EVOLUTION BY NATURAL SELECTION

Now, it's a straightforward matter to apply the above definition of a scientific theory to the Theory of Evolution by Natural Selection. After centuries of observation, there is no more serious intellectual debate about whether or not evolution itself has occurred. Any remaining dispute as to the <u>fact</u> of evolution having occurred is relegated to emotion, religious faith, faulty reasoning or denial. Every branch of science, whether it be biology, genetics, chemistry, physics, geology or astronomy has shown through the fossil record, microbiological genetics and countless independent, overlapping and interwoven scientific disciplines that evolution is a <u>fact</u>, species change their forms over time. As to the theories or models for <u>how</u> it occurred, there is always in science, the willingness to change to ever more accurate and all-encompassing theories in light of the latest discoveries.

The ancient Greeks, Romans and Chinese recognized that species evolved over time. Later, the science of medieval Islam concurred with this fact as well. With the Enlightenment, "natural philosophers" (the early forerunners of modern scientists) began to focus on the variability of species; with the emergence of the scientific disciplines of geology and paleontology, the concept of species extinction further undermined the prevailing views that nature had been created all at once and was static, unchanging. In the early 1800s, Jean-Baptiste Lamarck proposed his theory of the Transmutation of Species, one of the first fully formed theory of evolution. A classic example of Lamarck's theory is that since giraffes kept stretching their necks to reach ever higher branches on the tree, this forced their necks to grow longer and longer.

Then Alfred Russell Wallace and Charles Darwin came up with the theory of evolution by means of Natural Selection. From the further accumulated evidence of speciation and the fossil record,

251

they reasoned that all animals have a common ancestor. They even put forth the disconcerting idea that humans and other primates must have had a common ancestor; that in effect, the human species was merely a form of ape, a primate that had evolved a little further. Humanity obviously shared many physical features with primates and especially the great apes (orangutans, gorillas and chimpanzees), and startlingly enough, even some social similarities. This is where much of the contention arose between those who accepted the fact of evolution and those who didn't (as well as the earlier example of an individual's denial of a selected portion of science). The latter did not like thinking of themselves as "descended from a monkey" or "just an ape." However, what one wants to think or likes to think carries no weight in science; wishful thinking or personal discomfort doesn't alter facts. The kinship of *Homo sapiens sapiens* to apes, primates, mammals, vertebrates and chordates is not subject to "liking" or "disliking," it is enough to just accept the best established scientific facts, with no need to be embarrassed or proud of the fact, it is merely another truth.

But neither Wallace nor Darwin knew of the exact mechanism that drove Natural Selection, and they readily admitted to these missing pieces of the puzzle in their publications (as any good scientist does). By the 1960s, building upon the ground-breaking work of Gregor Mendel, there was enough molecular genetic detail discovered to show that chance mutations in the genome of a species can confer a reproductive or survival advantage (or at least not a disadvantage) to those with the mutation. In a large enough population, if enough individuals possess the same advantageous mutation, it will marginally increase the favorably mutated individual's reproductive success, and in that given ecological niche, an increased possibility of further speciation over time.

252

Most recently, DNA sequencing has led to molecular phylogenetics and the reorganization of the tree of life into the three-domain system by Carl Woese. In addition, the newly recognized factors of symbiogenesis and horizontal gene transfer introduced yet more detail into evolutionary theory. And epigenetics is a very new field where it has been demonstrated in some cases that non-genetic changes to an organism can be inherited and it has been suggested that such inheritance can help with adaptation to local conditions and affect evolution. Some have suggested that in some instances this epigenetic influence may result in a modified form of Lamarckian evolution. These evolutionary mechanisms (as well as others) may be in addition to Natural Selection, instead of NS or it may alternate over time with NS. Again, some puzzle pieces may have to be removed, and others added, but the overall picture improves, and the model's representation of reality, accuracy, predictive power and usefulness are always increasing. Irrespective of which mechanism(s) drive it, evolution occurs.

Nothing in biology makes sense except in the light of evolution.
—Theodosius Dobzhansky (d. 1975 Eastern Orthodox Christian geneticist and evolutionary biologist)

Still, any scientific theory, even one as useful and thoroughly tested as Natural Selection, must be approached daily with a healthy scientific skepticism (as opposed to denial). Humanity wouldn't have progressed in the biological sciences and medicine nearly as far as it has if Wallace/Darwin's theory was accepted as the final authoritarian word. Indeed, there was much contention among scientists about Natural Selection when it was initially proposed as the explanation of evolution. It took decades for NS to be accepted as the best current theory to explain evolution. Rival scientists (those with competing theories of their own) showed the necessary scientific skepticism and put Natural Selection to the test over and over and over again. And as history has shown, so far, Natural Selection has always withstood the onslaught.

But in the course of putting Natural Selection to the test, more recent additions to the evolution puzzle have been added, and the theory keeps getting better and gradually becomes a more accurate model of reality. This healthy scientific skepticism is vital to the advancement of science, and in scientific circles, it is expected and encouraged. In certain ideologies, skepticism of and questioning of its tenets and dogmas is not only ignored or frowned on, but it is also actively discouraged and sometimes, even punished! But one must ask just how weak does an ideology have to be that its believers insist that it not be tested or questioned?

Scientists not only expect questions about their ideas, but they also invite them, they want them. They are in essence saying, "Please put my hypothesis to the test; show me where I'm wrong, where I've been biased and where I've let my biases influence my conclusions, and I will return the favor when it is your turn to present your ideas." While it may not be the only way progress can be made (chance discoveries occasionally happen), peer review is currently the most consistent and reliable method available. It is the inevitable result of exercising CT; since you know you'll be dealing with humans, that means your going to be dealing with the biases in their brains, and therefore you've got to do everything in your power to discount those biases.

This by no means implies that human personalities never enter into science. Of course, wherever humans are concerned, there

254

are going to be heated rivalries due to the additional burden of human egos, even in science. Still, scientists aren't known for persecuting or killing rival colleagues that don't share their views. If a rival colleague shows you evidence that indicates that you are wrong about some aspect of science, out of sheer honesty and integrity, you have to admit your error and accept the facts as they are, no matter how angry, sad or disappointed it may make you. In order to find persecutions and killings that stem from disbelief in an idea that has no evidence, you must look to unquestioning religious faith.

However, one should never assume that the science is done, finished, and can now be espoused ad nauseum as if it were a mantra of some religious dogma. No area of science, no matter how exciting or seemingly promising or useful warrants admiration until it has withstood withering academic attack and then, only if it continues to prove itself day after day. The moment a theory has been refuted, even if it has been accepted for centuries, it must be discarded. Who would want to keep laboring under a delusion only because one has been used to repeating it over and over on a daily basis? Is the comfort of the daily repetition of a familiar pattern more important than discovering a better explanation, even if its an unfamiliar pattern that isn't as comforting? Doesn't humanity ultimately want to find the truth that benefits all?

Science will not come to an end because science is not merely a body of facts, it is a vitally necessary ongoing process for humanity to understand its world and universe better. Returning to the earlier analogy: The sculptor wishes to represent her subject in stone, and chips away at the block, removing the parts that don't resemble the subject, leaving behind a model that represents the original subject with gradually increasing accuracy. The sculpture or model is never perfect; it will always benefit from more detail, a bit more refining after the sculptor has taken a slightly closer look at the original subject. But the resulting masterpiece will still never be more than a representation/interpretation of the real thing, a facsimile to which the sculptor and her audience can relate. And so it is with both science and CT. Always chipping away at the biases, the fallacies, the false patterns that take away from the accurate model. Continued chipping leaves behind something slightly more accurate than what was there before. Never perfect, never finished, but hopefully a more accurate representation of the original truth.

Even though skepticism is needed in all areas of human thinking, one shouldn't make the mistake of confusing skepticism with denial. Skepticism is merely withholding judgment on a claim until more evidence is produced. Denial is making a judgment even though the evidence refutes the judgment. The skeptic of evolution may say, "The current theory is interesting, but despite all of the evidence, progress and usefulness of the theory, I still want it tested on a daily basis. There may be a better more complete theory coming in the future, and I will look forward to that, but since I must deal with reality in the meantime, I will go with the theory that has shown the most evidence, accuracy, predictability and usefulness. Today that is Natural Selection, whereas tomorrow it may be modified by symbiogenesis or epigenetics." The denier of evolution says, "Despite all of the evidence, progress and usefulness of the theory, I still say it isn't true." There is no way to rationally argue with denial because it shows such a shocking lack of CT.

Evolution is a natural process; it is not an agent with sentience; therefore, it can have no "intent"; it doesn't willfully change biological structures, let alone decide how to improve them. If a chance mutation confers some physical advantage to a percentage of a population, that percentage is slightly more likely to out-compete the remainder of the population and reproduce

256

more often than those without the advantage. Over a large enough span of time, the favorable mutation may, therefore, be spread to future generations; eventually, the numbers with the favorable mutation may no longer be the minority but actually become the majority. If a genetic line accumulates enough beneficial or benign mutations, eventually it becomes a new species, possibly even incapable of breeding with the original species from which it evolved. But evolution doesn't "make" this happen, it's merely the biological mechanism that allowed it to happen of its own accord.

With no intent, evolution can have no foresight, and it cannot create a useful organ or system from scratch. What evolution allows an organism to do is to respond to changes in an organism's environment by exploiting favorable mutations of existing structures. If a series of mutations lead to changes in a structure or system already present in the organism, and that altered structure or system confers a survival or reproductive advantage on that individual, over time, those changes are more likely to appear in the population as a whole. In other words, evolution simply makes do with whatever is already on hand within the animal, changing existing structures.

Need a moving jaw to improve predation because there is now an abundance of prey? Evolution allows the jaw to be fashioned from a gill arch of an early fish. Need inner ear bones to be able to hear better on dry land than your water-bound forefathers? Evolution allows the middle ear bones to be formed from the jaw. Are you gradually switching your diet from a strictly herbivorous one to an omnivorous to take advantage of a more dependable food source? Well then, you won't be needing your large cecum to digest a monotonous supply of plant matter anymore, but as your cecum shrinks over the millennia in response to its decreased herbivorous role, its vestigial remnant, the appendix would still make an excellent repository for bacteria that are beneficial to your colon, etc., etc.

A remarkable example of evolution's "modify what is already present" is demonstrated in the recurrent laryngeal nerve of the giraffe which traces the entire length of the giraffe's neck...not once but twice! If you trace the genetic lineage of giraffe's back to their primitive fish ancestors, you find the distance that this nerve had to traverse in the fish is on the order of a few centimeters, simply because fish ancestors had essentially no neck. But as evolution continued and some fish evolved into amphibians, then into land-dwelling reptiles, then into short-necked mammals, then into short-necked giraffe ancestors and finally into today's long-necked giraffes, the nerve was forced to elongate into an arguably ridiculous length of several meters! It originates near the giraffe's larynx just below its head, travels the entire length of the neck, loops down around an arch of a major cardiac blood vessel in the animal's chest, and then ascends back up to the giraffe's larynx along the entire length of the neck again, only to connect to a structure a few centimeters away from the nerve's origin.

It would be as if you wished to walk from one end of your bedroom to the other, but because there was no direct route, you had to walk out of one bedroom door, out of your house, down the street, walk around a tree, return down the same street, walk back into your house and re-enter your bedroom through a different door, all because whoever built your house didn't anticipate the need for any direct path between the two sides of your bedroom. No competent builder would construct anything so ludicrous. They would just start from the beginning and make sure there was a clear path from one end of your bedroom to another.

But as stated before, evolution is no intentional builder. It is merely a response to an environmental pressure. And when it responds, evolution can't create a brand new structure from the cellular level, even if such a new structure would greatly simplify the answer to the original pressure. It can't create a brand new nerve where one wasn't before. Evolution isn't a "blank slate" engineer; it is a passive modifier. It can only alter structures already present in the organism. And it can only do that when there's a chance mutation; and the mutation must result in some improvement (or at least no detriment) in the organism's structure that allows the organism to survive and thrive in the altered ecological niche. In the case of the recurrent laryngeal nerve, the nerve was already present in the fish, and due to the fish's anatomy, looping around the cardiac blood vessel was a reasonable, trivial distance for the nerve to travel. Evolution couldn't foresee that this nerve would have to elongate into seemingly absurd proportions to accommodate the elongation of the giraffe's neck. But since the mutation didn't confer any disadvantage in the species, it was perpetuated; the design was by no means perfect or even practical, but it was "good enough."

Some assume that because the human brain is arguably the "most advanced or complex" one on the planet that it must, by these very characteristics, be really good at thinking and reasoning, and that it may have even evolved for that purpose. But again, evolution has no purpose, no target to strive for; it is simply the process where less useful traits tend to be lost over time supplanted by more useful ones. For the human species, a large brain proved very useful, especially at helping survive and propagate the species. But a large, higher reasoning brain is hardly necessary to ensure the success and propagation of a species. If that were so, there would be far more species with large, complicated brains. But nature and evolution have shown that the success of a species is possible with much simpler brains; in the vast majority of cases, with no brain at all!

Arthropods include the most numerous class of animals, the insects. Most insects have brains so simple, they may be considered "swollen nerve nodes." Their structure allows them to respond to environmental stimuli and to find food and to mate and reproduce. Higher thinking isn't necessary for any of this (though when certain social species like ants, termites and bees work together as a kind of "extended organism," their organizational and constructional abilities can be impressive).

The most numerous beings known on the planet are bacteria, and they have no brain at all, not even a nerve network, yet they are arguably the most successful, long-lived species on the planet. They have evolved to occupy every ecological niche that humanity has discovered, and some places where the limit of human imagination didn't think it possible. Bacterial origins go back billions of years, and a bacterium has never had a single thought; it just wasn't necessary for their survival and reproduction. Intelligence may be an interesting option for an organism, but when considering the "success" of a species, intelligence is hardly the aim or even the epitome of evolution, it is merely a consequence. But if you're a human, you have the bias that your attributes are going to be the best, the highest, the most desirable. And unfortunately, you are also very likely to think that all of your thinking equipment is the most reliable, including that ultimate consequence of evolution, your brain. Even when, from the standpoint of evolution, the human brain is simply "good enough" in its environmental niche to assure propagation.

While the human brain has grown in size considerably over the last few million years and has arguably become better at higher reasoning skills during that time, as has been discussed earlier, it's also fraught with many inherent weaknesses, distortions as well as an unsettling propensity for non-CT. Early human brains were good at pattern-seeking, which helped humans avoid rain

260

when they heard the thunder. Later, humans reasoned when to plant seeds because they noted the pattern of the spring always following the winter. But if humans stay with the first interpretation that they think up when observing some new pattern, they are very often wrong. The face seen in the clouds is not an actual person, it's just the manifestation of a habit that a PSB practices all of the time. But this default setting of the human brain is too "hit and miss" to be reliable in the long-term.

You have no way of changing the default setting of your brain away from "I'm ready to be fooled." Because evolution has allowed your brain to be layered from the foundation of a fish brain at its core, to a reptilian brain layered above the fish, to mammalian brain layered above the reptilian and finally primate brain layered over all, the wiring is fairly well set. The default setting will likely always be the simplest, most readily available, most convenient, and worst of all, the habitual setting. And when one backs up and observes human society from the detached viewpoint of the visiting aliens, it is easy to feel pessimistic. It hurts to watch this species scurrying around on the face of the planet, waging war with each other for resources, imagining mythical beasts, swearing that they see ghosts, chanting faith-based mantras to stave off disaster, and inflicting deceit, oppression, and torture on one another for millennia. Humanity has the ability to scoff at reason and deny the best science that unrelenting human investigation have to offer. It is easy to feel like there is no hope.

CONCLUSION

Except that there is hope; humanity has an answer: A method of switching their questionable yet remarkable organ from its cumbersome, burdensome default setting to a far more admirable, impressive, useful, progressive, ethical setting:

Critical Thinking

And this potential accomplishment is achievable at virtually no cost (or little in the monetary sense).

First, the cost of admission: the individual's willingness to admit to the limitations of their own brain.

The only other substantial cost is increased use of the higher reasoning centers of the brain, through critical thinking. Yes, in the ultimate possible irony, the source of the malady can also be the source of its remedy.

THE END

SELECTED QUOTES BY CRITICAL THINKERS

(Each quote is followed by the name of the person to whom it is most often attributed, their pseudonym, or if the ultimate source is unknown, the place for a name is left blank)

The sleep of reason brings forth monsters.
—Francisco Goya (d. 1828 Painter and Printmaker)

Men create gods after their own image, not only with regard to their form but with regard to their mode of life.
—Aristotle (d. 322 BCE Philosopher and Practitioner of Science)

Beware of false knowledge; it is more dangerous than ignorance.
—George Bernard Shaw (Playwright d.1950)

Ignorance is nothing shameful; imposing ignorance is shameful. Most people are not to blame for their own ignorance, but if they willfully pass it on, they are to blame.
—Daniel Dennett (Cognitive Scientist and Philosopher)

I'm very down on authority, those who say, "Because I say this, you must accept it!" And at this point in my life, the authority that I'm down on the most is myself. I have to continually question what I think the truth is, that just because I thought of it, or because something I read agrees with what I already feel, that it must, therefore, be right. I must always be on guard against my own all-too-human brain misleading me.
—T. F. Hanlon

Liberty's chief foe is theology.
—Charles Bradlaugh (d. 1891 Political Activist, Founder of the National Secular Society)

There is no god and that's the simple truth. If every trace of any single religion died out and nothing were passed on, it would never be created exactly that way again. There might be some other nonsense in its place, but not that exact nonsense. If all of science were wiped out, it would still be true and someone would find a way to figure it all out again.
—Penn Jillette (Magician and Skeptic)

Certainty is the currency of fundamentalism.
—Neil Carter (Former fundamentalist church elder and seminarian)

Ubi dubium ibi libertas: Where there is doubt, there is freedom.

As you know, the best way to solve a problem is to identify the core belief that causes the problem; then mock that belief until the people who hold it insist that you heard them wrong.
—Scott Adams (Cartoonist and Satirist)

Religion is an insult to human dignity. Without it you would have good people doing good things and evil people doing evil things. But for good people to do evil things, that takes religion.
—Steven Weinberg (theoretical physicist, Nobel laureate in physics)

It's frightening that Skepticism has to be a movement, because you're just arguing that reality is reality. What a waste of energy in a way.
—Graham Linehan (Director and writer)

After listening to a proselytizer, an elderly lady asks, "Why should I be moral? Proselytizer: "Are you serious? Without morals nobody would be able to trust anyone else! Theft, rape, murder would be rampant...society would break down....without morals there would be anarchy!!" Old lady: "You know, you're absolutely right!....and you didn't have to mention god even once...."

If you think you see evidence of your faith all around you, & you feel it deeply, remember that those who have contradictory beliefs feel the same.
—Peter Boghossian (Philosophy Professor, Writer, CT Researcher)

A conclusion is the place where you got tired of thinking.
—Stephen Wright (Comedian)

Morals come from 1) Upbringing 2) Human Solidarity and 3) Empathy, not religion.

They must find it difficult...Those who have taken authority as the truth, Rather than truth as the authority.
—Gerald Massey (d. 1907 Poet and Writer)

No way of thinking or doing, however ancient, can be trusted without proof.
—Henry David Thoreau (d. 1862 Poet, Essayist, Philosopher and Historian)

If we have the truth, it cannot be harmed by investigation. If we have not the truth, it ought to be harmed.
—J. Reuben Clark (d. 1961 Attorney and Mormon leader)

If a believer demands that I, as a non-believer, observe his taboos in the public domain, he is not asking for my respect, but for my submission.
—Flemming Rose (Journalist, International Advocate of the freedom of speech, Culture Editor of the newspaper that in September 2005 published cartoons of Muhammad that led to an outcry from the religious)

You can sway a thousand men by appealing to their prejudices quicker than you can convince one man by logic.
—Robert A. Heinlein (d. 1988 Dean of Science Fiction Writers)

Cloaking your bigotry in religion doesn't make it any less bigoted. And calling you out on your bigotry isn't persecution, it's accountability.
—David Silverman (President American Atheists)

Facts do not cease to exist, because they are ignored.
—Aldous Huxley (d. 1963 Writer and Philosopher)

I would challenge anyone to think of a question upon which we once had a scientific answer, however inadequate, but for which now the best answer is a religious one.
—Sam Harris (Neuroscientist and Philosopher)

One of the great achievements of science has been, if not to make it impossible for intelligent people to be religious, then at least to make it possible for them not to be religious. We should not retreat from this accomplishment.
—Steven Weinberg (theoretical physicist, Nobel laureate in physics)

You don't see faith healers working in hospitals for the same reason you don't see psychics winning the lottery.

God is a sound people make when they're too tired to think anymore.
—Edward Abbey (d. 1989 Environmentalist, Author, Essayist)

There is no conflict between faith and science...until science starts to get all nitpicky with stuff like consistency and facts.

Faith: it is the perfection of virtual effort. It is the prelude to miscalculation and the raw material of disappointment.

Science has no enemy, save the ignorant.

Maybe if there were more atheists, there'd be fewer foxholes.
—Holly Franking

The idea that god is just, is directly contradicted by the idea that god is merciful. Perfect justice and any mercy are necessary directly in contradiction because mercy is the suspension of justice.
—Matt Dillahunty (Secular Humanist Advocate, Debater, Author and Speaker)

Religious faith has a certain appeal, it's because it tells lazy, gullible people exactly what they want to hear - - YOU DON'T HAVE TO THINK & YOU DON'T HAVE TO DIE.

Respecting human rights is more important than respecting cultures or beliefs...humans have rights, cultures and beliefs do not.
—Faisal Saeed Almutar (Founder of the Global Secular Humanist Movement)

A tyrant must put on the appearance of uncommon devotion to religion. Subjects are less apprehensive of illegal treatment from a ruler whom they consider god-fearing and pious. On the other hand, they do less easily move against him, believing that he has the gods on his side.
—Aristotle (d. 322 BCE Philosopher and Practitioner of Science)

Let me never fall into the vulgar mistake of dreaming that I am persecuted whenever I am contradicted.
—Ralph Waldo Emerson (d.1882 Essayist, Lecturer, Poet)

Peer pressure and social norms are powerful influences on behavior, and they are classic excuses.
—Andrew Lansley (Member of Parliament)

To learn who rules over you, simply find out who you are not allowed to criticize.
—Voltaire (d.1778 Writer, Historian, and Philosopher)

It is in the admission of ignorance and the admission of uncertainty that there is hope for the continuous motion of human beings in some direction that doesn't get confined, permanently blocked, as it has so many times before in various periods in the history of man.
—Richard Feynman (d. 1988 Nobel Laureate Theoretical Physicist)

So the universe is not quite as you thought it was. You'd better rearrange your beliefs, then. Because you certainly can't rearrange the universe.
—Isaac Asimov (d. 1992 Science Writer and Biochemist)

The line between perceiving and hallucinating is not as crisp as we like to think. In a sense, when we look at the world, we are hallucinating all the time. One could almost regard perception as the act of choosing the one hallucination that best fits the incoming data.
—V.S. Ramachandran (Neuroscientist)

If anyone can show me, and prove to me, that I am wrong in thought or deed, I will gladly change. I seek the truth, which never yet hurt anybody. It is only persistence in self-delusion and ignorance which does harm.
—Marcus Aurelius (d. 180 CE, Roman Emperor and Philosopher)

You must never feel bad about making mistakes as long as you take the trouble to learn from them. For you often learn more by being wrong for the right reasons than you do by being right for the wrong reasons.
—The Phantom Tollbooth by Norton Juster (Academic, Architect and Writer)

The Christian god is the only "all-loving" being who would torture you for eternity for simply being unconvinced.

I don't understand it any more than you do, but one thing I've learned is that you don't have to understand things for them to be.
—A Wrinkle in Time by Madeleine L'Engle (d. 2007 Writer)

There is no law stating that reality must match your level of ignorance.
—T. F. Hanlon

PRAYER: An act of doubt, not faith.

Teaching kids to ask magical beings to solve their problems in the form of prayers creates irresponsible adults who fail to find their own solutions.

When kids look up to great scientists the way they do to athletes and celebrities, civilization will jump to the next level.
— Brian Greene (Physicist, Author)

The trap that people fall into is to think "All the evidence I need is what I know in my head and feel in my heart and what I know to be true", but that isn't really evidence for it being true, that's just a statement about how much you believe it—and also how limiting your own perspective can be.
—Derren Brown (Illusionist and Mentalist)

No amount of belief makes something a fact.
—James Randi (Magician and Skeptic)

The more profoundly baffled you have been in your life, the more open your mind (should) become to new ideas.
—Neil Degrasse Tyson (Astrophysicist, Author and Science Communicator)

Take any religious faith, remove the mythology, the supernatural, the hurting/killing of those that aren't in your group and believing something without proof and you'll have humanism.

It is the mark of the mind untrained to take its own processes as valid for all men, and its own judgments for absolute truth.
—Aleister Crowley (d. 1947 Occultist, Magician, Poet, painter, Novelist and Mountaineer)

If you claim that things which cannot be explained must be the work of god: Does it mean if you don't understand something, and the community of physicists don't understand it, that means god did it? Is that how you want to play this game? Because if it is, there's a list of the things in the past that the physicists at the time didn't understand, and a talk show you might have conducted 200 years ago would have said, "The planets do retrograde motion? Can't understand that, must be a god". And we'd say, "You know, you're right". And then 10 years later we understand it, so what do you do? So if that's how you want to invoke your evidence for god, then god is an ever-receding pocket of scientific ignorance that's getting smaller and smaller and smaller as time moves on, so just be ready for that to happen if that's how you want to come at the problem.
—Neil Degrasse Tyson (Astrophysicist, Author and Science Communicator)

"Religion is the most malevolent of all mind viruses."
—Arthur C. Clarke (d. 2008 Science Writer, Futurist, Inventor and Undersea Explorer)

The idea of the sacred is quite simply the most conservative of notions in any culture, because it seeks to turn other ideas—uncertainty, progress, change-- into crimes.
—Salman Rushdie (Novelist and Essayist)

270

Most human beings have an almost infinite capacity for taking things for granted.
—Aldous Huxley (d. 1963 Writer and Philosopher)

The one permanent emotion of the inferior man is fear—fear of the unknown, the complex, the inexplicable. What he wants above everything else is safety.
—H.L. Mencken (d. 1956 Journalist, Satirist, Cultural Critic)

I would never die for my beliefs, because I might be wrong.
—Bertrand Russell (d. 1970 Philosopher, Logician, Mathematician, Historian, writer, Social Critic, Political Activist and Nobel Laureate)

Atheism leads a man to sense, to philosophy, to natural piety, to laws, to reputation, all which may be guides to an outward moral virtue, though religion were not but superstition dismounts all these, and erecteth an absolute monarchy in the minds of men.
—Sir Francis Bacon (d. 1626 Philosopher, Statesman, Scientist, Jurist, Orator, and Author---Father of the Scientific Method)

Is man merely a mistake of God's? Or God merely a mistake of man?
— Friedrich Nietzsche (d. 1900 Philosopher, Cultural Critic, Poet, Philologist and Latin /Greek Scholar)

Being a Humanist means trying to behave decently without expectation of rewards or punishment after you are dead.
— Kurt Vonnegut (d.2007 Writer)

Belief is the death of intelligence.
—Robert Anton Wilson (d. 2007 Author, Novelist, Essayist, Editor, Playwright, Poet and Futurist)

There is something infantile in the presumption that somebody else has a responsibility to give your life meaning and point. The truly adult view, by contrast, is that our life is as meaningful, as full and as wonderful as we choose to make it.
—Richard Dawkins (Evolutionary Biologist, Ethologist, Author)

A cult is a religion with no political power.
—Tom Wolfe (Author and Journalist)

Human decency is not derived from religion. It precedes it.
—Christopher Hitchens (d. 2011 author, columnist, essayist, orator, religious and literary critic, social critic, and journalist.)

Civilization will not attain to its perfection until the last stone from the last church falls on the last priest.
—Emile Zola (d. 1902 Novelist, Playwright, Journalist)

At least two-thirds of our miseries spring from human stupidity, human malice and those great motivators and justifiers of malice and stupidity: idealism, dogmatism and proselytizing zeal on behalf of religious or political ideas.
—Aldous Huxley (d. 1963 Writer and Philosopher)

I think it's much more interesting to live not knowing than to have answers which might be wrong. I have approximate answers and possible beliefs and different degrees of uncertainty about different things, but I am not absolutely sure of anything and there are many things I don't know anything about, such as whether it means anything to ask why we're here. I don't have to know an answer. I don't feel frightened not knowing things, by being lost in a Mysterious universe without any purpose, which is the way it really is as far as I can tell.
—Richard Feynman (d. 1988 Nobel Laureate Theoretical Physicist)

We have a choice. We have two options as human beings. We have a choice between conversation and war. That's it. Conversation and violence. And faith is a conversation stopper.
—Sam Harris (Neuroscientist and Philosopher)

Our belief is not a belief. Our principles are not a faith. We do not rely solely upon science and reason, because these are necessary rather than sufficient factors, but we distrust anything that contradicts science or outrages reason. We may differ on many things, but what we respect is free inquiry, open-mindedness, and the pursuit of ideas for their own sake.
—Christopher Hitchens (d. 2011 author, columnist, essayist, orator, religious and literary critic, social critic, and journalist.)

I feel that we should stop wasting our time trying to please the supernatural and concentrate on improving the welfare of human beings. I think that we should use our energy and our initiative to solve our problems, and stop relying on prayer and wishful thinking. If we have faith in ourselves, we won't have to have faith in gods.
—Ruth Hurmence Green (d. 1981 Author)

Those who cannot remember the past are condemned to repeat it. My atheism, like that of Spinoza , is true piety towards the universe and denies only gods fashioned by men in their own image, to be servants of their human interests.
—George Santayana (d. 1952 Philosopher, Essayist, Poet, and Novelist)

Religious moderation is the product of secular knowledge and scriptural ignorance.
—Sam Harris (Neuroscientist and Philosopher)

Religious bondage shackles and debilitates the mind, and unfits it for every noble enterprise, every expanded prospect.
—James Madison (d.1836 United States Founding Father, President and Father of the Constitution)

Religion is so absurd that it comes close to imbecility.
—H.L. Mencken (d. 1956 Journalist, Satirist, Cultural Critic)

How dismal it is to see present day Americans yearning for the very orthodoxy that their country was founded to escape.
—Christopher Hitchens (d. 2011 author, columnist, essayist, orator, religious and literary critic, social critic, and journalist.)

If you need a purpose-driven life, you are an actor in someone else's play. You are following a script and it's not even a good one. If your life only has a meaning while it is being directed in someone else's movie, you have no life of your own. You are being subjugated, cheated and robbed. You deserve better. You should emancipate yourself and reclaim your rightful property.
—Dan Barker, former evangelist

Faith means not wanting to know what is true.
—Friedrich Nietzsche (d. 1900 Philosopher, Cultural Critic, Poet, Philologist and Latin /Greek Scholar)

It is far better to grasp the Universe as it really is than to persist in delusion, however satisfying and reassuring.
—Carl Sagan (d. 1996 Astronomer, Cosmologist, Astrophysicist, Astrobiologist, Author, Science Popularizer and Communicator)

So far as religion of the day is concerned, it is a damned fake. Religion is all bunk. -
—Thomas Alva Edison (d. 1931 Inventor and Businessman)

274

The fact that a believer is happier than a skeptic is no more to the point than the fact that a drunken man is happier than a sober one.
— George Bernard Shaw (Playwright d. 1950)

Say what you will about the sweet miracle of unquestioning faith, I consider a capacity for it terrifying and absolutely vile.
— Kurt Vonnegut (d. 2007 Writer)

Man will never be free until the last king is strangled with the entrails of the last priest.
— Denis Diderot (d. 1784 Philosopher and Writer)

A man is accepted into a church for what he believes and he is turned out for what he knows.
— Samuel Clemens/Mark Twain (d. 1910 Writer, Humorist, Entrepreneur, Publisher, and Lecturer)

The problem with religion, because it's been sheltered from criticism, is that it allows people to believe en masse what only idiots or lunatics could believe in isolation.
—Sam Harris (Neuroscientist and Philosopher)

(On Religious faith) The whole thing is so patently infantile, so foreign to reality, that to anyone with a friendly attitude to humanity it is painful to think that the great majority of mortals will never be able to rise above this view of life.
— Sigmund Freud (d. 1939 Neurologist and Founder of Psychoanalysis)

The church says the Earth is flat, but I know that it is round, for I have seen the shadow on the moon, and I have more faith in a shadow than in the church.
— Ferdinand Magellan (d. 1521 Explorer)

It is difficult to reason someone out of a belief that they did not reason them self into.
—Jonathan Swift (D. 1745 Satirist, Essayist, Political Pamphleteer, Poet and Cleric)

It's an incredible con job when you think about it, to believe something now in exchange for something after death. Even corporations with their reward systems don't try to make it posthumous.
— Gloria Steinem (Feminist, Journalist, Social and Political Activist)

The bible and the church have been the greatest stumbling block in the way of women's emancipation. —Elizabeth Cady Stanton (d. 1902 Suffragist, Social Activist, Abolitionist)

While believing strongly, without evidence is considered a mark of madness or stupidity in any other area of our lives, faith in God still holds immense prestige in our society. Religion is the one area of our discourse where it is considered noble to pretend to be certain about things no human being could possibly be certain about. It is telling that this aura of nobility extends only to those faiths that still have many subscribers. Anyone caught worshiping Poseidon, even at sea, will be thought insane.
—Sam Harris (Neuroscientist and Philosopher)

I have always considered "Pascal's Wager" a questionable bet to place, since any God worth believing in would prefer an honest agnostic to a calculating hypocrite.
—Alan M. Dershowitz (Lawyer, Constitutional Jurist, and Author)

Once you've condoned faith in general, you've condoned any crazy shit done because of faith.
—Penn Jillette (Magician and Skeptic)

276

If god created man in his own image, how come I'm not invisible?
— David Powers

It is difficult to free fools from the chains they revere.
—Voltaire (d.1778 Writer, Historian, and Philosopher)

Religion doesn't just cloud our minds. It asks us to deliberately deceive ourselves-- to replace reason with its opposite, faith. And when men operate on faith, they can no longer be reasoned with, which makes them more dangerous than any sane man, good or evil.

— James L. Sutter (Author, Game Designer and Musician)

Angry atheists? Theocratic infringement on government, teaching creationism in public schools, compulsory male and female genital mutilation, scarring childhood psyches with threats of eternal damnation and hellfire, impugning my morality...yeah, excuse me if I'm a little thin-skinned.
—T. F. Hanlon

Anti-intellectualism has been a constant thread winding its way through our political and cultural life, nurtured by the false notion that democracy means that my ignorance is just as good as your knowledge.
—Isaac Asimov (d. 1992 Science Writer and Biochemist)

Never theorize before you have data. Invariably, you end up twisting facts to suit theories, instead of theories to suit facts.
—Sherlock Holmes (Sir Arthur Conan Doyle d. 1930 Physician and Writer)

By denying scientific principles, one may maintain any paradox.
—Galileo Galilei (d. 1642 Astronomer, Physicist, Engineer, Philosopher and Mathematician)

You can't convince a believer of anything: for their belief is not based on evidence, it's based on a deep-seated need to believe.
—Carl Sagan (d. 1996 Astronomer, Cosmologist, Astrophysicist, Astrobiologist, Author, Science Popularizer and Communicator)

Religion is notorious for conceiving an idea and then trying to make it true, either by propaganda or sometimes by force...while science makes a discovery and then immediately sets about trying to disprove it, just to make sure it's correct before everybody makes idiots of themselves.
—Seth McFarlane (Actor, Comedian, Filmmaker, and Singer)

What we do in every other area of our lives (other than religion), is, rather than respect somebody's beliefs, we evaluate their reasons.
—Sam Harris (Neuroscientist and Philosopher)

Remember, faith is the harbinger of chaos.
—Lionel Suggs (Author)

Religion is like drugs, it destroys the thinking mind.
—George Carlin (d. 2008 Comedian, Actor, Author and Social Critic)

Ultimately, totalitarianism is the only sort of politics that can truly serve the sky-god's purpose. Any movement of a liberal nature endangers his authority and that of his delegates on Earth. One God, one King, one Pope, one master in the factory, one father-leader in the family at home.
—Gore Vidal (d. 2012 Writer)

The Genesis story is just one that happened to have been adopted by one particular tribe of Middle Eastern herders. It has no more special status than the belief of a particular West African tribe that the world was created from the excrement of ants. —Richard Dawkins (Evolutionary Biologist, Ethologist, Author)

278

Books must follow sciences, and not sciences books.
—Sir Francis Bacon (d. 1626 Philosopher, Statesman, Scientist, Jurist, Orator, and Author---Father of the Scientific Method)

If we go back to the beginning we shall find that ignorance and fear created the gods; that fancy, enthusiasm, or deceit adorned or disfigured them; that weakness worships them; that credulity preserves them, and that custom, respect and tyranny support them in order to make the blindness of man serve its own interests.
—Baron D. Holbach (d. 1789 Author, Philosopher and Encyclopedist)

Essentially, almost all humans are born with a fear of the unknown. It casts a pall of anxiety which pushes us into the arms of religions and soothsayers and their made-up answers.
—Mario Stinger (Author)

If we subject religious claims to a lesser degree of scrutiny, we should not be surprised if religious people subject us to a greater degree of servitude.
—Stifyn Emrys (Author)

Religion was (is) always steps ahead of science; because religion lies and science can't.
—M.F. Moonzajer (Author)

Billions of years ago God was creating universes and life; thousands of years ago he was creating angry floods, sin-saving human sacrifices and audible burning bushes. Today he occasionally appears on a piece of toast. To state that God has become reclusive over the years would be an overwhelming understatement.
—Trevor Treharne (Author)

Nonbelievers are not anti-religious, they are anti-fraud and anti-deception.
—Steve Fowler

Prayer... panacea for some, placebo to others. I thought of it as an epidural administered through the soul to anesthetize the mind.
—Clyde Dsouza (Author)

I'll tell you what you did with Atheists for about 1500 years. You outlawed them from the universities or any teaching careers, besmirched their reputations, banned or burned their books or their writings of any kind, drove them into exile, humiliated them, seized their properties, arrested them for blasphemy. You dehumanized them with beatings and exquisite torture, gouged out their eyes, slit their tongues, stretched, crushed, or broke their limbs, tore off their breasts if they were women, crushed their scrotums if they were men, imprisoned them, stabbed them, disemboweled them, hanged them, burnt them alive. And you have nerve enough to complain to me that I laugh at you.
—Madalyn Murray O'Hair (d. 1995 Activist and Founder of American Atheists)

The greatest admission a human can make is that perhaps he does not have the intelligence, the vision, the grasp to fully understand the universe, and that perhaps no human ever will. To put it all down to some omnipotent deity is a cop-out. Factor in fairy tales of an afterlife and it becomes a comforting cop-out.
—Neal Asher (Science Fiction Writer)

The idea of god implies the abdication of human reason & justice; it is the most decisive negation of human liberty & necessarily ends in the enslavement of mankind both in theory & practice.
—Mikhail Bakunin (d. 1876 Founder of Collectivist Anarchism)

280

Someone with a fresh mind, one not conditioned by upbringing and environment, would doubtless look at science and the powerful reductionism that it inspires as overwhelmingly the better mode of understanding the world, and would doubtless scorn religion as sentimental wishful thinking. Would not that same uncluttered mind also see the attempts to reconcile science and religion by disparaging the reduction of the complex to the simple as attempts guided by muddle-headed sentiment and intellectually dishonest emotion?
—Peter Atkins (Author)

It's a strange myth that atheists have nothing to live for. It's the opposite. We have nothing to die for. We have everything to live for.
—Ricky Gervais (Comedian, Actor, Writer, Producer, Director, Singer, and Musician)

All children are atheists, they have no idea of God.
—Baron D. Holbach (d. 1789 Author, Philosopher and Encyclopedist)

Gods are fragile things, they may be killed by a whiff of science or a dose of common sense. They thrive on servility and shrink before independence. They feed upon worship as kings do upon flattery. That is why the cry of gods at all times is "Worship us or we perish." A dethroned monarch may retain some of his human dignity while driving a taxi for a living. But a god without his thunderbolt is a poor object.
—Chapman Cohen (d. 1954 Writer and Lecturer)

And what hypocrisy it is on the part of our Government to have the Bible in our courts of law for the culprit to take his oath upon and then be tried for the very crimes which the Bible itself sanctions.
— Joseph Lewis (d. 1968 Author and President of Freethinkers of America)

Either god exists or it doesn't exist. If a god does exist, it either interacts with the universe in some detectable way or it doesn't. If it doesn't, that god is indistinguishable from a non-existent god. That only leaves a god who interacts with the universe in some detectable way. But if science, which is the greatest realization of the use of our senses to, you know, detect things, hasn't found this god, that doesn't say much for individuals.

In short, the god you've created is, in fact, undetectable by science. The limits of science are not the province of religious knowledge. Where science is ignorant, so is religion. The only difference is that religion lacks the integrity of science.
—Matt Dillahunty (Secular Humanist Advocate, Debater, Author)

One of the main reasons and excuses behind every religious failure is a" FALSE PROMISE"
—M.F. Moonzajer (Author)

Consciously or unconsciously, most theists see in gods and devils, heaven and hell, reward and punishment, a whip to lash the people into obedience, meekness and contentment.... The philosophy of atheism expresses the expansion and growth of the human mind. The philosophy of theism, if we can call it a philosophy, is static and fixed.
— Emma Goldman (d. 1940 Political Activist and Writer)

It is a curious species that considers itself enlightened and advanced, yet finds it necessary to hold rallies for things such as reason and science and treating all members of the species equally.
—T. F. Hanlon

Children are born atheists. Then they are indoctrinated and abused by so-called 'God's representatives.' Innocents are scarred emotionally and psychologically by those who are sworn to protect them.
— C.J. Anderson (Author)

282

Yes, I'm a materialist. I'm willing to be shown wrong, but that has not happened — yet. And I admit that the reason I'm unable to accept the claims of psychic, occult, and/or supernatural wonders is because I'm locked into a world-view that demands evidence rather than blind faith, a view that insists upon the replication of all experiments — particularly those that appear to show violations of a rational world — and a view which requires open examination of the methods used to carry out those experiments.
—James Randi (Magician and Skeptic)

From the first day we have been fighting the wrong enemy; our common enemy is religion which dictates upon us division and partition.
— M.F. Moonzajer (Author)

A lively, disinterested, persistent liking for truth is extraordinarily rare. Action and faith enslave thought, both of them in order not to be troubled or inconvenienced by reflection, criticism or doubt.
—Henri Frédéric Amiel (d. 1881 Moral Philosopher, Poet, and Critic)
I guess it's true what they say: if we could reason with religious people, there would be no religious people.
— C.J. Anderson (Author)

The idea that things must have a beginning is really due to the poverty of our imagination.
—Bertrand Russell (d. 1970 Philosopher, Logician, Mathematician, Historian, writer, Social Critic, Political Activist and Nobel Laureate)

Truth can never be reached by just listening to the voice of an authority.
—Sir Francis Bacon (d. 1626 Philosopher, Statesman, Scientist, Jurist, Orator, and Author---Father of the Scientific Method)

Science has never killed or persecuted a single person for doubting or denying its teaching, and most of these teachings have been true; but religion has murdered millions for doubting or denying her dogmas and most of these dogmas have been false.

All stories about gods and devils, of heavens and hells, as they do not conform to nature, and are not apparent to sense, should be rejected without consideration. Beyond the universe there is nothing and within the universe the supernatural does not and cannot exist.

Of all deceivers who have plagued mankind, none are so deeply ruinous to human happiness as those impostors who pretend to lead by a light above nature.

The lips of the dead are closed forever. There comes no voice from the tomb. Christianity is responsible for having cast the fable of eternal fire over almost every grave.
—Gratis P. Spencer (d. 1908 Author)

If people are good only because they fear punishment, and hope for reward, then we are a sorry lot indeed.
—Albert Einstein (d. 1955 Nobel Laureate Theoretical Physicist)

Shrines! Shrines! Surely you don't believe in the gods. What's your argument? Where's your proof?
— Aristophanes (d. 386 BCE, Greek Playwright)

"Not only had I got rid of the theology and the supernatural, but I had found the truth of evolution."
— Andrew Carnegie, (d. 1919 Industrialist)

The world holds two classes of men--intelligent men without religion, and religious men without intelligence.
— Abu'l-Ala-Al-Ma'arri, (d.1057 Philosopher, Poet and Writer)

If God wants something from me, he would tell me. He wouldn't leave someone else to do this, as if an infinite being were short on time. And he would certainly not leave fallible, sinful humans to deliver an endless plethora of confused and contradictory messages. God would deliver the message himself, directly, to each and every one of us, and with such clarity as the most brilliant being in the universe could accomplish. We would all hear him out and shout "Eureka!" So obvious and well-demonstrated would his message be. It would be spoken to each of us in exactly those terms we would understand. And we would all agree on what that message was.
— Richard Carrier (Historian, Activist, Author, Lecturer)

It hurts so bad when you grow up and understand that everything you believed in and devoted yourself to were just fallacy and stupidity.
— M.F. Moonzajer (Author)

History does not record anywhere at any time a religion that has any rational basis. Religion is a crutch for people not strong enough to stand up to the unknown without help.
—Robert A. Heinlein (d. 1988 Dean of Science Fiction Writers)

Great minds think alike, but fools seldom differ.

For those in love with an illusion often refuse to accept reality.
— Sanal Edamaruku (Author, Rationalist and founder-president and editor of Rationalist International)

Religion is not a nice thing. It is potentially a very dangerous thing because it involves a heady complex of emotions, desires, yearnings and fears.
—Karen Armstrong (Former Catholic nun, Religious Scholar, Author and Commentator)

You keep believing, I'll keep evolving.

There is no doubt that we have defeated too many dictators; but we must not forget that the religion is still out there.
— M.F. Moonzajer (Author)

Two hands working can do more than a thousand clasped in prayer

Man created God in his image : intolerant, sexist, homophobic and violent.
—Attributed to Marie de France; coined by George Weinberg (Psychotherapist and Mathematician)

A belief is not true [simply] because it is useful.
—Henri Frédéric Amiel (d. 1881 moral philosopher, poet, and critic)

To surrender to ignorance and call it God has always been premature, and it remains premature today.
—Isaac Asimov (d. 1992 Science Writer and Biochemist)

The way to see by faith is to shut the eye of reason.
—Benjamin Franklin (d. 1790 Polymath, Author, Printer, Political Theorist, Politician, Scientist, Postmaster, Civic Activist, Statesman and Diplomat)

The sailor does not pray for wind, he learns to sail.
—Gustaf Lindborg (d. 1927?)

So you really think that God would plant a bunch of bones in the Earth to test your faith? Either you're in denial or God has some serious self-esteem issues.
—Coral Yoshi

Whatever we cannot easily understand we call God; this saves much wear and tear on the brain tissues.
—Edward Abbey (d. 1989 Environmentalist, Author, Essayist)

286

There are two things which cannot be attacked in front: ignorance and narrow-mindedness. They can only be shaken by the simple development of the contrary qualities. They will not bear discussion.
—Lord John Dalberg-Acton (d. 1902 Historian)

Those who invalidate reason ought seriously to consider whether they argue against reason or without reason; if with reason, then they establish the principle that they are laboring to dethrone: but if they argue without reason (which, in order to be consistent with themselves they must do), they are out of reach of rational conviction, nor do they deserve a rational argument.
—Ethan Allen (d. 1789 American Founding Father, Farmer, Businessman, Land Speculator, Philosopher, Writer, Lay Theologian, and Politician)

Every generation of humans believed it had all the answers it needed, except for a few mysteries they assumed would be solved at any moment. And they all believed their ancestors were simplistic and deluded. What are the odds that you are the first generation of humans who will understand reality?
—Scott Adams (Cartoonist and Satirist)

The biggest issue in this election is something called flip-flopping, and all candidates are accused of doing it. A strong leader is expected to maintain steadfast resolve in his opinion even if the environment changes or he gets new information. In any other context, that would be considered the first sign of a brain tumor. When presidents do it, it's called leadership, and frankly, we can't get enough of it.
—Scott Adams (Cartoonist and Satirist)

Any sufficiently advanced technology is indistinguishable from magic.
—Arthur C. Clarke (d. 2008 Science Writer, Futurist, Inventor and Undersea Explorer)

Thought means life, since those who do not think so do not live in any high or real sense.
—Amos Bronson Alcott (d. 1888 Teacher, Writer, Philosopher, Reformer , Abolitionist and Women's right's Advocate)

In those parts of the world where learning and science have prevailed, miracles have ceased; but in those parts of it as are barbarous and ignorant, miracles are still in vogue.
—Ethan Allen (d. 1789 American Founding Father, Farmer, Businessman, Land Speculator, Philosopher, Writer, Lay Theologian, and Politician)

We are always making God our accomplice so that we may legalize our own inequities. Every successful massacre is consecrated by a Te Deum, and the clergy have never been wanting in benedictions for any victorious enormity.
—Henri Frédéric Amiel (d. 1881 Moral Philosopher, Poet, and Critic)

Nothing defines humans better than their willingness to do irrational things in the pursuit of phenomenally unlucky payoffs. This is the principle of lotteries, dating and religion.
—Scott Adams (Cartoonist and Satirist)

With God, what is terrible is that one never knows whether it's not just a trick of the devil.
—Jean Anouilh (d. 1987 Dramatist)

To no form of religion is woman indebted for one impulse of freedom.
—Susan B Anthony (d.1906 Abolitionist, Social reformer and Women's Rights Activist)

"Theocracy" has always been the synonym for a bleak and narrow, if not a fierce and blood-stained, tyranny.
—William Archer

288

Prayers and sacrifices are of no avail.
—Aristotle (d. 322 BCE Philosopher and Practitioner of Science)

People go to church for the same reasons they go to a tavern: to stupefy themselves, to forget their misery, to imagine themselves, for a few minutes anyway, free and happy.
—Mikhail Bakunin (d. 1876 Founder of Collectivist Anarchism)

A God who kept tinkering with the universe was absurd; a God who interfered with human freedom and creativity was tyrant. If God is seen as a self in a world of his own, an ego that relates to a thought, a cause separate from its effect, "he" becomes a being, not Being itself. An omnipotent, all-knowing tyrant is not so different from Earthly dictators who make everything and everybody mere cogs in the machine which they controlled. An atheism that rejects such a God is amply justified.
—Karen Armstrong (Former Catholic nun, Religious Scholar, Author and Commentator)

Miracles are doomed; they will drop out like fairies and witchcraft, from among the matter which serious people believe.
—Matthew Arnold, (d.1888 Poet and Cultural Critic and School Inspector)

Imagine the people who believe such things and who are not ashamed to ignore, totally, all the patient findings of thinking minds through all the centuries since the (Holy Books) were written. And it is these ignorant people, the most uneducated, the most unimaginative, the most unthinking among us, who would make themselves the guides and leaders of us all; who would force their feeble and childish beliefs on us; who would invade our schools and libraries and homes. I personally resent it bitterly.
—Isaac Asimov (d. 1992 Science Writer and Biochemist)

If God has spoken, why is the world not convinced?
—Percy Bysshe Shelly (d. 1822 Poet)

Truth is the daughter of time, not of authority.
—Sir Francis Bacon (d. 1626 Philosopher, Statesman, Scientist, Jurist, Orator, and Author---Father of the Scientific Method)

All religions, with their gods, their demigods, and their prophets, their messiahs and their saints, were created by the prejudiced fancy of men who had not attained the full development and full possession of their faculties.
—Mikhail Bakunin (d. 1876 Founder of Collectivist Anarchism)

People everywhere enjoy believing things that they know are not true. It spares them the ordeal of thinking for themselves and taking responsibility for what they know.
—Brooks Atkinson (d. 1984 Theater Critic)

The philosopher aspires to explain away all mysteries, to dissolve them into light. Mystery, on the other hand, is demanded and pursued by the religious instinct; mystery constitutes the essence of worship.
—Henri Frédéric Amiel (d. 1881 Moral Philosopher, Poet, and Critic)

[When] church and state are separate, the effects are happy, and they do not at all interfere with each other: but where they have been confounded together, no tongue nor pen can fully describe the mischiefs that have ensued.
—Isaac Backus (d. 1806 Baptist Preacher and Champion of religious Freedom via Separationism)

Although the time of death is approaching me, I am not afraid of dying and going to Hell or (what would be considerably worse) going to the popularized version of Heaven. I expect death to be nothingness and, for removing me from all possible fears of death, I am thankful to atheism.
—Isaac Asimov (d. 1992 Science Writer and Biochemist)

290

He who desires to worship god must harbor no childish illusions about the matter but bravely renounce his liberty & humanity.
—Mikhail Bakunin (d. 1876 Founder of Collectivist Anarchism)

Perhaps the whole root of our trouble, the human trouble, is that we will sacrifice all the beauty of our lives, will imprison ourselves in totems, taboos, crosses, blood sacrifices, steeples, mosques, races, armies, flags, nations, in order to deny the fact of death, which is the only fact we have.
—James Arthur Baldwin (d. 1987 Writer)

Every religion manifests ideals such as do not steal, do not tell lies, and so on. These are the norms for any civilized society and they should not be linked to any religion or god.
—D. D. Bandist

Not thinking critically, I assumed that the successful prayers were proof that God answers prayer while the failures were proof that there was something wrong with me.
—Dan Barker (Musician and Former Preacher)

The most fatal illusion is the settled point of view. Since life is growth and motion, a fixed point of view kills anybody who has one.
—Brooks Atkinson (d. 1984 Theater Critic)

Freedom, morality, and the human dignity of the individual consists precisely in this; that he does good not because he is forced to do so, but because he freely conceives it, wants it, and loves it.
—Mikhail Bakunin (d. 1876 Founder of Collectivist Anarchism)

My favorite part of the bible is when god gives people free will and then kills everyone with a flood for not acting the way he wanted.
—Anonymous

Only two things are infinite: The universe and Human
Stupidity....and I'm not sure about the former.
—Attributed to Albert Einstein

Religious people will claim that everything happens for a reason
and that it's all part of some mysterious plan that god has for us,
while simultaneously asserting that suffering, sin and evil are a
result of free will. Huh?

Morality is doing what is right regardless of what you are told.
Religion is doing what you are told regardless of what's right.
Anonymous

The popularity of a belief is not an indication of its truth--if doubt
in the belief leads to torture, execution or eternal damnation, that
belief will become very popular.
—T. F. Hanlon

First the priests arrive. Then the conquistadors.
—James Clavell (Author)

A god made by man undoubtedly has need of man to make
himself known to man.
—Percy Bysshe Shelly

The difference between faith and insanity is that faith is the ability
to hold firmly to a conclusion that is incompatible with the
evidence, whereas insanity is the ability to hold firmly to a
conclusion that is incompatible with the evidence.
—William R. Harwood (Scientist and Author)

God, or rather the fiction of God, is thus the sanction and the
intellectual and moral cause of all the slavery on Earth, and the
liberty of men will not be complete, unless it will have completely
annihilated the inauspicious fiction of a heavenly master.
—Mikhail Bakunin (d. 1876 Founder of Collectivist Anarchism)

292

Let us account for all we see by the facts we know. If there are things for which we cannot account, let us wait for light. To account for anything by supernatural agencies is, in fact, to say that we do not know. Theology is not what we know about God, but what we do not know about Nature.
—Robert B. Ingersoll (d.1899 Lawyer, Politician, Orator "The Great Agnostic")

Whatever the final laws of nature may be, there is no reason to suppose that they are designed to make (you) happy.
—Steven Weinberg (theoretical physicist, Nobel laureate in physics)

Nothing draws people more quickly away from religion than an open mind.
—Hemant Mehta (Author)

Religion is fundamentally opposed to everything I hold in veneration--courage, clear thinking, honesty, fairness, and above all, love of the truth.
—H.L. Mencken (d. 1956 Journalist, Satirist, Cultural Critic)

Reality is what it is, not what you want it to be.
—Frank Zappa (d. 1993 Musician, Activist and Filmmaker)

God for you is where you sweep away all the mysteries of the world, all the challenges to our intelligence. You simply turn your mind off and say, "God did it".
—Carl Sagan (d. 1996 Astronomer, Cosmologist, Astrophysicist, Astrobiologist, Author, Science Popularizer and Communicator)

I distrust those people who know so well what God wants them to do because I notice it always coincides with their own desires.
—Susan B Anthony (d.1906 Abolitionist, Social reformer and Women's Rights Activist)

I do not feel obliged to believe that the same God who has endowed us with sense, reason and intellect has intended us to forgo their use.
—Galileo Galilei (d. 1642 Astronomer, Physicist, Engineer, Philosopher and Mathematician)

Religion: A daughter of Hope and Fear, explaining to Ignorance the nature of the Unknowable.
—Ambrose Bierce (d.1914 Writer)

I'm proud to be an atheist--it helps me stand for so much more and fall for so much less.
—Dan Barker (Musician and Former Preacher)

Just because you believe in something does not mean that it is true.
—Albert Einstein (d. 1955 Nobel Laureate Theoretical Physicist)

All religions have been made by men.
—Napoleon Bonaparte (d.1821 General and Emperor)

The human brain is excellent at maximizing the convenience of its beliefs. TFM

We are all atheists about most of the gods that societies have ever believed in. Some of us just go one god further.
—Richard Dawkins (Evolutionary Biologist, Ethologist, Author)

Atheism is a requirement for a complete human being. Religion is a crutch that is shackled to you, one you never really needed in the first place, but were convinced by others that you couldn't live without. Once you discover it's all an illusion, that it's not even a real crutch, you discard it gladly.
—Brent Yaciw

The invisible and the non-existent look very much alike.
—Huang Po (d. 850 CE, Zen Buddhist Master)

294

If there is a God, atheism must seem to Him as less of an insult than religion.
—Edmond de Goncourt (c. 1896 Writer, Literary Critic, Art critic and publisher)

We can judge our progress by the courage of our questions and the depth of our answers, our willingness to embrace what is true rather than what feels good.
—Carl Sagan (d. 1996 Astronomer, Cosmologist, Astrophysicist, Astrobiologist, Author, Science Popularize and Communicator)

Faith is intellectual bankruptcy. If the only way you can accept an assertion is by faith, then you are conceding that it can't be taken on its own merits.
—Dan Barker (Musician and Former Preacher)

Religion is excellent stuff for keeping people quiet.
—Napoleon Bonaparte (d.1821 General and Emperor)

Hence today, I believe I am acting in accordance with the will of the Almighty Creator.
—Adolf Hitler, Mein Kampf (d. 1945 Der Fuhrer of Nazi Germany, responsible for the Holocaust)

One man's theology is another man's belly laugh.
—Robert A. Heinlein (d. 1988 Dean of Science Fiction Writers)

The theologian says the philosopher resembles a blind man, in a dark room, looking for a black cat that isn't there. The philosopher says the theologian would find it.

I'd rather have a mind opened by wonder than one closed by belief.
—Gerry Spencer (Lawyer and Writer)

Philosophy is questions that may never be answered. Religion is answers that may never be questioned.

Those who can make you believe absurdities can make you commit atrocities.
—Voltaire (d.1778 Writer, Historian, and Philosopher)

Men never do evil so completely and cheerfully as when they do it from a religious conviction.
—Blaise Pascal (d. 1662 Mathematician, Physicist, Inventor, Writer and Theologian)

I don't know if God exists, but it would be better for his reputation if He didn't.
—Jules Renard (d. 1910 Author)

All the biblical miracles will at last disappear with the progress of science.
—Matthew Arnold (d.1888 Poet and Cultural Critic and School Inspector)

Men rarely (if ever) manage to dream up a God superior to themselves. Most Gods have the manners and morals of a spoiled child.
—Robert A. Heinlein (d. 1988 Dean of Science Fiction Writers)

He that will not reason is a bigot; he that cannot reason is a fool; he that dares not reason is a slave.
—William Drummond (d. 1828 Diplomat and Member of Parliament, Poet and philosopher)

Religion does three things quite effectively: Divides people, Controls people, Deludes people.
—Carlespie Mary Alice McKinney (Author)

Faith does not give you the answers, it just stops you asking the questions.
—Frater Ravus

296

We would be 1500 years ahead if it hadn't been for religion dragging science back by its coattails and burning our best minds at the stake.
—Catherine Fahringer (d. 2008 activist for the separation of church and state)

A myth is a religion in which no one any longer believes.
—James K. Feibleman (Author)

The family that prays together...is brainwashing their children.
—Albert Einstein (d. 1955 Nobel Laureate Theoretical Physicist)

Faith is the fatigue resulting from the attempt to preserve God's integrity instead of one's own.
—Matt Berry (Author)

All thinking men are atheists.
—Ernest Hemingway (d. 1961 Writer and Journalist)

Lighthouses are more helpful than churches.
—Benjamin Franklin (d. 1790 Polymath, Author, Printer, Political Theorist, Politician, Scientist, Postmaster, Civic Activist, Statesman and Diplomat)

This would be the best of all possible worlds if there were no religion in it.
—John Adams (d. 1826 President/Vice President of U.S., lawyer, diplomat, statesman, political theorist, diarist and correspondent)

Why is it often that, when someone points out the lies of another person, the person who lied gets angry, rather than abashed. Never is this more apparent than when the lie pointed out is a lie to oneself, and the anger never more fierce than when the lie is one of religion.
—G. Scott Wells

People who don't like their beliefs being laughed at shouldn't have such funny beliefs.

Freedom of religion allows me to interpret religious texts exactly how it fits my worldview already.
—Stephen Colbert (Comedian, Television Host, and Author)

If you're a person of faith, and you make the distinction that your "moderate faith" means that you're not as crazy or dangerous as the fundamentalist or the extremist, aren't you saying that what makes you safer is your distance from total belief on the spectrum of religious certainty and your relative proximity to the secular?
—T. F. Hanlon

The people are beginning to think, to reason and to investigate. Slowly, painfully, but surely, the gods are being driven from the Earth.
—Robert B. Ingersoll (d.1899 Lawyer, Politician, Orator "The Great Agnostic")

The evolutionary future of religion is extinction; while it might take several hundred years, belief in supernatural beings and in supernatural forces that affect nature without obeying nature's laws will erode and become only an interesting historical memory.
—Anthony F.C. Wallace (d. 2015 Cultural Anthropologist)

Blind belief in authority is the greatest enemy of truth.
—Albert Einstein (d. 1955 Nobel Laureate Theoretical Physicist)

CLOSING THOUGHT

By being born and developing to your current stage, you have borrowed from the universe, a particular collection of molecules, chemicals, and atoms. Through the intricacies of physical, chemical and biological interactions, your particular collection of these substances have combined into something totally unique: your body, your mind, your very thoughts, ideas, emotions and memories. Your particular combination has even varied over time as you developed and aged; certain cells were lost, shed, converted or modified, as were the molecules that constituted them.

Upon your final demise, in one way or another, the chemicals, molecules, atoms, quarks and energy contained within your cells will all be returned, in some form or other to the Earth and the universe as a whole. Your borrowing of these substances, from your conception to your expiration, will come to an end. Your lease on life will come to maturity, and the cosmic bank will ask for final deposit. Your atoms and energy will now, once again, be made available for some other aspect of the universe, perhaps for a different collection of chemicals that turn into a tree or a wasp, or an underground fungus, or a bacterium, perhaps a rock or soil, or quite likely, a combination of many seemingly disparate and mundane things.

Hopefully, you will have done something with your loan during the time that you possessed it. Did you merely exist as a vessel using up surrounding energy and molecules as resources to see to your needs, to satisfy your hungers and to fulfill your desires? Consider that the odds are far, far more likely that you could have been born as some other form of life, perhaps a wildebeest or a frog or an ant or a small patch of ivy. But as luck would have it, you won the cosmic lottery, and you were born a human and received the ultimate jackpot: a human brain. Yet for some reason, you've decided not to open up this gift and use it. It's too much trouble; it will take too long to set it up and learn how to use it. After all, you've made it this far in life comfortably without opening the package and putting the contents to the test, why make your life more complicated? After all, you've managed your life fairly well so far without opening it.

At the same time, the other 99.9% of all life peers through a window envying your fortune, salivating at the opportunity with which you've been awarded, wishing that it had been their fortune to receive such a treasure. Yet the gift sits in the corner of a room, gathering dust, it's potential lost, squandered in disuse; the 99.9% of life gape in disbelief and mutter to themselves, "Why won't they open it?" And yet, their parting thought, "What might have been..." doesn't even occur to you. Hopefully, before too much time has passed, you will come across your gift and finally decide to open it and learn to use it properly, marveling at the new abilities that it now imparts to you, the progress and productivity that it enables, simplifies and expedites. Perhaps you will even be slightly chagrined or even embarrassed at how you'd been going through life unnecessarily burdened, slowed down by your thinking's relative inefficiency before opening the gift.

And beyond improving your own lot in life, maybe you will have actively sought out ways to make other things better, healthier, wiser, happier, even if they're outside of your own particular collection of molecules. After all is said and done, your collection of atoms is merely a baton in a relay race; and as you tire and fade from the competition, dying away, succumbing to entropy, your atoms and energy are handed off to some other entity or entities down the lane, which will take off running for a while until they too eventually fade; only for their energy and atoms to be handed off to something else still further down the lane.

300

Perhaps, you will find it within yourself to put forth your best effort in using your gift, trying to advance as far as possible as quickly as possible during your leg of the race, if only to pass on your baton to whatever runs the next leg in the relay.

T.F.H.

ABOUT THE AUTHOR

Traditionally, by supplying the reader some of the author's background, this section of a book gives the reader an idea of the mind/mindset of the author, possibly to suggest at least some reasons why the author has come to the conclusions that they have. As a child, the informal education of the current author included the absence of being told what to think or believe. Their formal education involved receiving a Bachelor's Degree in Biology, a Master's Degree in Neuroscience and a Doctorate in Vision Science, none of which affects the validity of the ideas contained within this volume. The truth of ideas should hold true regardless of the upbringing, education or experiences of the author or the reader. A more salient inclusion in any book would be:

ABOUT THE READER

Please list the aspects of your upbringing, education and life experiences that are likely to bias your interpretation, acceptance or rejection of the ideas included within.

303

www.ingramcontent.com/pod-product-compliance
Lightning Source LLC
Chambersburg PA
CBHW060836280326
41934CB00007B/810